DEADLY
CONSEQUENCES

DEADLY CONSEQUENCES

Deborah Prothrow-Stith, M.D.

with Michaele Weissman

HarperPerennial

A Division of HarperCollins*Publishers*

A hardcover edition of this book was published in 1991 by HarperCollins Publishers.

HarperCollins books may be purchased for educational, business, or sales promotional use. For information please write: Special Markets Department,
NY 10022.

First HarperPerennial edition published 1993.

The Library of Congress has catalogued the hardcover edition as follows:
Prothrow-Stith, Deborah, 1954–
   Deadly consequences : how violence is destroying our teenage population and a plan to begin solving the problem / Deborah Prothrow-Stith; with Michaele Weissman.
      p.   cm.
   Includes bibliographical references and index.
   ISBN 0-06-016344-5
   1. Teenagers—United States—Crime against.   2. Juvenile delinquency—United States.   3. Violence—United States—Prevention.
I. Weissman, Michaele.   II. Title.
HV6250.4.Y68P76   1991
364.3'6'0973—dc20   90-55938

ISBN 0-06-092402-0 (pbk.)

93 94 95 96 97 RRD 10 9 8 7 6 5 4 3 2 1

PERMISSIONS

CONTENTS

Foreword   xi

Acknowledgments   xiii

Introduction   xvii

1   Free-Floating Anger   1

2   An American Tragedy   11

3   Teaching Our Kids to Kill   29

4   Adolescence: The Dangerous Passage   48

5   An Endangered Species—Young Men of Color Living
    in Poverty   64

6   What the Kids Say   80

7   Gangs   95

8   Drugs, Gangs, Guns, and Cops   111

9   The Public Health Approach   130

10 Helping Families Prevent Violence   145

11 Helping Schools Prevent Violence   161

12 Helping Communities Prevent Violence   184

Notes   204

Appendix I: Public Health and Criminal Justice Chart   226

Appendix II: State-by-State Organizations   227

Index   262

FOREWORD

DEADLY CONSEQUENCES IS AN IMPORTANT, PERSUASIVE, and well-written study of adolescent violence. Dr. Prothrow-Stith, a physician and public health official, recognizes that insights on adolescent violence and aggression from the disciplines of criminal justice, mental health, and biological science can only take us so far. Therefore, she (with Michaele Weissman) brilliantly incorporates materials from the social and behavioral sciences to address "questions about the social context in which violence occurs." *Deadly Consequences* pursues these and other questions by focusing on the problem of adolescent violence in disadvantaged neighborhoods.

Poor youngsters in nonpoor neighborhoods tend to have significantly different experiences than those in inner-city ghetto neighborhoods. Adolescents who live in neighborhoods that have limited legitimate employment opportunities, high rates of joblessness and poverty, poor schools, inadequate job information networks, and few conventional role models are far more likely to be exposed to or exhibit violent and aggressive behavior.

Adolescents in ghetto neighborhoods are not only influenced by restricted opportunities in the broader society that confront all disadvantaged families, they are also influenced by the behavior of other poor families and individuals who face these same constraints. The latter influence is one of culture—that is, the extent to which individuals follow their inclinations as they have been developed by learning or influence from other members of the community. As the anthropologist Ulf Hannerz has observed, ghetto-specific practices such as overt emphasis on sexuality, idleness, and public drinking are often denounced by those who reside in inner-city ghetto neighborhoods. However, since such practices occur much more frequently there than in middle-class society, due in major part to social organizational forces, the transmission of these modes of behavior by precept, as in role modeling, is more easily facilitated.

The transmission of such beliefs is part of what I have called "concentration effects," that is, the effects of living in a neighborhood that is overwhelmingly impoverished. In my book, *The Truly Disadvantaged*, I argue that these concentration effects, reflected in a range of outcomes from weak labor force-attachment to social dispositions, are created by the constraints or restricted opportunities that the residents of the inner-city neighborhoods face in terms of access to jobs and job networks, involvement in quality schools, availability of marriageable partners, and exposure to conventional role models.

In these neighborhoods, as Dr. Prothrow-Stith so clearly shows, youngsters are more likely to see violence as a way of life. They are more likely to witness violent acts, be taught to be violent by exhortation, and have role models who do not adequately control their own violent impulses or restrain their own anger. Accordingly, given the availability of and easy access to firearms, knives, and other weapons, adolescent experiments with macho behavior often have deadly consequences.

The problems of psychological development faced by all adolescents are magnified in the inner-city ghetto setting. And this is especially true of the young black males. In too many cases, as revealed in *Deadly Consequences*, their families are unable to provide for them, their schools do not believe they can learn, do not teach them to learn, and blame them for their lack of academic achievement. The jobs for which they qualify have been severely reduced by economic restructuring and periodic recessions and their incomes have declined precipitously. For all these reasons, when they become fathers they are not in a position to support their children or to play a positive and major role in a new family. In short, they are denied a meaningful role in mainstream society and therefore frequently end up as thugs or deviants.

Working from a public health perspective, Dr. Prothrow-Stith believes that we can change the climate of violence in many of these high-risk neighborhoods. What is required, she maintains, "is a broad array of strategies, strategies that teach new ways of coping with angry and aggressive feelings." She believes that we can and must mobilize every organized unit in American society—government, churches, schools, the media, community organizations, industry—to disseminate the message that "anger can be managed and aggressive impulses controlled." After reading this thoughtful book, I am persuaded that we should seriously consider her proposed program. I also feel that a good start in mobilizing organizations and individuals in a fight to reduce adolescent violence would be to recommend strongly that they read *Deadly Consequences*.

—William Julius Wilson

ACKNOWLEDGMENTS

THERE ARE MANY COLLEAGUES, CO-WORKERS, FRIENDS and supporters to thank. Michaele Weissman, my partner in the writing of this book, and I both feel that without the willingness of so many people to help, our writing efforts would not have succeeded.

Some of my "thank yous" are really mine alone and I will list them first. John Auerbach has earned my gratitude and affection during many years of shared duty. It is he who convinced me to write this book and he who helped write the initial proposal. He has been a cheerleader for this project throughout.

There are two people with whom I worked early on who added depth to my understanding of the issue of violence. Psychologist Hussein Bulhan taught me how racism, poverty and oppression can lead to violence. Pediatrician Howard Spivak, too, helped shape my thinking. Howard was convinced that violence was a public health problem when few other physicians were paying attention to the data. Together Howard and I founded and ran the Violence Prevention Project at Boston City Hospital. He is my colleague and my comrade. I am grateful for his friendship.

I want to acknowledge the encouragement and support of three physician/mentors—Alvin Poussaint, John Noble, and George A. Lamb. In the early years of my public health career all were generous with ideas, with funding, and with creative supervision. They helped shape my thinking and my career.

Mark Rosenberg, Director of the Division of Injury Control and the Centers for Disease Control in Atlanta has been a driving force in the national effort to win recognition of violence as a legitimate public health concern and to reduce the incidence of violence in American life. From the beginning, Mark has championed my intervention efforts. I value his respect and am grateful for his support.

The "Curriculum to Prevent Adolescent Violence" was the result of my collaboration with mediation specialist and writer Bill Kreidler and Renee Wilson-Brewer and Cheryl Vince from the Educational Development Corporation. The creativity and dedication of these three and many others at EDC has had a huge impact in the fields of violence prevention and childhood injury. I want especially to thank Renee—no matter what, she has always been there, wise and worldly, to help get the job done.

And then there are my dear friends and special colleagues from the Violence Prevention Project. Alice Hausman, Joanne Taupier, Paul Bracy, Mark Bukuras and Jim Roeper, all were present during the exciting days when we were inventing a new public health intervention—violence prevention. These wonderful professionals were willing to stake their careers on the idea that public health strategies could be used to combat violence. The spade work they did and the seeds they planted are still bearing fruit at the Violence Prevention Project where these "old hands" have been joined by a new team of talented individuals—Executive Director Linda Hudson, Vaughn Simpkins and Rebecca Atnafou.

My public health colleagues—Carl Bell, John Waller, Beverly Coleman-Miller, Lisa Porche, Jeanne Taylor, Woody Meyers, Reed Tuckson, Nollie Wood, Omwale Amuleru Marshall—all have my admiration for the fine quality of their work and my gratitude for their help and never-ending support. They have been an inspiration.

I have one concluding acknowledgment that is mine alone. Three years ago, Michaele Weissman was a writer helping me with a book. Today, she is my friend, my co-author, and a colleague in violence prevention. She has done an outstanding job, and I am truly indebted to her.

Together, Michaele and I have many people to thank. Our agent Doe Coover has had a commitment to this book that goes beyond professional. She's been a driving force behind this project, nurturing it when it appeared it might not flourish. Thank you. And thanks to our editor, Marshall DeBruhl, who believed in this book not once, but twice.

Hundreds of people at Cathedral High School and at the Jeremiah E. Burke High School have helped me over the years and have helped us write this book. It is impossible to name all the teachers, administrators and students at these schools who have shared their insight and wisdom with us. Four names must not go unmentioned—Ann Bishop, formerly the nurse and health teacher at Cathedral High; Sister Pat Keaveney, principal of Cathedral High School; Albert Holland, Principal at the Burke School and Lawrence Whitfield, the Burke health teacher. Special thanks to these four for their dedication, their wisdom and their willingness to open their classrooms to the violence prevention curriculum.

Then there are all the kids at these schools. The kids who opened themselves to the curriculum and in so doing taught me so very much. The kids who entered our essay contest on "Surviving in a Violent World." The kids from the Burke football team who shared their thoughts and feelings with Michaele and me. We don't just thank you. We love you.

There is a long list of "experts" who generously shared their knowledge with us, helping make this a deeper and more comprehensive book. Each one of them possesses books-full of knowledge. Mark Moore, Ron Ferguson, Glen Pierce, Mickey Roach, Mohamed Seedat, Ron Slaby, Jeff Howard and the team at the Efficacy Institute, Lester Grinspoon, Peter Stringham, Leon Dash, Petra Hesse, Gerald Patterson, Marion Forgatch, Vernon Mark—all shared their valuable time and their wisdom and we are deeply grateful.

We are grateful to Zita Jackson for her logistical help and her lovely composure and to Wendy Larson who prepared the resource list at the end of this book and whose capacity to thrive amidst our madness has been a gift. Thanks, too, to Andrea Sargent of HarperCollins who held down the fort, not an easy task on this project.

To our husbands, children, stepdaughters, nephews, parents and in-laws, we have only this to say: We are endlessly grateful for your support and love and limitless capacity to eat pizza for dinner.

To all who have helped, again our thanks. Much of the wisdom in this book belongs to you. The errors are ours alone.

DEBORAH PROTHROW-STITH
and MICHAELE WEISSMAN
February 1991

INTRODUCTION

IN 1984, WHILE SERVING AS THE SURGEON GENERAL OF THIS nation, I startled a great number of Americans, including health professionals, when I declared that violence is as much a public health issue for physicians today as small pox, tuberculosis, and syphilis were for my predecessors in the last two centuries.

Seven years ago, few regarded the 20,000 Americans who die each year in homicides and the hundreds of thousands who are injured in assaults as victims of a condition that falls within the purview of public health. Few saw the relevance of prevention to violence. Even fewer appreciated that sophisticated systems of data collection and analysis and complex prevention strategies can postpone or prevent the deadly moment when one individual raises his arm against another.

In the years since 1984, many inside and outside the public health establishment have changed their thinking. The idea that intra-family violence (child abuse, spouse abuse, elder abuse) is the legitimate concern of health care professionals is now universally embraced. We understand that it is the responsibility of those who provide health care to identify those at risk and try to prevent assaults within the family. We understand that we must reduce the incidence of injury and death, and interrupt the terrible cycle in which children who observe of fall victim to violence so often become its perpetrators.

We have learned, too, that violence that explodes between individuals who know each other, but are not members of the same family, must also command our interest and concern. This form of violence, as Dr. Prothrow-Stith teaches us, has a terrible poignancy—those it carries off in greatest number are our young. Too many young men, often poor, often black- and brown-skinned, are dying in homicides that erupt in a moment of rage between two people who know each other, who drink or take drugs, who argue—and at least one of whom has a handgun. Half of the homicides that occur each year in the United States fit this essentially non-criminal profile. Just as we health care professionals are learning to identify and to offer treatment to the victims of family violence when they appear in our offices and in our emergency rooms, so we must learn to identify and to treat the potential perpetrators of acquaintance violence.

Dr. Prothrow-Stith and her co-author Michaele Weissman have looked at the issue of acquaintance violence, particularly homicide among young males, clearly and comprehensively. Their excellent book will lead you to believe that *the discipline of* public health possesses the solution to the mounting toll of violence in this country. The public health approach seeks to prevent tragedy; it seeks to identify and treat young males who are at risk for violence before their lives and the lives of those around them are ruined. The discipline of public health provides strategies to stop violence before it maims and kills.

Deadly Consequences is a road map designed to help us lead our children and our communities out of the tragic morass in which so many are succumbing. The authors provide us with a new understanding of and a new response to violence—one that is sensible, doable, and one that we can put into action today. We need only take the first steps.

C. Everett Koop, M.D., Sc.D.
Surgeon General
United States Public Health Service 1981–1989

1

FREE-FLOATING ANGER

I FIRST BECAME AWARE OF VIOLENCE AS A MAJOR THREAT to young people during my third year at Harvard Medical School.

The third year is the clinical year, the time when frightened students begin to practice medicine on living patients. For me and for many, the third year is a crash course in real life. Every hospital room we enter teaches new lessons about the bad things that can happen to people.

In late January of 1978, as part of my third-year training, I did a six week surgical rotation at Boston's Brigham and Women Hospital. I didn't like surgery. My husband and I were expecting our first child. In those early months of pregnancy, everything nauseated me, especially the sights and the smells of the operating room. During my six weeks at the Brigham, I probably dashed out of more rooms and vomited in more hallways than any other student in the school's history.

The surgical rotation included an extended stint in the emergency room. On a typical night the doors to the Brigham E.R. would swing open to admit every imaginable kind of case. There were people with abdominal pain and urinary tract infections. There were people pulled from car wrecks. People with sore throats, broken bones, infected toes. Kids who had swallowed their parents' pills. And teenagers—an endless parade of teens; cut, shot, bleeding, dead, the victims of would-be or actual homicides.

The pace in the emergency room was fast and the pressure was almost always on. During one twelve-hour shift, the surgical resident looking over my shoulder decided that I was ready; my lesson for the night would be suturing. For several weeks I had been practicing. Using a surgical needle and thread, I had closed great juicy gashes slashed in navel oranges. I had practiced taking small, neat stitches on artificial skin. But nothing prepared me for the moment when I thrust a needle through the resistant skin of a squirming person.

That night I treated all the patients who arrived needing stitches. I explained to each that I was a student just learning to suture and that my work would be closely supervised by a resident. My stitching was slow, but competent. The resident praised my efforts and I was feeling pretty good.

At around 3 A.M., a young man not yet 20 years old arrived pressing a blood-stained shirt to a laceration over his eyebrow. I told him I was a student and that got us talking. As I cleaned and stitched his wound, the patient told me what had happened. He'd been to a party. He had had quite a lot to drink. A throw-away comment from a guy he barely knew ignited his anger. An argument erupted. Insults were shouted. A crowd of excited on-lookers gathered and began to egg the disputants on. A shove was given, and then a punch was thrown. A knife flashed across the young man's brow. An inch lower and he would have lost his eye.

I could see that the young man's anger had not cooled down one bit in the hour since the fight. As I taped a clean bandage over his stitches, he told me with a swagger, "Don't go to sleep because the guy who did this to me is going to be in here in about an hour and you'll get all the practice stitching you need!"

I chuckled and went to bed, but I was filled with a sense of foreboding. Technically speaking, my work was finished. In the crisis-driven atmosphere of the emergency room, a doctor's job is to "stitch 'em up and send 'em out." That response, though medically correct, seemed woefully inadequate.

Suppose the patient had arrived in the emergency room after taking an overdose of barbituates. We would have lavaged his stomach and then, if we were successful, we would have declared him medically stable. Our job would not have been done, however, until we had determined that he was no longer a threat to himself. Had he said, "Don't go to bed, because I am going home to take more pills," we would have been required to intervene. Standard practice mandates that a mental health provider be consulted when a patient is at risk for suicide. Moreover, if a patient appears to be a danger to himself, his physician has the medical and legal power to order a ten-day hospital stay for observation—even if the patient objects.

My emergency room patient was threatening to harm someone other than himself. Despite the fact that his anger imperiled many lives (including his own), I had no medically-recognized options. There was no standard practice mandating that I intervene. There was no prescribed treatment for anger that might explode into violence. I had no way to protect my patient or the community from an outburst of rage I had every reason to suspect would be deadly. Anger and violence were outside my jurisdiction.

In the weeks and months that followed, I thought a great deal about this patient and other young males like him. I wanted to understand the forces that sent so many of them to the emergency room—cut up, shot up, bleeding, and dead. Why were so many young males striking out with knives and guns? What could be done to stop the carnage? These questions motivated me to learn about violence.

I learned that this country has many more assaults and murders than any other industrialized nation, and that most of these incidents occur among the poor.* I learned that violence takes the lives of thousands of our young each year; that homicide is the leading cause of death of young black males and the second or third leading cause of death (depending on the year) of young white males. I learned that half of all the victims of homicide are African-American, which is astonishing when you consider that blacks constitute only 12 percent of the American population.

The more I learned, the more perturbed I became. I could not understand the blindness of my profession. How could doctors ignore a problem that killed and maimed so many young, healthy patients? I knew that physicians spend a great deal of their time trying to prevent what are called behavioral illnesses—heart disease, suicide, obesity; conditions that result from a patient's own behavior. Yet violence, a grievous condition that surely stemmed from behavior, was overlooked. Why? Could the lack of interest be related to the race and economic status of the victims? Could it be that no one really cared about the pointless deaths each year of thousands of young men, most of them poor, half of them black? Well, I cared. I had a new son, a beautiful black baby boy with whom I was already madly in love. To me the lives of young males, black and white, were not expendable.

I began to ponder ways that medicine could intervene to reduce the number of young victims of violence. I was looking for an approach that would provide an unexplored perspective. My thinking centered on public health, the area of medicine most concerned with education and prevention. Twenty thousand homicide deaths a year convinced me that violence was a public health problem. To me it seemed self-evident: an "ailment" that killed so many ought to have the full attention of physicians and others concerned with improving health.

Seniors at Harvard Medical School were required to do special projects. For mine I decided to create a public health intervention to

---

* References throughout will be discussed in the Notes section following the text.

combat adolescent violence. My "intervention" was educational. I created a violence prevention curriculum to teach young males at risk for violence that they *were* at risk for violence, and to introduce them to ways of managing anger constructively. That early piece of work was far from complete. I still had a great deal to learn about violence, but at least I had made a start. Later I would refine this course and teach it in two of Boston's troubled high schools. A much later version of the curriculum was eventually prepared and marketed, and is now being used in schools in 324 cities in 45 states, as well as in Canada, England, Israel, and American Samoa.

Designing the first version of the curriculum forced me to find out about different disciplines that have traditionally been concerned with interpersonal violence. There were at least three separate professions to be considered—criminal justice, mental health, and the biological sciences. I needed to know what each of these disciplines could teach me about violence and violence prevention, and I needed to figure out where my thinking diverged from that of the experts in each of these fields.

Criminal justice is the vast mechanism created by local, state, and federal governments to apprehend criminal suspects, adjudicate their guilt or innocence, punish (and perhaps rehabilitate) the guilty, and eventually oversee their reintroduction into society. Police officers, prosecutors, judges, lawyers, forensic psychiatrists, prison officials, prison guards, and probation officers are all part of the criminal justice establishment.

Our criminal justice system is the offspring of English Common Law. Fundamental to this ancient code is the assumption that when a crime occurs there is an assailant who is guilty of the crime and a victim who is innocent. The job of the criminal justice system is to find an appropriate criminal suspect for every crime, to determine his guilt or innocence without trampling his constitutional rights, and, if he is found guilty, to punish him. In contrast to the idea of punishment, the far more modern and controversial idea that convicted criminals can and should be rehabilitated during incarceration is an idea to which our society has only occasionally been committed, although there is some evidence that rehabilitation programs can reduce rates of recidivism among young offenders.

Many people who work within the criminal justice system believe that punishment, in addition to being an appropriate social response to major offenses, serves as a deterrent to crime. They see punishment, if swift and sure, as a form of crime prevention. This is an idea that is passionately defended, but difficult to prove. I very much doubt that it is true. Today we have more people in prison than ever before. If punishment were a deterrent, then the number of crimes being committed in our society ought to be declining. FBI statistics indicate just the opposite.

A dozen years ago, as I explored these ideas, several gaps in the criminal justice approach to violence became apparent to me. First, the criminal justice system is fundamentally reactive. Little happens until a crime has occurred. By then, it is too late for prevention strategies. There is another, more subtle problem with the criminal justice approach. Many, perhaps most, homicides and assaults do not readily fit into the model that assigns total blame to one party and total innocence to the other. The majority of violent incidents occur between family members, friends, and acquaintances, following an argument. Under such circumstances blame may well be shared. What I, as a physician, wanted was to find ways to intervene *before* blame was necessary; *before* a homicide was committed.

My skepticism of the criminal justice approach had yet another origin. As a black person I could not help but be aware of the lack of trust that pervades the relationship between blacks and the police. African-Americans are acutely aware of the many instances in which young men of color have been shot by police officers under suspicious circumstances. (So common are these kinds of shootings that many black Americans erroneously blame the police for the high homicide rate in the black community.) The suspicion between blacks and police officers no doubt played a part in directing me toward strategies to combat violence outside the scope of the criminal justice system. I did not, however, deny the important role the criminal justice system plays apprehending and punishing criminals after real crimes have been committed.

Learning what the mental health professions teach about violence supported my intuitive belief that anger is a normal emotion that each of us feels when our desires are not satisfied. From the psychological perspective, anger is neither a good, nor a bad thing. What is "good" or "bad" is the way we handle the anger that we feel. Many people retaliate by using aggression when they feel angry. Aggression means physically or verbally hurting other people. If my husband says he will meet me at 7:00 in front of the movie theater, and he arrives half an hour late, what I feel is anger, but what I enact when I berate him is my aggression. A person whose aggression is out of control might hit or kick in similar circumstances.

In orthodox psychiatric terms, anger and aggression originate within a small child when his basic needs are not met or when his basic drives are thwarted. The anger each of us feels in the present is said to be fired by the fuel of past angers and disappointments within our families. Aggression explodes when anger grows great and individuals do not have strong enough internal "defenses" to control it. In other words, when my husband arrives late and we miss our movie, I do not kick him in the shins, because my internal "defenses" against my own aggression prevent me from doing what I know is stupid and destructive—retaliating physically because I am angry.

The psychiatric approach is individualistic. Difficulty controlling aggressive outbursts is described in the context of one individual in relation to one family. Within this framework the impact of events and conditions external to the family are more or less ignored. This privatistic approach did not seem adequate to me to describe the experience of the many poor, young, non-white people I saw in the emergency room. I could think of many reasons, in addition to difficult family situations, that might make young trauma patients angry. Being poor in America, a nation that admires wealth almost beyond all else, could certainly make a young person angry. Being the victim of racism could certainly trigger angry feelings, as could attending a school where students' intelligence levels are pre-conceived, or facing a future of joblessness. All are good reasons why a young person or any person might feel angry. I intuitively believed that the social context was as important as the family setting. Moreover, I sensed that the social setting could play a role in a young person's failing to develop adequate ways to handle his own aggression. Living in a violent environment in which aggressive outbursts were common, I tended to think, could encourage displays of aggression that in another, more peaceful environment might well have been contained.

I was disturbed by the lack of social vision in the mental health approach. How could it be that so many people with inadequate "defenses" against aggression just happened to be poor? And black? Were all poor parents failing their children? I knew that to be false. Were all black babies born angry and aggressive? If that was so, how could the infant in my own arms be so sweet-natured and peaceable? Surely something in the environment was feeding the anger and aggression that carried off so many poor young males, black and white.

"Black self-hatred" is one explanation of this environmental "something" that has often been suggested to explain the violence in poor black communities. Those who hold to this view say that racism has taught poor black males to hate themselves. Because they hate themselves, they assault and murder others whom they resemble. Blacks in the mental health professions find this theory improbable and unhelpful, and so do I. More satisfying to me is an idea suggested by psychologist Louis Ramey which I think can be extended to apply to poor whites. Black males living in poverty, Ramey suggested, are awash in what he called "free-floating anger." This generalized anger, accompanied by feelings of frustration and helplessness, results from a feeling that the deck is stacked against them—that the double whammy of class and race places them so far outside the economic and social mainstream that they can never find a place inside. Disenfranchised, they are perpetually irritable, like a person who wakes up on the wrong side of the bed day after day. Their free-floating, non-specific feelings of anger are easy to ignite. Any small provocation can cause an explosion. Then black males strike out at the nearest target, displacing their pent up, "free-floating" anger on the nearest target, usually another male just like themselves.

The mental health approach to violence did not provide a social context through which individual acts of violence could be understood and addressed, but it did offer something extremely important—faith in the capacity of young patients to change their aggressive behavior. Mental health providers believe that the right therapeutic intervention can teach individuals new ways of behaving and relating. The newer, behaviorally oriented therapies which are of great interest to me have research data showing precisely to what extent a specific course of therapy alters attitudes and behavior. To someone like me, who is trained to look at quantitative evidence, these findings are extremely exciting, pointing the way toward standardized interventions that one day might help redirect the large number of our young males who are at risk for violence.

I approached my exploration of the biological origins of violence with a sinking feeling in my stomach. Too often biology has been used to "prove" that "some people are just born that way." African-Americans, women, Jews, Asians, and others, all have been hurt when science is trotted out to "prove" that their inferior position in society results from their imagined biological inferiority.

My fears were not entirely founded. The discussion of the impact of biology on human behavior is more sophisticated than I had thought. The old nature versus nurture argument that pitted biology against the environment has not been thrown out, but it has been downgraded. Many scientists no longer believe that a single biological factor can explain a complex social phenomena such as violence. Instead of seeing nature versus nurture, the most imaginative scientists talk about the interplay of nature and nurture, the interplay of biology and environment. Much of their talk, however, is speculative. So far, I am sorry to say, little truly interdisciplinary research has been undertaken; research that would, for example, study the impact of the environment on the biochemistry of the brain.

Medical ethics limits the biological investigation of aggression in human subjects. As a result, much that we know about brain function and aggression comes not from humans, but from laboratory experiments with rats, cats, and monkeys. The limbic system is a portion of the mammalian brain; in humans the limbic system controls some of our emotional responses, including aggression. Electrically stimulating parts of the limbic system will trigger an explosive, violent reaction in animals that resembles aggression in humans. Certain chemicals can increase or decrease the amount of violence displayed after the limbic system is electrically stimulated. Haloperidol (an antipsychotic agent in humans) and metenkephalin (a heroin-like substance produced naturally in the human brain) all suppress the violent response that follows the electric stimulation of the brain. Each of these agents poses tantalizing questions to researchers about the possibility of creating anti-violence drugs. Nalox (a narcotic antagonist) enhances violent response.

Human studies of aggression lack the scope of animal studies and have produced fewer generally accepted conclusions. Even the definition and function of aggression and violence in humans are subjects of debate. Most biologists agree that aggression in animals is necessary to their survival. In humans, biologists have difficulty distinguishing between adaptive (necessary to survival) aggression and maladaptive aggression. Some extremists believe all human aggression works against the survival of our species. I find this assertion, which denies the necessity of protecting oneself, one's children, or one's home absurd. My own view is a pragmatic one. I believe that as a society we in the United States have too much violence, too many homicides, and that this extreme amount of violence is maladaptive.

Invasive studies of the human brain are done infrequently and only on patients with severe brain abnormalities. Such investigations carried out in the past have established the similarity between human and animal subjects. When the limbic systems of aggressive humans with epilepsy or traumatic brain injury were electrically stimulated, humans, too, responded violently. Surgically removing portions of the limbic systems of violent human subjects whose aggressive behavior was related to epilepsy or brain injury resulted in a reduction of the symptoms of aggression. Nowadays, non-invasive imaging techniques such as MRI, CAT, and PET scans that provide cross-sectional views of internal organs are usually used to study the brains of human research subjects.

Much brain/violence research in humans focuses on groups of patients who are thought to be at risk for aggressive outbursts. Many studies have focused on schizophrenic patients, but have failed to establish a conclusive link between this tragically common mental disorder and violence. Other studies have attempted to establish a link between seizure disorders and violence. Again, no conclusive connection has been established, although I continue to be intrigued by some work done in the 1960s by Drs. Vernon Mark and Frank Ervin. For this study, the researchers surgically implanted electrodes deep in the limbic systems of the brains of violent patients with seizures and/or brain injury. They detected electrical abnormalities that had not been diagnosed by the standard test. In several patients, they were able to trigger attack behavior when abnormal areas of the brain were stimulated with a weak electrical current. They theorized that it was this seizure activity in a remote portion of the brain that triggered violent outbursts. Seizures can be caused by head trauma, insufficient oxygen, infection, etc. The researchers speculated that phenomena such as poverty, malnutrition, and child abuse, particularly when associated with brain injury, also could have caused the violence-inducing seizures they detected.

The chemical most often associated with human aggression is alcohol. No one knows precisely why alcohol triggers violence. As a brain depressant, alcohol appears to suppress inhibitions against violence in some people, increasing the likelihood of violence. Some illicit drugs, most especially PCP and ICE (metaphetamines) are very strongly associated with displays of aggression. These drugs are understood to directly trigger violent explosions, much as if the limbic system had been electrically stimulated. Cocaine, in fact, stimulates epileptic electrical outbursts often followed by uncontrollable aggression in the deep limbic brains of epileptic patients.

Severe head injury has also been associated with violence. The medical charts of many of the most violent juvenile and adult offenders in our prisons describe incidents of severe head trauma in childhood caused by accidents and beatings. Whether brain damage from serious childhood head trauma causes later violence or whether repeated abuse, which includes head injury, causes violence is not clear.

While much about human aggression is not known, one fact is indisputable: Among all races, all classes, and in every corner of the globe men are more violent than women. This truth has led researchers to look for a particular male substance that explains violent outbursts. Discredited work done in the 1970s attempted, but failed, to establish the presence in violent males of an extra Y chromosome. Researchers today believe it is the male hormone testosterone that causes male violence. Testosterone courses through the bloodstream of all males. Do violent males have more testosterone than peaceful ones? This question has not yet been fully answered, but according to a small study done by the respected Swedish psychologist Dan Olweus, they do. "Testosterone poisoning," is the term Olweus uses to describe displays of male aggression. What is not clear, however, is whether testosterone causes violence or whether aggressive feelings and violent acts cause increased amounts of testosterone to be produced.

I think there is a likelihood that testosterone plays some not yet fully understood role in male sex role differentiation and aggression. However, I feel certain that neither this hormone, nor any hormone, is totally responsible. Presumably males in all nations possess reasonably equal amounts of testosterone, and yet rates of violence are far from equal worldwide. Socialization is the factor that differs from place to place. Some societies, like our own, clearly encourage young males to enact their violent feelings. Other societies convey to their young that non-violent outlets must be found for aggressive feelings.

My own belief is that socialization plays a large part in explaining the excess aggression of boys as compared to girls. I do not deny that the two sexes have different biologies, each of which has an impact on behavior. I am merely emphasizing how differently boys and girls are raised. Researchers in one particularly interesting study observed the hitting, pushing, kicking, and grabbing behaviors of toddlers between 12 and 16 months old. At this age girls and boys often exhibited these "aggressive" behaviors equally. What differed for the two was the response of their caregivers. Adults ignored the "aggressive" behavior of the female babies 80 percent of the time. They paid attention to the "aggressive" behavior of the boy babies 80 percent of the time. As every nursery school teacher knows, any attention, including negative attention, can reinforce negative behavior. As the boys in the study grew up, they were significantly more aggressive than the girls.

My exploration of the way violence is understood by the criminal justice system, the mental health professions, and the biological sciences taught me a great deal. The worldview of each of these disciplines helped to shape my own thinking about violence and aggression. For me, however, each of these professions left too many questions unanswered—questions about the social context in which violence occurs. The more I learned, the more I was convinced that a new multi-disciplinary approach to violence, one beginning with the perception that violence is an assault on the public health, was required to save the endangered lives of our young.

2

AN AMERICAN TRAGEDY

TEENAGER SLAIN TRYING
TO SHIELD BROTHER FROM BULLIES

Arnulfo Williams Jr. was the kind of big brother most children would love. He watched out for his two younger brothers, drove them to school in the morning and stood by them when they were threatened by other teenagers on the violent streets of South Jamaica, Queens.

Yesterday, his sense of duty cost him his life. Trying to shield his slightly built brother from three bullies at a school bus stop, Mr. Williams was shot in the chest and killed, the police said. His brother, 15-year-old Johnny, was shot twice but survived.

The 19-year-old Mr. Williams had taken special care to protect his little brother yesterday. On Wednesday, his family said, three bullies beat up Johnny in the halls of Bayside High School. With rumors circulating that the youths would attack again, Mr. Willams rose early and went with his brother to the bus stop at 168th Street and Archer Avenue . . .

The brothers drove to the bus stop in Mr. Williams' 1982 Plymouth, parked a half a block away and walked to the corner, where at least 50 students were milling around in the cold clear morning air . . .

The three young men who had attacked Johnny were there and began insulting him . . .

—James C. McKinley, Jr.
The New York Times,
Dec. 2, 1989

Good kids like Arnulfo Williams are not supposed to die in homicides. Guys who grow up in neat white houses with mothers and fathers who work hard to support their families are not supposed to wind up in body bags with their parents weeping over a tragedy that is too great and too final ever to overcome. Nor are youngsters like

Johnny Williams supposed to endure their adolescence choking on the guilt and desire for revenge that comes when you watch your brother shot down by a bullet meant for you. But in New York City, as in many American cities, a bloodbath is drowning thousands of young men who are supposed to live good, productive lives—long lives.

Maybe we should erect a black marble slab and start compiling the names of all those like Arnulfo Williams whose lives are wasted by volence. Covering the slab with names will not take long. Every day more than 60 Americans die in homicides. About 450 a week. About 1900 a month. 23,000 a year. 46,000 in two years.

In two years we would have a solemn memorial covered with names, just like the Vietnam Memorial in Washington, D.C. Mourners could come and weep. Mothers and fathers could express their anguish. Children could find a legacy, small but powerful, as they trace their fingers over the names of the fathers taken from them. Only this memorial would be different. Very soon the names would spill over, and you would need another memorial and another and another to report the names of the endless stream of fatalities.

We can start now recording the names of the young men who have died. Along with Arnulfo Williams in the section reserved for names beginning with "W" is 21-year-old Carl West. Carl has a lot in common with Arnulfo. Both were New Yorkers, shot to death trying to protect their younger brothers. Carl was killed in 1988 following a fist fight with a man who had tried to take a fake gold ring from 15-year-old Percy West. The other guy was armed with a .22 caliber weapon. He fired two bullets into Carl's head, killing him instantly.

There is 16-year-old Richard Bailey from Boston who was stabbed to death in 1988 after he bested a rival in a fist fight. Following Richard's death, his mother was so distraught that she could not admit that he was dead. For weeks she sat near the spot where he died saying her son had joined the armed services. "Why would they kill my son?" she would ask her sister. "He's a good boy. He's off in the Air Force."

There is 19-year-old Raymond Tersignis from Cooper City, Florida, who was shot to death by his best friend in his own home at a party during which both had been drinking. Sean Stemmerman says the death was an accident, but he was charged with manslaughter and will serve a four-year prison sentence. A year after his death, Peter Tersignis' parents have not removed a black wreath from their door. The Tersignis' do not forgive Stemmerman. "I want him to suffer as we have suffered," says Peter's mother. "I have to walk around and see a blood-stained floor."

There is 17-year-old Donald White, an honors student from Hollis, Queens who left the apartment he shared with his mother one Sunday morning to go to the laundromat. He never returned. An un-known assailant shot him twice in the chest and head with a 9-millimeter pistol. A neighbor says Donald was the son parents in the neighborhood held up as a role model. He was kind. He was diligent, and he was going places. Donald's father, with whom the college-bound boy was close, speaks as if his son were still alive. "Donald," says his father, "gives a true reflection on everything I ever hoped to be myself."

There is 13-year-old Thomas Viens of South Boston who was shot to death by his pal, another 13-year-old whose name was withheld because of his age. The assailant ate supper at the house of the victim the night before the murder. The victim's father, Robert Viens, spoke about his own son and all the sons who die so senselessly. "He's not a number," said the grieving father. "Anyone out there that reads this, none of them are numbers. None of them. They are just kids. . . ."

The list of homicide victims is endless. Endless names. Endless tragedies. An endless stream struck down in barrage after barrage of gun fire. Grandmothers and college students, prowling street kids and small babies in their walkers, neighbors chatting on city streets, young mothers getting ready for work. Sometimes bullets kill those at whom they are aimed; sometimes victims are annihilated by bullets meant for others.

The statistics are relentless. In the United States in 1989, the most recent year for which complete statistics are available, the Federal Bureau of Investigation (FBI) reported that 21,500 Americans died the victims of homicides. That translated into a national homicide rate of 8.7 per 100,000 population. In the first six months of 1990, the FBI reported an 8 percent increase in homicides. While FBI figures for 1990 were not yet available as this book went to print, the Senate Judiciary Committee predicted that the homicide rate for the 1990 would rise to 10.5 per 100,000 Americans, meaning that 23,220 people would die in homicides in 1990. Senator Joseph Biden chairman of the committee said the 1990 would be "the bloodiest year in American history." The dire predictions for 1990 were confirmed at the end of the year in New York City, Washington, D.C., Dallas, Phoenix, San Antonio, Memphis, Milwaukee and Boston, my home, as individual police departments revealed that record-breaking numbers of homi-cides had occurred in their cities.

While no group is exempt from the carnage, a disproportionate number of American homicide victims are young males. A major new study published in the Journal of the American Medical Association that looked at the homicide rates of young males in the United States and abroad revealed the magnitude of the American problem. In the United States in 1986, 4,223 young men between the ages of 15 and 24

HOMICIDE RATES FOR YOUNG MEN 15 TO 24
IN DEVELOPED NATIONS

Young Men at Risk

Killings per 100,000 men 15 through 24 years old for 1986 or 1987.

0.3 Austria	1.4 Greece	3.0 Finland
0.5 Japan	1.4 France	3.3 Norway
1.0 W. Germany	1.4 Switzerland	3.7 Israel
1.0 Denmark	1.4 Netherlands	4.4 New Zealand
1.0 Portugal	1.7 Belgium	5.0 Scotland
1.2 England	2.3 Sweden	**United States 21.9**
1.2 Poland	2.5 Australia	
1.3 Ireland	2.9 Canada	

SOURCE: Journal of the American Medical Association

died in homicides. That worked out to a homicide rate of 21.9 per 100,000 for young males 15 to 24.

The homicide rate for young black males in this age bracket was a staggering 85.6 per 100,000—making homicide the leading cause of death for young men of color. Young blacks die in homicides seven times more frequently than young whites, and there is reason to believe that the percentage of black victims is increasing. Still, homicide is not just a problem for African-Americans. The homicide rate for young white males in the United States was 11.2 per 100,000 in 1986—twice as high as the rate for young men in any other industrialized nation. From year to year in the United States homicides and suicides leapfrog back and forth as the second and third most common causes of death for young white males. Auto accidents, another form of violence, are the most common cause of death for these young men.

The overall homicide rate of 21.9 per 100,000 for young males in the United States was between 4 and 73 times higher than the homicide rate for young males in any other industrialized nation. In Austria, for example, the homicide rate for young males was .3. In Japan the figure was .5. In Germany, Denmark and Portugal the figure was 1.0—less than one-twentieth of the American figure. The highest number of homicides among young males outside of the United States was recorded in Scotland with a rate of 5.0 per 100,000. Interestingly, firearms were used in none of the Scottish homicides. Handguns, rifles, and other firearms were used in less than one-quarter of the young male homicides in Europe and Japan. In the United States firearms were used in three-quarters of the homicides involving young males (see the chart at the top of page 15).

The difference between the number of firearm-related homicides in the United States and in the rest of the industrialized world are startling. Handguns alone killed over 8,000 Americans young and old in 1985:

HANDGUN DEATHS IN 1985

United States	8,092
Japan	46
Switzerland	31
Israel	18
Great Britain	8
Australia	5

It is tempting to blame the dramatic disparity in handgun deaths on the easy availability of handguns in the United States. While access to handguns plays a significant role in the American homicide rate, other factors are also at work. Weapons possession alone does not drive up a nation's homicide. In Switzerland, all adult males in the country remain in the military reserves until age fifty and are required by law to bear arms. As a result, nearly every Swiss household contains firearms, and most Swiss citizens, have access to guns. Still, few Swiss use handguns or other weapons to kill each other. The same is true in Israel where large portions of the population are armed members of the military and the military reserves.

In the United States, death by homicide is distributed geographically. Using data from 1987, for young black males, Michigan had the highest death rate—232 per 100,000 population. Most of these deaths were concentrated in Detroit. California, with a homicide rate of 155, had the second highest homicide rate for blacks. The District of Columbia, with a rate of 139 homicides per 100,000 population, was third, and New York, with a rate of 137 per 100,000, was a close fourth.

For whites, California was the most dangerous state with a homicide rate for young males of 22 per 100,000 population. This figure is less than one-tenth of the Michigan rate for young blacks. Texas, New York, and Arizona, next most dangerous states for whites, had homicide rates of 21, 18, and 17 respectively.

The American homicide rate for all races and age groups was 8.4 per 100,000 population in 1988. This figure, too, is anomalous. In England, for example, according to Interpol, the international police agency, the overall homicide rate in 1988 was slightly less than 2 per 100,000 population. In Spain, Interpol pegs the homicide rate at slightly over 2 per 100,000 population. Using 1980 data from the United Nations, World Health Organization the American homicide rate was the fifth highest in the world, topped only by Guatemala, Thailand, and Puerto Rico (a commonwealth of the United States),

CHART OF TEN CITIES
WITH THE HIGHEST HOMICIDE RATE IN 1988

Homicide rate per 100,000 population

Detroit	68.6	Houston	29.2
Washington, D.C.	60.0*	Memphis	28.0
Dallas	36.8	New York City	25.7
Jacksonville	33.0	Philadelphia	24.5
Baltimore	31.2	Los Angeles	23.4

* up from 36.2 in 1987

and Brazil. These international figures, however, should be viewed with some skepticism. Many politically repressive regimes, such as the governments of South Africa and Iran, do not publish sensitive homicide data. Other governments may accidentally or purposefully falsify information relating to homicide.

Homicide within the United States is growing more frequent. From 1950 to 1980 homicide increased 300 percent for young black men. Looking at figures for the entire population, homicide has increased 100 percent since 1960. Thirty years ago, five out of every 100,000 Americans died the victim of a homicide. Even then, ours was the highest homicide rate of any of the twenty most industrialized countries. By 1980 that figure had doubled. In the mid-1980s the homicide rate declined, apparently due to a drop in the number of young males in their teens and twenties. It has since returned to its previous high.

Who are the over 20,000 Americans who die each year in homicides? They are young men. Nearly 70 percent of homicide victims are male. Nearly 60 percent are young males between the ages of 15 and 34. Each year these premature deaths result in hundreds of thousands of years of potential life lost. Homicide, which is the eleventh most common cause of death, ranks fourth when years of lost life are computed.

Class and race often determine who will die. Most homicide victims are poor. Half the victims are white and half are black, although blacks comprise only 12 percent of the population. Of the young victims 15 to 24, blacks outnumber whites by four to one.

Black males face the greatest risk, of course, but black females are also vulnerable. In fact, black females are significantly more at risk for homicide over a lifetime than white males. According to figures compiled by the Centers for Disease Control in Atlanta, a black male infant born in 1989 has one chance in 27 of dying in a homicide. A black female has one chance in 117 of dying in a homicide. A white male, on the other hand, born in 1989 faces a lifetime risk of 1 in 205. Over the course of her lifetime a white female faces one chance in 496 of being murdered:

group	lifetime risk	computed risk
white female	1/496	1
white male	1/205	2.4
black female	1/117	4.2
black male	1/27	18.4

Numerous studies point to the fact that it is poverty rather than race that makes victims vulnerable to homicide. (Half of the poor people in America are black.) Influential new scholarship by the sociologist William Julius Wilson and his colleagues at the University of Chicago has established that homicide rates soar in neighborhoods where men have no jobs or job prospects, children are raised without fathers, and social institutions are in disarray. White and black young men living in neighborhoods with these terrible problems are equally vulnerable to dying young, the victims of homicide.

Similar results establishing poverty as the root cause of violence were achieved by the noted public health researcher Brandon Centerwall when he looked at domestic homicides in Atlanta. Centerwall found that white spouses and black spouses at the same socioeconomic level murdered each other at the same rate. The poorer the family, black or white, the more likely spouses were to murder one another. Other studies indicate that high homicide rates are related to high rates of male unemployment.

The correlation between poverty and violence is well established in social science literature. The meaning of this correlation is far from obvious. Poverty means not having enough money to maintain a satisfactory standard of living—that in itself is significant and debilitating. Poverty in America often means more than the lack of funds, however. Individuals, families, whole communities can thrive when money is short, but they may not be able to overcome the secondary effects of poverty. Increasingly, being poor in America means living in a devastated, crime-ridden neighborhood. It often means growing up in a family without a father and going to schools where most students fail and most are expected to fail. It is hard to measure the exact impact of these phenomena on the homicide rate, but surely the impact is great.

HANDGUNS: THE WEAPONS OF CHOICE

THE TIME WHEN YOUNG MEN COULD FIGHT WITH THEIR fists, risking little more than their front teeth, is gone. One young man in Detroit put it this way. "There are no more fights in Detroit," he said. "It's just guns now." Law enforcement officials say hand-guns have rewritten the script. The number of handguns available has doubled in recent years. The deadly consequence of this increase is all too familiar. Each year 1,400 Americans are killed when hand-guns are fired *accidentally*. Add to this the astonishing number of intentional injuries. Americans too often resolve their trivial argu-ments by shooting one another to death. Often the victims and the perpetrators are too young to even realize that death is not a televi-sion stunt—to be done and undone in a twinkling.

That a connection exists between the proliferation of handguns and the mounting homicide rate seems hard to deny. To prove this point, researchers in the U.S. and Canada examined the homicide statistics for Seattle and Vancouver between 1980 and 1986. These two cities, located only 140 miles apart, are similar in size, rates of unem-ployment, and income. Seattle had 388 homicides during the six years, Vancouver had 204 homicides. In both cities, the number of homicides from non-handgun violence—including knife attacks—was about the same. What was different was the number of handgun deaths. In Seattle, where handguns are freely available, 139 people were shot to death. In Vancouver, with restrictive handgun laws, 25 people were shot to death during the same time period.

It is estimated that fifty million handguns are now in circulation in the United States. The key word is "circulation." Guns don't stay where their owners put them. When the Massachusetts Department of Public Health and the Boston Police Department organized a task force to combat adolescent violence, kids bragged to the members how easy guns are to obtain. They said they get guns at home—not surprising when half the households in the nation contain firearms. The kids said they take guns off the top of their parents' dresser or out of the bureau drawer. They said they borrow them, steal them, or buy them for twenty dollars.

Statistics confirm that young people in cities and suburbs through-out the nation have no trouble obtaining guns. Firearms are used in more than 80 percent of the homicides among young black males under 25 and in nearly 70 percent of the homicides involving young whites. It's noteworthy that firearms are even more common in ho-micides involving young people than in the mass of homicides. This fact says a great deal about how easily young people obtain handguns and other firearms.

Routine searches of young people yield an abundance of weap-onry that leaves police officers shaken. Many complain that young suspects carry more sophisticated arms than the police. Powerful semi-automatic weapons such as the 9-millimeter are common. Kids dealing drugs have escalated the arms race even further, introducing military style assault weapons like the AK-47 and the UZI into the urban arsenal. All these weapons are far more lethal than the small, cheap handguns called "Saturday night specials" kids and grown-ups used five or ten years ago. The bullets of these powerful weapons tear people apart. Those few who survive sustain injuries that are permanent and crippling. Urban police, with reason, fear these heavily armed young. Riding with Boston police I have seen the caution with which even veteran police officers approach young males. Every interaction is perceived as a scene of potential violence and even death.

In many of our nation's cities, carrying a weapon has come to be defined as "normal" behavior for adults and especially for kids. Guns are not just for drug dealers and gang members. "Good kids" as well as "bad" feel compelled to protect themselves with a firearm. In a survey of high school students conducted by a Boston commission to study school safety, 37 percent of boys and 17 percent of girls reported carrying a weapon to school at least once. These figures may be inflated, but the mere fact that a child would brag about carrying a weapon to school is reason enough for alarm. A national student health survey conducted in 1987 among eighth and tenth grade students in twenty states found that nearly 2 percent of the 11,000 students asked had carried a handgun to school at least once in the previous year. Extrapolating nationally from the survey results, that would add up to 338,000 armed students, a third of whom report carrying a handgun every day. Eight times as many students reported carrying knives.

In New York City, Chicago, Los Angeles, Detroit, and Washington, D.C., metal detectors are becoming standard equipment in junior and senior high schools. In New York City's Bronx County the arming of the young has gone even further. In one usually peaceful primary school, a five-year-old kindergarten student arrived one morning carrying a fully loaded .25 caliber pistol. That child did not use his weapon. Not yet. Many other children, only a few years older, have already pulled the trigger. According to the Crime Control Institute, a Washington-based research group the number of 10 to 17 year olds charged with homicide doubled between 1984 and 1989, rising to 10 per 100,000 population nationwide.

Overall, firearms are used in about two-thirds of all American homicides. Nearly half of these are caused by handguns, and another 17 percent are caused by other firearms—rifles and so forth. Firearms are not the only weapons used, however. A week after that five-year-old in the Bronx surprised his teacher with a gun, a first grader arrived at the same Bronx school carrying a butcher knife. Knives and other sharp objects cause 20 percent of homicide deaths.

Knives are not as efficient as guns. An attack with a gun is five times more likely than a stabbing to end in death. This does not mean that people who use knives as weapons are less aggressive than people who use guns. An assailant who uses a gun appears to be no more intent on killing than one who uses a knife. Guns, however, are more lethal as they do not require proximity, strength, or skill to use.

ASSAULT

WE KNOW QUITE A BIT ABOUT HOMICIDE. WE CAN SEE ITS victims and count them. The FBI gathers reliable data on homicide, especially the victims of homicide. (There is a great deal we do not know about assailants.) When we are looking at violence, however, homicide is just the tip of the iceberg.

We know relatively little about the large number of assaults that injure, but do not kill. What we do "know" tends to be an approximation, an educated guess. The National Safety Council, for example, estimates that for every one person killed with a gun, five are injured. Since 20,000 are killed in homicides each year, the Safety Council's five to one ratio would suggest that 100,000 Americans are injured in non-lethal firearm incidents annually.

A major study done in Northeastern Ohio indicates that the total ratio of all kinds of assaults to homicides is about 100 to one. Again, working back from the 20,000 or so homicides that take place each year, we can estimate that some 2 million assaults occur that are violent enough to require an emergency room visit. We know nothing of the fights that do not send the participants to the hospital. Another finding of this important Ohio study was that only one in four of the assaults that arrived at the emergency room were reported to the police. Clearly, most of the violence occurring in our society is unseen and unknown by the police.

The cost of treating these injured Americans, whatever their exact number, is astronomical. A study published in the *Journal of the American Medical Association* suggested that we spend 1 billion dollars a year treating gunshot wounds in the United States. (This statistic includes fatal and non-fatal incidents.) Of this cost, 85 percent is underwritten by taxpayers. Dr. Mark Rosenberg, Director of the Centers for Disease Control's Injury Division estimates that each year violent injuries cost our nation somewhere in the region of 60 billion dollars. Sixty billions, not millions! Within this figure is included the cost of caring for those who are injured and disabled by violence and the lost productivity of those who are injured and disabled. Of course, this statistic is a guestimate, but it gives, I think, some sense of the magnitude of the problem.

When it comes to assault, what we do not know far outweighs what we do know. There are no routinely collected national statistics detailing the number of emergency room visits and hospital stays of people injured in fights, including non-lethal knife and gun battles. We do not know who the people are who fight and injure one another. Are they friends? Relatives? Spouses? We do not know how many days of work are lost because of injuries received in fights. We do not know how many people are permanently disabled. We do not know how many young people spend their lives in wheelchairs after sustaining a spinal cord injury in a shootout.

TWO PEOPLE WHO KNOW EACH OTHER

MANY PEOPLE WHO READ NEWSPAPERS AND WATCH television presume that they know all about the murder of one American by another. They presume that most homicides occur during the commission of a crime—a robbery, a rape, a drug deal. They presume "victim" and "assailant" are strangers, separated by the vast chasm that separates good from evil. And they presume that the slain and the slayer often come from different races.

All of these presumptions are incorrect. While these kinds of homicides certainly do occur, they do not predominate. Less than 1 in 6 (16 percent of all homicides) occurs during the commission of another crime. Half the time people kill people they know, either family members (16 percent) or friends and acquaintances (33 percent). Victim and assailant are of the same race 90 percent of the time.

As a physician and public health official, my main concern is reducing the incidence of homicide and violence in our society. I believe the most effective way to do this is by focusing on the homicides— half of the total—that occur between acquaintances, not just the small percentage that occur during the commission of another felony. I say this, knowing that the distinctions between what is criminal and what is not are not always clear. Is a 13-year-old with a single vial of crack in his jeans a criminal? If he earns fifty dollars as a drug dealer's lookout, what then? When the dealer gives him a gun to carry—does he then become a criminal? The police and the courts need to make these distinctions, but I do not. I am undertaking to propose solutions for reducing the calamitous incidence of violence in our society.

The homicides I believe to be the most preventable are the "typical" ones, the ones that follow a pattern every cop on the beat and emergency room doctor can recite by heart. These typical homicides occur so frequently they seem pre-ordained:

> Two people know each other. They drink and then argue. At least one person is armed. Violence flashes. In the aftermath, one person is dead and the life of the other is destroyed.

Police call one participant in a fight like this the victim and the other the criminal aggressor, but these words are inaccurate. In fact, except for the outcome, victim and aggressor are often indistinguishable. The study of homicide and violence has pinpointed dozens of traits the victim and aggressor in a homicide may share with one another.

Both are likely to be young and male.

Both are likely to be of the same race.

Both are likely to be poor.

Both are likely to have been exposed to violence in the past—to have seen violence inflicted, often on their mother or siblings, or to have been the victim of violence themselves.

Both may be depressed, although very few persons who commit homicide are truly mentally unbalanced.

Both may use or abuse alcohol.

Both may use drugs.

Both are likely to see themselves as persons under attack, threatened, needing protection. As a result, each is likely to describe his weapon-carrying behavior in defensive terms. The bad guys in the project, on the street, or at school are "packing something" (a handgun) and he, too, needs "something" as a form of protection.

I might add that rarely have I heard of an adolescent who says he is carrying a gun for a reason other than self-protection. No doubt this statement is self-serving. Still, it illuminates the psychological reality of many of the kids who are killing each other. Inside, kids carrying guns do not feel strong. They feel weak and vulnerable. The gun they carry is their compensation.

TEACHING OUR KIDS TO KILL

"VICTIM" AND "AGGRESSOR" ARE OFTEN LIKELY TO SHARE another profoundly important trait. Each is likely to believe that fighting is his only choice. Chances are he learned this lesson at home. Almost without exception, adolescents and young adults who grow up to be violent learn to lash out aggressively when young, often in their families. Parents teach their children to be violent by example and by exhortation. Parents are violent with each other and with their children. They teach their children to resolve their disputes with other children by using brute force. One study of middle-class sons who became delinquent found that their parents had openly encouraged them to behave violently. These parents routinely threatened to punish their sons for not fighting; they advised them how to fight; they labelled not fighting as babyish and unmasculine; and they allowed fights to continue long after other parents would have intervened.

As a physician I have been amazed by what parents teach their children about fighting. The mother of a teenage girl suspended from school after a fist fight applauded her child's action. "Well, you wouldn't let someone call you names, would you?" she asked me. Even the most peaceful parents often feel compelled to goad their sons into aggressive behavior, fearing that a non-aggressive male must be a "wimp." "Go out there and fight. Go out there and teach that so and so a lesson." "My parents will beat me unless I beat him," is the way one young boy explained his parents' fighting philosophy to me.

The result of parental indoctrination may be the creation of children who do not know how to cope with angry feelings in ways that are not violent. Counting to ten; walking away from an argument; using words instead of punches and making a joke to cut the tension are all helpful devices unavailable to untaught young people. Instead, their anger may all too quickly become violent aggression, particularly if in the past they themselves have been the object of someone else's rage. Children are not to blame for their inability to handle anger in non-lethal ways. We as parents, as teachers, as clergy, as health care providers have failed to teach them this most basic survival skill.

TEENS AND VIOLENCE

A CERTAIN ATTRACTION TO VIOLENCE IS PROBABLY A normal adolescent trait, from a developmental viewpoint. The insecurity adolescents feel—their need to take risks; their abundant energy; their sense of invincibility—propel them toward behavior adults might label foolhardy. Teaching violence prevention to poor urban tenth graders in Boston brought this lesson home to me. In an informal classroom survey, nearly three-quarters of the students—72 percent of those present—told me that a person ought to fight if challenged to fight. No matter what the provocation, or how great they sensed the danger to be, they could imagine no way out once a rival had dared them to fight.

The students in this class were knowledgeable about the violence surrounding them in Boston. They knew better than I about the rising death toll on the streets. They knew that their peers were armed and that every dispute was only a trigger squeeze away from death. Repeatedly during the ten-session courses I taught, the students expressed grave fears about their own safety. They wanted help. They wanted their world to be different, less dangerous, less frightening. They wanted to learn tactics for avoiding fights. Still, despite their fears and their eagerness to learn, they had trouble going against the unwritten rules that say you must fight to protect your mother's honor, your girlfriend's fidelity, your reputation. They had no faith that fighting could be prevented, and they were fearful of looking cowardly in the eyes of their peers.

I think we need to recognize how fatalistic many teenagers, especially inner city teens, feel about violence. Firearms, physical force, injury, and death are intimately known to these kids. Many poor, black, inner city kids are living surrounded by an amount of violence that even those of us who are experts in "intentional injury" find astounding. What you and I read about in the headlines, hundreds of thousands of ordinary kids are living every day, often without the protection or guidance of any adult. Researchers at the University of Maryland discovered just how violence-plagued the everyday world of many African-American youngsters is when they talked about victimization to 168 teens at a health clinic. Of the health clinic patients, 24 percent had witnessed a murder, 72 percent knew someone who had been shot. On average, these young people had been victimized one and a half times by some sort of violence. Each had witnessed five serious crimes taking place. One out of five had had their lives threatened. One in eleven of the survey participants had been raped. (Because of the kind of care being offered at the Baltimore clinic, 80 percent of those who took part in this survey were female.)

GANGS AND DRUGS

MANY OF US PREFER TO BLAME GANGS AND DRUGS FOR ALL the violence that kill and injure our young people. It's comforting to think that only "bad" kids resort to violence, that only evil drug dealers and vicious gangsters are responsible for the slaughter in our streets. Unfortunately this is not true. In Milwaukee, drug-related homicides declined in the first six months of 1990; still, homicides increased by 16 percent. Gangs and drugs are serious and terrible social problems, but outside of a few cities they are not the sole or even the major causes of homicide among young males. In most parts of the country, gang-activity and gang-related homicides are relatively uncommon. The FBI estimated that homicides by youth gang members in 1988 constituted less than 2 percent of homicides.

In 1987, again according to the FBI, approximately 6 percent of homicides were related to the use or the sale of drugs. In some cities, of course, the impact of drug dealing and use is catastrophic. In Washington, D.C., Houston, Miami, Philadelphia, and New York—all cities that have seen a substantial increase in their homicide statistics—police attribute much of the rising number of deaths to drugs. In Washington, D.C., according to data gathered by the medical examiner, the bodies of 80 percent of homicide victims contained residues of cocaine. In New York City where homicides increased almost 18 percent between 1987 and 1988, police estimate that drugs played a part in 40 percent of all homicides. These figures, it should be noted, include very different kinds of deaths—from the premeditated murder of one drug dealer by another to the impulsive murder of one 15-year-old by another during an argument after using crack.

Gang- and drug-related homicides have had a psychological impact on the nation beyond their numbers. Daily reports of viciousness by cold blooded young killers have made each and every one of us feel endangered, even when we live far from the scenes of these crimes. The violence from a gang-style shootout in which innocent bystanders die is not contained within one neighborhood, or even within one city. Violence like this bleeds into the rest of society, destroying the feeling of trust and safety that holds society together. Moreover, highly publicized cases of brutality tend to lower the threshold of violence in those most susceptible to committing violence. The drug dealer, for example, who kills his rival with cold impunity does more than consolidate his market. He also provides a dangerous example to others, primarily adolescents, who are especially susceptible to deviant role models.

I would add, however, that we make a serious mistake if we try to separate gang and drug violence from the overall violent context of American life. It is my view, one that is supported by a growing number of police officials in New York City, Washington, D.C. and elsewhere, that gang and drug violence are manifestations not causes of our nation's terrible problem with violence. Gang and drug dealers are not vastly different from many other young Americans when they resolve their disputes violently. You might say they are like other Americans—only more so. They have learned the violence-embracing lessons taught in many of our homes and glorified in our mass media only too well.

LIVING ON THESE MEAN STREETS

MEDIA REPORTS FOCUS ON THE VIOLENCE COMMITTED BY kids who appear to be beyond feeling. We read about gang members on rooftops who shoot aimlessly at strangers to assert their dominance on this corner, in that project. We read about "mushrooms," the innocent bystanders to gang and drug violence who are shot down without thought or care. The acts these people commit are incomprehensible to us. Occasionally, however, we read something that reveals to us the desperation out of which many violent acts grow:

> You'd probably pick Napier Traylor as a victim, not a perpetrator. And you'd be right. According to his attorney, the 16-year-old was the victim of bullying that went on for many months. A gang of kids from his new school in Boston's Roslindale section harassed Napier, following him to and from school each day, threatening to beat him up, calling his house so often that his mother had the telephone number changed.
>
> In February 1988, the gang chased Napier home and again threatened to beat him. Napier and his mother went to the Boston Police Department and complained. The Boston police referred them to the school police. Later that same day the gang members attacked Napier near his house. His mother, standing on the porch, threw a stick to her son, exhorting him to fight.
>
> Napier took a knife out of his gym bag. Prosecutors say he stabbed 15-year-old Jeffrey Buttler in the heart and fled. Napier, who has been charged with manslaughter, says Buttler's death was accidental.
>
> Napier's lawyer says her client is a kid who had run out of options: "The system wasn't available to him," the lawyer told a reporter. "The system didn't protect him."*

Napier's lawyer is surely correct when she says "the system" didn't protect her client. In a world full of teachers, principals, clergy, city police, and school police, no one was able or willing to help Napier Traylor find a non-violent way out of his predicament. No one offered to help. No adults suggested that his argument with his tormenters be submitted for mediation, even though this widely publicized technique for setting disputes has been used very successfully in other violence-plagued communities. Bullies tormented him. Professionals failed him. His mother urged him to fight. The streets offered him a weapon. Now a young boy is dead and another boy's life is in shambles. Those of us who view violence from the perspective of public health believe that this tragedy could and should have been prevented. We are saddened and we are enraged that so much meaningless violence is polluting the life of our cities and destroying the lives of our young.

THE PUBLIC HEALTH APPROACH

AS A PUBLIC HEALTH EDUCATOR, AS THE FORMER PUBLIC health commissioner of Massachusetts, as a physician, as a parent, as

* As reported by Sally Jacobs in the *Boston Sunday Globe*, February 21, 1988.

a black American, and as an inner city resident, I have attended scores of community meetings called to discuss the epidemic of homicide in our cities. At these meetings, distraught and angry citizens call out for more police on patrol, for more arrests, for more judges to hear cases, for more jail cells to house convicted criminals, for more teenagers in jail. I share my neighbors' concerns. I share their fear; the fear we all feel for our children. However, I am convinced that more police will not solve the problem of homicide in America. More police in patrol cars, more street lights, stiffer sentences, and new prisons will not, I believe, prevent two young people from settling their differences with a firearm.

Many of my colleagues in public health and many police officials around the nation have come to believe that in order to reduce violence we must design imaginative new strategies; strategies that will augment, not replace police work. As Boston's Police Commissioner Francis M. Roache, a former patrolman, says often, violence is bigger than the police. What he means is this: The impulse to hurt others cannot be controlled by a police officer called to the scene after a crime has been committed. This same conviction was expressed most forcibly by the premier police department in the United States, the FBI, in a 1981 report on homicide. "Criminal homicide is primarily a societal problem over which law enforcement has little or no control."

As the FBI recognizes, homicide most often is caused by failed human relationships—tragic breaches between people who know one another, sometimes intimately, sometimes not, who cannot surmount their differences. The arguments that lead to homicide can be as profound and fundamental as the decades-long struggle of a husband to control and dominate his wife, or as transitory as an argument over what television channel to watch. Whatever the cause, conflict coupled with the inability to control anger leads to catastrophe.

Lee Brown, the police commissioner of New York City, echoed the FBI view when in early 1990 he commented on the record number of homicides (1,905) that occurred in his city in 1989. Although many of these homicides involved drug use or drug dealing, Commissioner Brown did not call for a stepped up "war on drugs." Instead, he called for a whole new approach to violence and especially to homicide. Commissioner Brown called upon our schools to educate students to solve disputes without violence. He called on our churches to instill moral values. He called on the medical profession to study possible physiological and psychological causes of violence. The Commissioner is a convert to the growing movement to define homicide as a public health problem.

A decade ago the Surgeon General of the United States placed violence on his short list of major American health problems. Thousands of deaths and millions of injuries were the factors that impelled him to classify violence as a health problem. The Surgeon General's move gave credence, support, and legitimacy to the fledgling efforts of a small band of physicians and public health experts who were redefining violence as a problem that needs to be studied and addressed as a gross assault on the public health.

When most people think about public health, they think of inoculations to prevent polio, small pox, and diphtheria. They think of hygienic practices to prevent tuberculosis and typhoid. It's difficult for many to fit the prevention of violence into what they know about this field. It is true that preventing violence (and other destructive behaviors) does indeed represent an expansion of the public health agenda.

My own view is a pragmatic one. To me a problem that destroys health by causing so much injury and death is a health problem. Like most physicians, I am practical by nature. What interests me is action—doing something, saving lives. I am drawn to the public health approach because it has worked in the past. Over time, employing an array of interventions, the public health approach can change people's attitudes, and in the long run, their destructive behavior. We have done this with cigarettes. Following a massive twenty-year public health campaign the incidence of smoking has decreased by 30 percent. We have done this with drunk driving. Americans no longer believe it is all right to drive when intoxicated or to allow a friend to drive home when intoxicated. We have done this with exercise and diet, convincing millions of Americans to adopt more healthful lifestyles in order to reduce their risk of heart disease and stroke. I believe that we can do the same thing for violence.

I am convinced we can change public attitudes toward violence and that we can change violent behavior. What is required is a broad array of strategies; strategies that teach new ways of coping with anger and aggressive feelings. I believe we can and we must mobilize schools, the media, industry, government, churches, community organizations, and every organized unit within our society to deliver the message that anger can be managed and aggressive impulses controlled. We must also redefine the physician's role and the role of the emergency room. We need to use the health care system to create an early warning network that will identify young people at risk for violence and offer them treatment before they become victims or perpetrators. Until we begin to teach physicians' and emergency room patients that they have choices besides "finding the guy who did this to me and doing worse to him," I fear our homicide rate will not decline.

3

TEACHING OUR KIDS TO KILL

NOW AT A THEATER NEAR YOU:
A SKYROCKETING BODY COUNT

In "Die Hard 2" the new film that is less a sequel to than a remake of the 1988 hit "Die Hard," Bruce Willis uses an icicle to stab a man in the brain via the eye socket. Later, another unfortunate man is sucked into a 747's jet engine and comes out the other end looking like borscht.

"Robocop 2" continues the adventures of the half-man, half-machine Detroit police officer introduced in "Robocop." Among other things featured in Robocop's newest campaign for law and order are a 12-year-old boy who is a drug lord, a new drug-of-choice called nuke (self-administered through a needle gun held against the neck) and dozens of dazzling deaths. . . .

Among the on-screen superdeaths in "Total Recall" are those of several people who explode when tossed out into the vacuum that is the natural environment of Mars. The death of a supervillain suits his station in the plot. At the climactic moment in his fight with Mr. Schwarzenegger, on the open platform of a moving elevator, this man is sideswiped by an obstruction. He falls to his death while Mr. Schwarzenegger is left holding the man's severed arms. . . .

—Vincent Canby,
The New York Times,
July 16, 1990

A KALEIDOSCOPE OF VIOLENCE

JUST AS OUR NATION HAS MORE VIOLENT CRIME THAN ANY other industrialized nation, so, too, is our popular culture more violent than that of other countries. Our movies, our broadcast talk, our television drama, our children's T.V., our toys, our sports, our music for adolescents, our print and broadcast news are awash in violent words and violent pictures. In the media world, brutality is portrayed as ordinary and amusing.

Often we do not even notice. We are inured to the violence in our mass media. We take it for granted. When we go to the movies to see recent hits like *Total Recall, Robocop, Another 48 Hours, Die Hard II*, also known as *Die Harder*, we do not even notice that a single weirdly invincible hero is responsible for hundreds of deaths. The critic Vincent Canby counted 74 dead in *Total Recall*, 81 dead in *Robocop 2*, 106 dead in *Rambo III*, and 264 dead in *Die Hard II*. All these deaths interfere with the director's ability to tell his story, but then, no one goes to these movies to watch a well-crafted story unfold. They go to see blood and gore. Each time they go, they have learned to expect the blood to be bloodier and the gore gorier.

Janet Maslin, another *New York Times* critic, described the creative process of the producers and directors who make these movies. They spend their time, she wrote, "thinking up ever more facile and cynical excuses for mayhem, then devoting vast and distracting amounts of technological expertise to the problem of making that mayhem look good." It does look "good," or at least realistic. All that is missing is the element associated with violence that humanizes its portrayal— emotion.

When the producers of these "adventure" movies come up with a really imaginative way to hurt people, the audience cheers and applauds. They stomp and whistle when Bruce Willis uses that icicle to mash the brains of an enemy and when another foe is turned into technicolor hamburger. Arguably the favorite scene in all these films occurred in *Total Recall* when the stolid Arnold Schwarzenegger shoots his gorgeous blond wife in the head. This is the same woman to whom the audience saw him make love earlier in the movie. After Schwarzenegger kills his mate, he turns to her corpse and says, to the audience's delight, "I guess you can consider this a divorce."

In all these movies, bystanders, subway riders, ordinary people get caught in shootouts, crossfires, explosions, and other violent incidents. The action moves on quickly. We're not supposed to even think about the dead and dying left behind. By ignoring "details" like this, the filmmakers exhibit a morality that is more or less equivalent to that of young gang members in Los Angeles who ignore the "mushrooms" they injure and kill in their drive-by shootings.

Perhaps we are meant to believe that the hero's cause is so just and right that no price is too high to pay for his victory. Americans used to reject the idea that the ends justify the means, but apparently, they do not anymore. At least not in the movies. In the movies, violence is limitless, and it is fun. In the same spirit as President

Reagan when he urged the Libyans to "make my day," by attacking, the violent hero cannot wait for the opportunity to, in the words of our most recent President Bush, "kick ass."

Why shouldn't the movie hero enjoy using violence? Why not, indeed, when only bad guys, never heroes, get hurt. You won't see Bruce Willis or Arnold Schwarzenegger shot through the spine, a quadriplegic, a paraplegic, a young man without sexual function, a young man with a permanent breathing tube who can only whisper his words from a hospital bed where he will pass the rest of his life. Who, then, if not the mass media, will tell our young that these are the true consequences of violence?

Perhaps I ought to say, I do not oppose the showing of all violence on television or in the movies—what I oppose is gratuitous violence. Sometimes showing violence is needed to tell a story. This struck me when I saw the movie, *Glory* which is about the 54th Massachusetts Infantry, the first "Negro" regiment to fight in the Civil War. The bravery of this doomed regiment, led by Colonel Robert Gould Shaw, changed the attitude of the North towards African-American fighting men and led to the more equal treatment of thousands of black soldiers in the Union army. *Glory* is a very violent movie that does not exploit its audience's hunger for gore. The violence is realistic and exists within an emotional context. We do not watch abstract bodies absorb the blows of war, we watch people whom we have grown to understand and admire suffer injury and death. This is not, I might say, the kind of violence my 11-year-old son likes seeing. Perhaps, however, it is the kind of violence he ought to see.

To understand how pervasive and surreal the violence in our mass media has become, we need to step back and look at our own culture as if we were outsiders:

—A couple of seasons back *People* magazine featured a picture of Cher on its cover. The cover copy noted that Cher was a big star with a new hit movie and a new young boyfriend. The final lines of copy proclaimed that Cher is tough enough to stand up for herself under any circumstances. "Mess with me and I'll kill you," the magazine quoted her as saying, right on its cover.

—One of the top novelty toys of a recent Christmas season was a small black box called the Revenger. This crowd pleaser provides drivers with a weapon for symbolically annihilating other motorists. Angered by the guy in the next car, a motorist, with the push of a button, can zap him with a flash of light and the sound of a machine gun, a grenade launcher, or a death ray.

—Harvard School of Education psychologist Ron Slaby says that among many young people, watching the documentary like *Faces of Death* has become a party game. The winner is the last to become nauseous. This gruesome, plotless movie shows scene after scene of real life deaths—dead and bloody animal carcasses, dead, mutilated people. Slaby and other experts say repeated doses to these grossly explicit movies are like repeated visits to a slaughter house. After a while the natural human aversion to cruelty and gore is swept away.

—You can rent or buy an 88-minute videocassette, "The Confessions of Bernhard Goetz," at your neighborhood video store. This tape shows Goetz's tortured, real life performance as he confessed to New Hampshire police that he was the assailant who had shot and seriously injured four young black men in a New York City subway. Posters advertising this videocassette were posted in New York City subway cars and stations.

—The cameras kept rolling during a taping of "Geraldo," a talk show hosted by Geraldo Rivera, when the host and his guests began to fight. Later T.V.'s millions were able to watch three grown men smash and hammer away at one another. Rivera, his nose broken, was proud of his performance. "At least I got a couple of real good shots in," he said afterward.

—There was a notorious tape broadcast on the Fox network of convicted murderer Robert Chambers cavorting at a party with several female friends. Chambers, who was found guilty of strangling an 18-year-old woman to death during a sexual encounter in New York City's Central Park, is shown on the tape knocking the head off a small doll and saying, "Oops, I think I killed it."

Television, our most popular form of entertainment, is arguably the most violent. The old-time formula in which one murder could busy two detectives for an hour has yielded to a high volume/high tech form of violence with kinky overtones. A quiet evening at home presents an ordinary viewer with a cornucopia of political, criminal, and psychopathological deviance. Some of the violent acts shown on television are so arcane that they were once familiar only to hardened big city cops. Prostitution—child and adult, heterosexual and homosexual. Child molestation and kidnapping. Sadomasochism. Fetishism. Devil-worship. Neo-nazi extremism. Rape. All these mingle with the more conventional styles of violence such as international terrorism, drug dealing, and gang warfare to make up a "normal" weeknight fare in an average American home.

Throughout our mass media, taboos about what can be said and what can be shown are collapsing. The NBC miniseries *Favorite Son*, broadcast in October, 1988 showed sadomasochistic bondage, near-explicit masturbation, and a dog lapping the blood of a murder victim. Nor are shocking sights the exclusive domain of "entertainment" divisions. Television newscasters are every bit as disturbing as an episode of *Night Caller*, only these are broadcast at 6:00 P.M. when the smallest children are watching. Television journalists are no longer content to show bodybags following plane crashes and other disasters. Now the contents of those bags must be displayed. When in January, 1990 an Avianca jetliner en route to New York from Colombia crashed in Cove Neck, Long Island, all three television networks broadcast rescue efforts live. There was no effort made to shield viewers from the grisly sight of burned and dismembered bodies. The networks say no one complained about the coverage.

Nor were television viewers and newspaper readers protected from the blood-splattered picture of a young pregnant Bostonian who had been shot in the head in the most widely publicized crime story of 1989. The victim was Carol Stuart. Her husband, Charles Stuart, was shot in the stomach. He told police that a black male had forced his way into the couple's car and shot them both during a robbery. For weeks the story of Carol Stuart's murder was headline news all over the country. The coverage shared a single theme. Story after story told the white, middle-class that it was now threatened by the violence consuming the black community. The angle turned out to be a gross distortion. Carol Stuart was not killed by a black male. She was killed, as the vast majority of white female homicide victims are, by her white husband. In December, Charles Stuart committed suicide after his brother implicated him in his wife's murder. His stomach wound, police now believe, was self-inflicted.

My friend Glen Pierce Director of Northeastern University's Center of Applied Social Research, was struck by the publicity surrounding the Stuart case. He wondered why the press paid so much attention to this one case when so many young blacks in Massachusetts are dying. He did some fairly simple math and discovered that the likelihood of a white woman in Massachusetts being shot to death by a black man she did not know is one in four million. That's the same risk a white woman runs of being hit by lightning. Pierce thought it odd that journalists, who must know that almost all homicides in this state are intra-racial, reported the Stuart case as they did. He believes that consciously or unconsciously, reporters used the deaths of Carol Stuart and her unborn child to increase ratings and boost sales. He is profoundly concerned about the long-term, political impact of this kind of journalism. He believes that by misrepresenting the crime problem, reporters are frightening the electorate and driving them to the right. It is his view that white voters, erroneously believing their own safety to be threatened, are growing more conservative and punitive in their politics. Their fear blinds them to the terrible fact that it is poor communities and poor minority citizens who are most often the victims of crime.

As in the Stuart case, much of the violence we see in the mass media merges sex and violence. Television dramas depicting lurid crimes committed against children and young women are as common as cowboy stories were a few decades ago. Slow motion reenactments of real life crimes of passion are the speciality of a whole new genre of television programs that some refer to as "tabloid television" or "trash T.V." *A Current Affair, America's Most Wanted, Unsolved Mysteries*—all of these programs recreate in gory detail real life crimes, often of a sexual nature. It was on one of these programs, Fox's *A Current Affair*, that the home movie of Robert Chambers' playing with his girlfriends was broadcast. These series, which blithely merge reality and fantasy, play to the inability of viewers, especially young viewers, to discriminate between what is true and what is untrue.

Even violence that has nothing to do with sex tends to be sexualized on film and videotape. Directors use the tricks of their trade to make violence look glamorous and sexy. Hot music, fast cuts, lots of action, energy and movement titillate and seduce the viewer. Camera effects alter the emotional content of what is being shown. Scenes depicting horrifying events appear to be dramatic and thrilling. The camera after all has no moral point of view. The camera loves action, especially violent action, because that is what it captures most successfully.

The mass media lie about the physical and the emotional realities of violence. As a graduate of the emergency room I know better than most that in real life, mashed and mangled bodies are not attractive. Neither is the emotional pain that violence causes. The remorse of those who resort to violence, even justifiably; the rage and humiliation of victims; the life-destroying impact of permanent injury; the endless grief of family members; the smashed psyches of children who lose parents—these crucial elements of the story are usually left untold on television and in the movies. In real life, the impact of a moment of violence reverberates through time. Years later, parents are still mourning the loss of a child, children are still mourning the loss of a parent, a police officer may still feel anguish that he was required to use deadly force, even to save his own life. On film or videotape violence begins and ends in a moment. "Bang bang, you're dead." Then the death is over. This sense of action-without-consequences replicates and reinforces the dangerous "magical" way many children think. Do the 12- and 14-year-olds who are shooting each other to death in Los Angeles, Chicago, Washington, D.C. really understand that death is permanent, unalterable, final, tragic? Television certainly is not telling them so.

Particularly disturbing to me is the violent material created exclusively for children. The 1990 hit movie for children, *Teenage Mutant Ninja Turtles*, tells tiny viewers that the world is brutal and dangerous. The movie is set in New York City where an unprecedented crime wave is terrorizing the populace. The first scene shows a young woman being surrounded by a gang of teenage street toughs who are trying to rob her. One of the muggers jumps up and knocks out the street light shining down on the crime scene. Something terrible is about to happen. The victim of the assault is not a puppet or animated figure, she is a person, which makes the violence against her especially frightening. Eventually, the heroine is rescued by the four human-sized turtles named in the movie's title. Much of the rest of the film is a sort of pint-sized martial arts epic in which numerous fight sequences are intercut with sequences of the young Ninja warriors learning the moral lessons taught by their master, Splinter. This movie is not without its charms and positive qualities. The turtles are required to learn discipline and self-control. One angry and rebellious boy learns kindness and compassion from the Ninja master. Still, I cannot help wondering why it is that our youngest children—many still toddlers—are thought to be an appropriate market for a film in which fighting and killing is every bit as common as in *Total Recall*.

Teenage Mutant Ninja Turtles was a television show before it was a movie. The Ninja Turtle T.V. series is the most recent of the "superhero" programs that dominated children's T.V. in the 1980s. The "superhero" programs, including Ninja Turtles, were created to sell toys. For programs such as Rambo, Transformers, G.I. Joe, Ghostbusters, She-Ra—the toys came first, although not always before movies of the same name. These programs were not created by storytellers; they were created by marketing specialists.

Children use the numerous superhero toys they convince their parents to buy for them to enact the good-guy-versus-bad-guy dramas they see on T.V. What's most notable about these episodes is that they never go anywhere. The hero confronts the same war-loving villain week after week. No one ever learns his lesson, or changes, or grows or develops, or even dies. Instead what children watch is a mindless repetition of an archetypal, heavily technological stand-off between "good guys" and "the forces of evil." These same elements are showing up in children's play say educator and authors Nancy Carlsson-Paige and Diane Levin in their book *The War Play Dilemma*. Many pre-school and kindergarten teachers complained to these authors about the autistic-like repetitiveness and lack of imagination they see on the playground from children immersed in these and other violent television programs. Too much play with war toys seems to denude children's imaginations. Some kids get stuck in a groove shooting down enemies who pop right up again and cannot recover the spontaneity of free-form play.

Some researchers at Harvard University have looked very carefully at the content of the superhero programs. These cartoons, says psychologist Petra Hesse, teach children that the world is a threatening place. On children's television, enemies look like animals, they wear frightening masks and they speak with foreign accents. These characters are so mean that they even mistreat their own friends. No compromise or negotiation is possible with enemies like this, enemies who proclaim regularly that they love war and destruction. The only response possible to a television enemy is total war. The traits of the enemy in the superhero programs are the same inhuman traits as the bad guys in violent adult movies like *Total Recall* and *Robocop* possess.

Petra Hesse and her colleagues believe that superhero programs teach our kids an outdated political ideology of hate and fear in which people different from ourselves come across as barely human, or not human at all. Developmentally this plays into the polarized, all-black-and-white-and-no-gray way many young children look at the world. Instead of helping them move toward a more forgiving and complex view of the world, superhero television encourages children to hold onto a destructive ethnocentrism, one that is completely unreconcilable with the realities of the post-cold war age. Dr. Hesse and her colleague, Dr. John Mack, speak about the necessity of creating new stories to reflect our new world; stories, for example, in which the hero would "fight" to save the earth from devastation instead of creating the earth's devastation by fighting.

HEAVY METAL AND RAP

CONDEMNING CHILDREN'S TELEVISION IS EASY. IT IS EASY to be angry at the adults who are making huge profits by teaching our children that war is fun. Condemning the popular music business that is at least partially driven by adolescent and young-adult talent is more difficult. Whatever we think of the violence in music marketed to teenagers, we cannot deny that to some extent at least, it represents the way young performers see the world. (To what degree adults manipulate the content of popular music to increase profits is impossible to know.)

Heavy metal is a kind of loud, driving rock and roll made most often by young white males. The subjects of heavy metal songs are sex, violence, death, satan, and alienation. A kind of thumb-your-nose nihilism pervades this music. Heavy metal exploits the feelings of isolation and despair that are common among adolescents. Lyrics tend to proclaim that life is nasty and brutish, violence and death are clean and pure. Many of the songs are satirical, although as adults we may find little comfort knowing that a song about raping your mother is "only a joke."

The creators of heavy metal and rap are the world's first television generation, the first generation nurtured on television's steady diet of fictional and nonfictional mayhem. One critic has suggested that what these performers do in their music is feed back the violence consumed by them during years and years before the "tube." Be that as it may, adults, and perhaps young people as well, are at a loss to know what to think when they hear the popular heavy metal group Guns N'Roses proclaiming in song that they "used to love her," but that they had to kill her because she complained a lot. The violence in this song is utterly pointless—lacking reason, lacking passion, even lacking energy. It is violence—murder—as the last possible diversion of the bored and naughty.

Rap is primarily the music of young, black, urban males. This music is all rhythm and repetition. Melody is gone. Sex, violence, and black pride—a particularly assertive male style of black pride—are the most common subjects of rap. As in heavy metal, women are sex objects and the objects of rage:

Now back on the street and
my records are clean
I creeped on my bitch with my UZI machine
went to the house and kicked
down the door
Unloaded like hell, cold
smoked the ho'.

"Eazy Duz It," by Eazy E

The sexism in this music is truly alarming, as is the self-congratulatory quality of the violence. In rap song after rap song, young black men brag about owning guns, using guns and killing:

Here's a murder rap to keep ya dancin'
With a crime record like Charles Manson
AK-47 is the tool
Don't make me act a motherf—in fool

"Straight Outta Compton," by N.W.A.

Back up dancers for another group, Public Enemy, carry plastic UZIs on stage.

Police are often the target of rapper's violent fantasies. The most infamous violent rap song is "F— tha Police" by the California group N.W.A. (Niggers With Attitude). This song about killing police officers so enraged the FBI that higher-ups took the unusual step of writing a critical letter about the song to the group and its record company. Some of its inflammatory lyrics threaten police with a black armaggedon:

Ice Cube will swarm
on any M—F—er in a blue uniform
A young nigger on the warpath
And when I finish it's gonna be a blood-bath

Not all rap songs or rap artists advocate violence against police officers or anyone else. There is, in fact, a Stop The Violence movement among rap artists and a Stop the Violence rap song, the profits of which have been donated to the Urban League. Still, it's impossible to deny that celebrating violence is a central theme in rap music. Rap artists defend their music, saying that they do not originate the violence in their communities. Eazy-E calls himself and his fellow rappers "underground reporters . . . telling it like it is."

Nelson George, the rock critic who helped start the Stop the Violence movement in rap, agrees with Eazy-E's assessment. He says rap records catalogue pop culture and reflect the rebel attitudes of young black males. These songs are powerful, he says, because they "slap you in the face" with the disturbing events taking place in black communities. Moreover, he says, the violence in rap music reflects the attitudes of the audience, the attitudes of everyday black people.

I am very disturbed by the violent content in rap music. Urging young black males to challenge the authority of the police in their communities is, to my way of thinking, a way of encouraging black suicide. I do not agree with those who call for the censoring of this music, however. For philosophical and for practical reasons, I do not believe in censorship. Nor do I entirely agree with Nelson George when he says that rappers represent what ordinary black people think. No doubt many ordinary blacks, especially ones who are young and male, advocate violence, but many more do not.

In response to the pro-violence message that rap proclaims, we in the black community who oppose violence need to provide countermessages. We need to support the artistic and musical efforts of those who turn away from violence, and we need to convince record companies who have grown rich on rap music that they have a responsibility to develop a broad spectrum of black talent with varying points of view. I would take this one step further. I think the record companies have a responsibility to return some of the profits they have earned to black communities to support a diversity of black cultural and artistic programs, especially those aimed at children. We cannot silence the voices that we do not like hearing. We can, however, do everything in our power to make certain that other voices are heard.

THE CHILDREN ARE WATCHING

Paul Bracy administers the violence prevention effort at the Massachusetts Department of Health. Paul, who is black, recalls a scene from his school years in Boston, more than twenty years ago. He had gone to a basketball game at a stadium in a white, working class neighborhood. Racial tensions were high back then in Boston. Not yet committed to non-violence, Paul did what many teens do today. He carried a weapon—a black jack, which is a kind of small, easily concealed club.

As the crowd surged out after the game, Paul saw a young white man maybe ten feet away brandishing a knife. For a moment the two eyed each other. Menace glinted between them. Then the moment passed. The crowd swept both young men along. Nothing happened.

Today such an incident might have deadly consequences. Today, the slender thread of restraint that contained Paul and his nameless adversary might snap apart.

Twenty years ago, why did these two flee instead of fighting? Why did they walk away unharmed when so many young men today cannot resist the impulse to strike out? What narrow margin differentiates a look or a threat from a bloody confrontation?

Many experts say that heavy viewing of violence-saturated television may account for this difference. The youth of Paul's generation were not reared on T.V. violence. Paul's family did not even own a television when he was young. For young people today, exposure to violence on television begins at the age of two or three—years before a child can begin to discriminate fantasy from reality and continues through adolescence.

Researchers have established that years of ingesting television's violent repast may promote aggression. And no wonder! Look what television teaches: *Good guys use violence as a first resort. Any amount of killing is all right, so long as one's cause is just. Violence is a hero's way to solve problems.* In a world permeated with violence, these dangerous lessons learned during a decade or more of watching may be the incendiary cap that ignites a confrontation. And instead of walking away, two hot-headed young men, armed with deadly weapons, may choose to stay and fight.

No reasonably alert observer could doubt that there is a great deal of violence in our popular arts, but what does that mean? Some would say that the violence in our mass media, particularly television, merely reflects the violence in our society. Is that the case? Or does the violence in our mass media *promote* violence in our society? Does heavy television watching, for example, cause children to behave more aggressively than they might otherwise?

We are focusing on television because of its preeminence. Almost since its inception, television has been the most pervasive and powerful mass medium. The availability of new ways of watching television—subscribing to Cable, for example, or hooking up to a

VCR—has only increased television's cultural dominance. Network television, meantime, remains the conduit for our national culture. Day-time and prime-time network dramas shape how Americans view conflict between individuals. Network news programs define the way most Americans view the world. The networks broadcast our sports and our great public spectacles, such as inaugurations and state funerals. Network television even broadcasts our movies, although in recent years, many viewers have been switching to Cable for movies and for music, especially the hard rock broadcast on the Music Television Video (MTV).

For most children, television in its several guises is as much an influence as school or church—maybe more so. Most American children spend more hours watching television than they spend on any other waking activity, including going to school. From preschool until around seven years of age, the average young child watches between two and three hours of television a day. By the age of eight most children are watching four hours of T.V. daily—that's twenty-eight hours a week. Later, in mid-adolescence, viewing declines by an hour or so a day. Of course, some children watch less television than the average, and others, most often those growing up in poverty, watch much more.

Many adults view television as what psychologist Ron Slaby calls "a children's medium," and, I might add, a good babysitter. Rarely do parents control what children watch or how much they watch. In families with two televisions, parent and child often do not watch together. Nor do parents talk to children about what they see. Experts say this is especially unfortunate as watching together and talking can help children understand and interpret what is broadcast.

For decades critics have been saying that the twenty, twenty-five, or thirty hours a week our children are spending in front of the television is damaging them and undermining our society. Violence, as every parent knows, is not the only problem. I myself am particularly concerned with the time-consuming aspect of television. Children who are watching T.V. are not playing ball, practicing the piano, or doing their homework. Nor are they reading books! One Canadian study documented the impact on children's reading skills when multi-channel television arrived at their remote mountain town in the 1970s. Within a year the reading comprehension of the children had declined. Children who are watching *Three's Company* are not reading books.

Also, there is the issue of violence. A rancorous debate has surrounded the question of television's impact on aggression for thirty years. Television executives have used all their energy and resources to prove that television-viewing does not teach children to behave violently. Scores of psychologists and university professors, on the other hand, have produced a huge body of research concluding that a causal connection does indeed exist between violent behavior and television. They believe, and the evidence seems to indicate, that some of the violence today would not take place were violence to disappear from the airwaves.

While the case is not air-tight, two Surgeon Generals have publicly supported the thesis that an overdose of media violence can trigger aggressive behavior. This view has also been championed by the American Medical Association, the American Pediatric Association, the American Academy of Child Psychiatry, and the American Psychological Association. I, too, believe that violence on television is one of the factors that causes some young people to behave violently. I base my opinion not only on research but also on common sense. For me the issue of television's impact on children's behavior was settled when my own son and daughter were old enough to prefer one pair of blue jeans to another. Each pair of pants was made of 100 percent cotton denim, each had the same stitching, the same snaps; but they had different labels. One brand had been advertised on television, the other had not. Of course, my kids wanted the jeans they had seen advertised on television. Manufacturers spend hundreds of millions of dollars a year advertising their products on television because of T.V.'s impact on behavior. If television did not have an impact on the behavior of consumers, manufacturers would use other advertising media.

STUDYING AGGRESSION

—In 1981, in Washington, D.C., John Hinckley shot and nearly killed President Ronald Reagan. Hinckley, who was found to be insane, told authorities that he had seen *Taxi Driver*, a film about psychotic violence, hundreds of times.

—In 1988, outside of Boston, 14-year-old Rod Matthews stalked and murdered a junior high classmate. At his trial, a psychiatrist testified that Matthews might have been "inspired" by the documentary *Faces of Death* which he had seen on videocassette shortly before the murder.

—In 1977, 15-year-old Ronald Zamora of Miami Beach shot and killed his elderly neighbor when she threatened to call the police during a bungled robbery attempt in her home. Zamora's parents testified during his trial that their son was a "T.V. Addict," who watched six hours of cops and robbers violence each day. A psychiatrist for the defense testified that Zamora compared the shooting to a "Kojak" episode in which a woman who was shot later got up and walked away.

—In 1974, in San Francisco, three girls and a boy attacked a 9-year-old and raped her with a bottle. Four days prior to the attack, a similar crime had been explicitly shown during an NBC movie set in a girls' reform school.

Most of the time when we think about the impact of media violence, we think about cases in which disturbed young people are "inspired" to commit violent acts by what they see on the large or small screen. Researchers have established that copy-cat events are not an anomaly. Statistically-speaking, they are rare, but predictable, occurrences. Television shows, movies, novels—all can trigger copycat violence. Sensational news stories also may be copied. In the weeks after a major prize fight, for example, the homicide rate all over the country temporarily rises. Following the suicide of Marilyn Monroe, 300 Americans committed suicide who were statistically predicted to remain alive.

It's not just movie stars that can "inspire" people to commit violence against themselves. My friend Dr. Mark Rosenberg, of the federal Center for Disease Control in Atlanta, tells the story about a woman in Atlanta who committed suicide by shooting herself. Inside her purse next to her body was the story of another woman in Atlanta who had shot herself to death. The clipping revealed where the first victim had bought the gun she turned on herself. The second victim had gone to the same store to buy a gun.

We are a suggestible species. We learn how to behave from each other. When we see one of our species act, their act becomes a model for us to emulate. In this way, we sometimes make the unthinkable thinkable, the undoable doable. We can learn how to kill a president from a movie. We can learn how to commit suicide from each other. We can also learn how to commit mass murder. The Northeastern University researchers Jamie Fox and Jack Levin have studied the phenomena of mass murder. They looked at incidents during the past three decades in which assailants opened fire, usually in crowded public places—schools, offices, restaurants—killing large numbers of people. These incidents, they discovered, have increased significantly over the years. In the past they were rare occurrences. Now two to three mass murders happen each month.

No one knows all the reasons why these incidents are becoming so common, but Professors Fox and Levin believe the publicity that surrounds them is one of a series of reasons. The attention focused on mass murder may make this crime seem like a glamorous and powerful way to demand the world's attention and to exact retribution for wrongs, real and imagined. And then there is the copycat aspect; one act encourages another. Publicity alone does not "cause" a person to commit mass murder. Perhaps, however, constant exposure to information about violence and mass murder can plant and legitimate the idea that killing one or more persons is an acceptable way to avenge oneself. Deviance, like other human phenomena, exists within a social framework. In a very peaceful society, even the angriest and most seriously disturbed people will behave non-violently most of the time. A few rare violent incidents will occur. In a very violent society like ours many angry and disturbed people are prompted to behave violently.

The teenager dressed like Rambo who slaughters his family will get an avalanche of publicity. Reading about this crime we may be filled with fear and a sick feeling that our modern, technological life is slipping out of control. That does not make Rambo lookalikes the primary or even the secondary cause of the nation's rising homicide rate, however. The scores of psychologists who study television violence have interests that go far beyond the relatively small sensational homicides that dominate the headlines. These academics seek to discover the impact of video violence on the more than 20,000 homicides that occur each year, on the millions of assaults and on the tens of millions of American children for whom television is a daily habit. Their work is of particular interest now, when the first generations of young people reared on a heavy diet of television have come of age.

Leonard D. Eron is the researcher whose name is most associated with this effort. Eron and his numerous collaborators have carried out a series of long-term studies investigating aggression in school children. Hundreds of young people have been followed for thirty years at ten year intervals, beginning at age eight. The authors' most illuminating finding is that aggression tends to be a stable characteristic, one that is established early and remains in effect unless some form of intervention is successfully applied. In other words, the 8-year-old who gets in trouble for bullying has a disproportionately great chance of growing into the 19-year-old who robs and mugs and the 30-year-old sentenced to a lengthy prison term for assault, or even murder.

Eron and his colleagues established a quantifiable link between television watching and aggression. Among the hundreds of boys who were followed, a preference for T.V. violence turned out to be a key warning sign of later trouble. In fact, the leading predictor of how aggressive a young male would be at nineteen turned out to be the violence of the television he preferred at age eight. This does not mean that years of viewing violent television will make a 19-year-old behave violently, but there is reason to believe that television can be a key factor. Eron himself has written that what a child watches can make the difference between a child who strikes out at others and one who does not. So convinced is he of the negative impact of violent television that he lists massive exposure to violent television programs ahead of parenting practices as a factor in the creation of antisocial young adults.

Another interesting element of Eron's research relates to church-going. Retrospectively, Eron and his colleagues searched for the factors that seemed to inoculate children against trouble in later life. They looked at the aggressive 8-year-olds who did *not* grow up to have trouble with the law. Church-going turned out to be a significant factor. Aggressive 8-year-olds who were taken to church were less likely to grow up to have trouble with the law than those who did not go. As the wife of a minister, this finding makes perfect sense to me. The way I see it, religious services and Sunday school provide a setting for children to learn non-violent conflict resolution. If they are Christian, they are taught to turn the other cheek. Whatever their religion, however, they are taught to set high moral and ethical standards for themselves.

A LEARNED BEHAVIOR

I SHARE THE VIEW OF ERON AND MOST NON-FREUDIAN PSY-chologists that aggression is a learned behavior, one that can be unlearned. Like many psychologists I believe that the family and social environment can teach children to use violence to solve problems. The basic set of ideas that describe how this learning takes place is called social learning theory. The underlying assumption in this theory is that children learn how to behave from their social environment.

According to social learning theory, children learn how to behave aggressively by watching others use violence to their advantage and then imitating what they have seen. This process is called "modeling." Parents who have seen their three- or four-year-old watch a newcomer at the playground and then later reproduce the newcomer's unpleasant habit—throwing sand at other children, for example,—know how powerful a learning tool modeling is. Modeling is only part of the picture, however. The modeled behavior will become a part of the child's standard repertoire only if it is reinforced. That means if the child gets some sort of reward—control of his brother's truck, say—when he exhibits a new behavior, he will use that new behavior often. How to sit still in the classroom. How to comfort a crying baby. How to talk to adults and other children. How to hit and punch to get what you want. These are all "skills" that children develop by the subtle interaction of modeling plus reinforcements.

The social learning process operates regardless of whether the observed behavior is seen on T.V. or in person. Through research in the field, psychologists have repeatedly shown how this process works. In numerous experiments based at pre-schools, researchers have observed children at play before and after seeing violent television programs. Following the violent program the children's play is invariably more aggressive. They are much more likely to hit, punch, kick, and grab to get their way. In other words, television teaches children how to use aggression for personal gain. The environment, then, reinforces this behavior. Moreover, in follow-up studies, researchers have learned that the greater the amount of violent television a child watches, the more violent his or her interaction with peers is likely to become, and these effects linger.

It ought to be noted, however, that not all of television's lessons are violent ones. Social learning does not just involve the modeling of negative behaviors. Researchers have shown that positive behaviors can be modeled, too. The people who produce *Sesame Street* and *Mr. Rogers* do a great job of providing models of desirable social behavior for young kids to emulate. Concern for others. The willingness to delay gratification. The capacity to compromise. All these behaviors and many more are made available to small children who watch these programs. These lessons will not become patterns of behavior, however, unless home and schools provide reinforcement. When a child sees another child sharing on *Sesame Street* and then tries sharing at home, parents need to be vigilant. Positive behavior needs reinforcement or it will not reoccur. It is not enough for parents to say all the don'ts. "Don't hit your brother." "Don't take his toys." They must provide positive praise. "Gee, that was good sharing." "You did a good job helping your brother." "I know it's hard to share, but I can see you are really trying." The kind words, a friendly pat, and a smile reinforce and help cement the child's fledgling efforts to be a good citizen.

THE MEAN WORLD

IF YOU SHOW A 20-YEAR-OLD MALE A ROMANTIC MOVIE AND then ask him about a rape, he will probably empathize with the rape victim. But if you show him a violent movie—*The Texas Chainsaw Massacre*, say—and then ask him about a rape, he is likely to tell you that the rape victim deserved what she got. She was a vicious tease. She was asking for it. The process at work is called disinhibition. Repeated exposure to real life or fictional violence can make violence seem normal and acceptable.

Similarly, children who watch a great deal of violent T.V. are desensitized to the wrongness of what they are seeing. Television tells them that violence is an everyday occurrence, a justified form of self-defense. Teens who live in communities where violence is endemic are particularly vulnerable. T.V. reinforces the seeming ordinariness and rightness of the violence that confronts them daily. The violence these children see on television tells them that the violence in which they live is expected and normal—when in fact it is neither.

People who watch a great deal of television violence are more fearful than other people, and they overestimate the amount of violence in their environment. George Gerbner, Director of the Annenberg School of Communications at the University of Pennsylvania has studied the worldview of heavy television viewers. Rich or poor, young or old, those who watch four hours or more of T.V. a day share a common disillusionment. Gerbner calls this phenomenon the "mean world syndrome." This affliction, he says, besets heavy television watchers, who in time cease to differentiate between the world portrayed on television, where half the inhabitants are police officers and the other half are violent criminals and news stories about crime are replayed endlessly, from the real world. Those suffering from the "mean world syndrome" are filled with feelings of danger, mistrust, intolerance, gloom and hopelessness. They erroneously assume that the perverse and violent world portrayed on commercial television accurately reflects reality. When asked by researchers to describe the dimension of the crime problem, they grossly overestimate the incidence of crime and violence. The mental universe heavy T.V. viewers inhabit is the sensational, predatory, lowest-common-denominator world portrayed on "the tube." The world they look out upon is perpetually framed by television's version of human events.

Gerbner has also done interesting work with children. He discovered that children are especially vulnerable to the underlying assumptions television makes. Years before children are capable of making moral judgements, television provides them with a view of how the world is and how the world should be. Even when children understand that the plots of television dramas are fiction, they tend to accept as real the rest that television portrays—the relationships, the material wealth, the settings. How should people treat each other? When should violence be used? What kind of car and house and clothing must a person have to be happy? How long does it take to get what you want in life? Who is a hero? Who is a chump? These are the kinds of sophisticated questions television answers. Our children watch, and they learn.

THE CHILDREN MOST AT RISK

TELEVISION'S PORTRAYAL OF VIOLENCE AS A GLAMOROUS, successful, and entertaining method of resolving disputes is a problem for most children and most parents. All of our children are being dosed, overdosed I would say, by these messages. But some children are more vulnerable than others to television's violence-promoting message. Boys and men who are poor, who are urban, and who have witnessed or been victimized by violence in their families are more at risk for the dangerous lessons television teaches.

At a conference in Philadelphia, which I attended one of the participants, a probation officer, shed some light on those at greatest risk. He suggested and I agree with him that young males growing up in poverty, in homes that lack non-violent male role models, are the most vulnerable to television's violence-promoting message. Boys like this may never get to see an adult man restrain his own anger or control his own violent impulses. They may never experience non-violent discipline. They may never have the chance to see an adult man, or a woman, resolve disputes effectively and assertively, using non-violent strategies. Boys living in these circumstances are the ones most susceptible to television's message that heroes use violence to serve their purposes.

Emmett Folgert, a youth worker in Boston's Dorchester Youth Collaborative who is close to scores of young, poor fatherless males has elaborated on this thought. Boys without fathers who grow up in impoverished, female-headed households, Folgert believes, identify with the violent heroes on television to a degree that other young boys do not. Folgert, trained as a social worker, labels this kind of identification "clinical." The imaginary relationship such boys have with their T.V. heroes has great emotional meaning. Desperately hungry for fathering, such boys transform their television heroes into imaginary fathers. They talk to these pretend fathers. They make up long stories about what their T.V. heroes would do if they lived in Boston in a poor neighborhood. They ask their imaginary heroes for advice. What should they do? How should they handle themselves? Folgert says the answer they receive is always the same. Their heroes tell them to be tough. Their heroes tell them to fight.

We teach our children to kill, and some children are more vulnerable than others to this deadly lesson.

4

ADOLESCENCE: THE DANGEROUS PASSAGE

GROWING UP

NO ONE GETS TO STAND STILL FOR LONG.

One of the most interesting perceptions of modern developmental psychology is that life, from birth to death, is a flux. As soon as we master the tasks associated with one phase of life, the next phase begins, challenging us yet again. The baby who has just learned to walk has no time to rest. Now she must learn to talk. Similarly, the young adults who have just mastered the skills of independent living do not stop growing and changing. An intimate relationship, a new marriage, present them with complicated new adjustments that must be made, and so it goes through every phase of life. Rarely do we have time to congratulate ourselves on our psychological and maturational achievements.

Still, no period of life requires quite so much adjustment as adolescence. In fact, in adolescence almost nothing stays the same. *Bodies change and grow.* Suddenly we are taller, larger. Our bodies have taken on startling new forms—unmistakably male, unmistakably female. Very quickly an array of sexual choices present themselves. *Feelings change—drastically.* Our response is either love or hate; rarely are we neutral. *Relationships change.* We no longer know ourselves, or our family, or our peers. Even with our friends, we sometimes do not feel confident. A new set of rules governs how we are supposed to talk, and walk and be, but no one tells us what these new rules are. *Ideas about the world change.* The line separating good from bad, the truth from lies, is suddenly hard to see. What is right and what is wrong? What do we believe in? At the moment when we have more choices than ever before, we have no answers, no answers at all.

Often parents are not able to help teenagers find their way through these adolescent minefields. I learned during my years as the director of adolescent medicine at a neighborhood health center that many parents feel as ill-prepared to cope with their children's adolescence as their children do. The child's normal need to assert independence often feels like a betrayal to his parents. A daughter's or son's lack of responsibility enrages parents. Parents miss the pre-adolescent child with whom life was so (relatively) simple, and many parents, most I would say, have decidedly mixed feelings about their children's burgeoning sexuality. They fear and dread the consequences of choices thoughtlessly made. They feel uncomfortable with their daughters' womanhood, their son's manhood. They may feel they no longer know how to be close to this child with an adult's body.

The adult ambivalence toward adolescence that I have been describing has particularly powerful ramifications for young males. The kindness most adults show small children is often withdrawn from teenage boys whose challenging attitude toward authority and growing physical prowess are seen as threatening by men and frightening by women. Fathers, teachers, principals, police officers, and others feel compelled to show young males who is boss. Whether they deserve to be or not, young men are treated as juvenile delinquents who need to be "taught a lesson." This response cuts across racial and socio-economic lines, but tends to fall most harshly on poor non-whites. A brown-skinned East Indian social worker I know says every time she and her 13-year-old son enter the corner store in the affluent suburb where they live, the storekeeper looks alarmed. Her son is followed throughout his entire stay. The storekeeper assumes he is a thief, or worse. In poor neighborhoods young males are routinely treated as criminals. Most damaging, of course, is the interaction between minority youth and police. Given the state of fear in Roxbury, Massachusetts, where I live, and in many poor, urban minority neighborhoods, police feel they must stop and search young people for weapons. These interchanges seethe with barely suppressed feelings. Young black males and young male police officers, white as well as black, are like two poles of a magnet. A dangerous current runs back and forth as dark-skinned youths, suspects by virtue of race and age, are ordered to lie down, faces on the pavement, while they are searched for weapons by police officers. In many neighborhoods, including mine, this interaction is common, occurring as often as a young man leaves his home. The fears of police and community that trigger these searches are legitimate, but that does not take away the hurt of young black men who daily confront the assumption that they are bad and dangerous.

Adolescence itself is like a long tunnel connecting two quite disparate phases of life. A child enters one end. An adult exits the other.

What happens inside the tunnel? What processes occur to alter the way a child thinks and feels, to turn him into a young adult? Psychologists talk about four "developmental tasks" that adolescents in our culture must accomplish in order to become healthy, functioning adults. These four can be summed up in the following way:

1. Separating from family
2. Forging a healthy sexual identity
3. Preparing for the future
4. Forging a moral value system

Each of these "tasks" requires a major effort and much time to complete. All involve struggle through many interim steps in the years spanning age 12 to age 20, and each task, I believe, makes a young person vulnerable to attitudes and behavior that are potentially dangerous.

Every child who begins this process follows his own unique timetable. Some 12- and 13-year-olds are still very young, both physically and emotionally. These are the late bloomers who will not begin to grapple with the developmental issues of adolescence until age 14 or later. By age 15 or 16, other young people are remarkably mature in all or most regards. In general, by age 18 most young people have taken major steps toward completing all these tasks—meaning that most of the time they can be expected to exhibit a certain degree of maturity and independence. Most of us, however, are not really mature at 18. In our society, entry into the adult world of work and responsibility is usually postponed until young people have completed their education, by which time they may be well along in their twenties.

Adolescence is a normal phase of life, not a form of pathology. Recent research into the adolescent years has wisely emphasized the capacity of most adolescents to achieve adulthood without destroying themselves or their families. The research indicates that most teenagers grow up to become adults with lifestyles, beliefs, and values surprisingly similar to their parents. We are naive, however, if we fail to acknowledge that adolescence strains family relationships. We are naive, too, if we fail to understand that the changing shape of American families—half of all children spend at least part of their childhood in a family headed by a single parent—has an impact on the struggle of young people to mature. When families are more complicated, children have a harder time sorting out family relationships, figuring out who they are, and breaking away constructively. Under these circumstances, the teenage years may be especially wrenching and difficult.

Adolescence is about changing your relationship to your parents and to the world at large. An adolescent renounces parental care in favor of his own independence. This is one way that he or she prepares for adulthood. In order to successfully complete the process of adolescence, children must receive a certain amount of basic nurturing (not perfect parenting but good enough parenting) during their pre-adolescent years. Sadly, however, during the first twelve years of life many children do not receive the basic love and attention they need. These kids enter adolescence without the basic building blocks; for them, the entire developmental process is handicapped. Children who have been deprived of the basics have a very difficult time becoming emotionally balanced, competent adults.

There is one other preliminary point that needs to be made: Adolescence barely exists as a concept outside highly industrialized nations like our own. In some rural societies there is no formal period of adolescence. Young people take on adult responsibilities as soon as they are physically mature and pass through some sort of ritual ceremony. Other societies in which adolescence is seen as part of the life-cycle may have ideas very different from ours about how the adolescent years are to be spent. For example, some societies discourage contact between adolescent males and females. Sexual experimentation is outlawed and all grown children, males and females, remain in the homes of their parents until they wed. In America, we tend to believe that the way our culture is organized is the way all cultures are or should be organized, but of course this is not so. Each society is unique. The way we describe adolescence, the way we experience it, and the predisposition of our adolescents toward violence is peculiar to our own American culture.

INDIVIDUATION/SEPARATION FROM FAMILY

IN ADOLESCENCE, CHILDREN BEGIN TO SEE THEMSELVES AS persons separate from their parents and siblings. They begin to develop independent identities, learning to think for themselves, and to make decisions for themselves. This process, which takes years, is called individuation and separation. When it is complete, adult children see themselves as independent individuals whose relationships with parents are different from the ones they had in the past.

No one calls his parents up on the telephone and announce that he is separating from them. Separation is a process, not an event. Many small rifts, insults, challenges, and confrontations, and reconciliations shape the long years during which adolescents struggle to alter their relationships to their parents. All these are normal. What is not normal are abrupt and dramatic separations that may drive permanent or long-lasting wedges between teenagers and their parents.

Our society does little to help adolescents mature and separate. We have remarkably few rites of passage that mark the stages of life. We have few ceremonies and tests to determine eligibility for specific adult privileges. Getting your driver's license, graduating from high school, reaching the 21-year-old legal age for drinking are among the few that exist. Nor do we have many generally agreed upon social dictums. When is the right age to begin dating? What is a reasonable curfew? Should an 18-year-old be allowed to stay out all night? There are few areas of general agreement. Every family makes up its own rules, influenced, but uninstructed, by the society at large. Many families have a great deal of difficulty with this process.

The desire for self determination—what psychologists call autonomy—comes long before adolescence. Observing my own children when they were small, I was amazed at how soon and how vociferously they expressed the need to be in control of their own feeding, their own play, their own moving about. The small child's desire for autonomy, however, exists within the context of his overwhelming need for his parents. He or she cannot survive without the shelter, the food, the clothes, the love that the parents provide. The desire for independence, then, is tempered by the need for care. Not so with the adolescent. The adolescent is someone who needs little or no physical care, someone who has begun to imagine that he or she can survive very well without the interference of adults, someone quite blind to his own continuing need for adult support and guidance.

For many teenagers and their parents the adolescent years are filled with intense emotional struggle. Parent and child face each other again and again in an unrelenting round of skirmishes. The arguments are usually about freedom, responsibility, and control; the teenager's coming and going, the hours he keeps, the money he earns and the money he spends. The amount of labor he expends on chores, his school performance, whether or not he drinks or takes drugs. The language he uses, his access to the car, the music he prefers, the friends he chooses, what he wears. All these highly charged issues are hashed and rehashed. Exacerbating these disputes is the contemptuous attitude toward authority exhibited by many teenagers. Wordless signals emanate from adolescents challenging all comers to try and make me. This swaggering denial of adult power fuels the generational conflict, sometimes for years.

Of course, some families handle generational conflict better than others. Some parents have an easier time loosening the reins without abandoning the child. Some teenagers are more responsible in their behavior and more reasonable in their demands. Some parents do a good job of picking their fights, struggling over only those few issues that really matter. Some teenagers are more persuasive and can convince parents that they are capable of handling more freedom. Even under the best of circumstances, however, adolescence is an assault on the family power structure established during a child's first twelve years.

Questions of loyalty are paramount in the adolescent's struggle. His tactic for discovering his own identity often involves rejecting what his parents value in favor of what his peers value. Parents are cast as hopelessly old-fashioned, hypercritical know-nothings. Parents, in turn, worry about their children's futures, while criticizing everything adolescents like—their clothes, their music, and their friends. Both sides feel betrayed and confused. Where did the boundless love of small child for parent, parent for small child disappear to?

Peers replace parents in the teenager's hierarchy of important people. Teenagers use their peers to help them orient themselves in the world. Is this what I should wear? Is this what I should think? Is this what I should do? Peers create the standard against which behavior and taste is judged. The need for peers and the pressure peers exert is normal. The peer group is a refuge providing approval, warmth, friendship, sustenance, and fun, but the refuge can become an unsafe haven. To measure up, a young person may be required to think and act in lockstep. The group may propel him in dangerous and illegal directions. The more conflict there is at home, the more a young person depends on the approval of the peer group and the more difficulty he may have extricating himself. Moreover, when the adolescent can see no healthy future awaiting, the peer group takes on a disproportionate importance.

No one has better described the potentially vicious effect of peer pressure than Claude Brown, whose classic book about ghetto life, *Manchild in the Promised Land* was published in 1965. Recalling his early adolescence (arrived at after a childhood spent stealing, vandalizing, and cutting school), Brown describes his horror as he realized what was supposed to come next: "I was growing up now, and . . . I would soon be expected to kill a nigger if he mistreated me, like (my friends) Rock, Bubba Williams, and Dewdrop had. . . . I knew now that I had to keep up with these cats; if I didn't I would lose my respect in the neighborhood . . . I knew that I was going to have to get a gun sooner or later and that I was going to have to make my new rep and take my place along with the bad niggers of the community. . . ."

What I find so interesting about Claude Brown's anguished words is their rationality. Claude Brown was not crazy. He was not going to become a killer because he was crazy, but because he lived in an environment that expected him to become a killer. My sense is that many of the kids committing violence today are similar to Claude

Brown in that they are normal kids trying to survive in violent, unhealthy circumstances. Sadly, though, many do not do as well as Claude Brown, who found a way to escape. He gave himself up to the authorities knowing that he would be sent away to a detention facility. A 14-year-old when he returned, Claude Brown got a job, enrolled in night school, rented a small room downtown and left Harlem. If Claude Brown were growing up today, when violence has crossed over into nearly every neighborhood, I am not so sure he would ever have known the pleasure of creating a non-violent life for himself.

FORGING A HEALTHY SEXUAL IDENTITY

NO EXPERIENCE IN LIFE IS QUITE AS OVERPOWERING AS THE feelings of romantic attraction we feel as teenagers. Male and female alike, we believe that we could die of love, or die for love, and, in a way, we want to, because we want the outcome of our emotions to be as melodramatic as our emotions themselves.

In real life, instead of dying for love, young people are expected to learn how to manage their romantic and their sexual feelings. That's one of their most important developmental jobs. They are also expected to learn to value and relate to members of the opposite sex. Developmentally-speaking, young romance is supposed to be a preparation for mature romance and for marriage. By observing the adults around them, and through their own experiences, young people are supposed to learn how to create satisfying, non-violent, permanent relationships. The high incidence of teenage pregnancy, single-parent families, domestic violence, divorce, and sexually transmitted disease within our society, indicates that often what is "supposed" to happen is not, and what isn't "supposed" to happen, is. The fact is that when it comes to sex we teach our children one lesson, but expect them to learn another. They are indoctrinated by the electronic media to view sex as a kind of candy-store commodity. Yum, yum. I'll try this today. Yum, yum. I'll try that tomorrow. Imprinted on their minds practically from infancy are video images of gorgeous bodies, instant gratification, and the easy getaway. At home, meantime, the message heard most often regarding all sexual subjects is silence, utter silence. Yet somehow parents manage to be surprised when their children are ignorant of the emotional and practical responsibilities that every sexual relationship ought to entail.

Few teens accomplish the task of "finding themselves" as sexual beings without suffering bouts of self-consciousness and self doubt. At no other time in life are we so afraid of doing the wrong thing, or

saying the wrong thing, or looking the wrong way as when we take
our first steps toward members of the opposite sex. Teenagers com-
pensate by spending hours preening and grooming. They brood
about blemishes and flaws invisible to the naked eye, and have a
difficult time seeing the world beyond the bubble of their self-concern.
They cannot easily imagine that others feel as they feel, or that some
people have problems far worse than they.

Young teens are like the actor in the joke who says, "Enough
about me. Let's talk about you. What do you think of me?" They see
themselves in technicolor and the rest of the world in black and
white. The psychological term for this phenomenon is narcissism. I
believe that narcissism, though a normal and necessary part of adolescent sexual development, puts teenagers at risk for violence. Narcissistic feelings impair judgement, preventing young people—
especially young men—from perceiving and fleeing from dangerous
circumstances. Moreover, even if he perceives a risk, an adolescent's
overdeveloped narcissistic pride may compel him to fight each hot-
headed rival. In communities where the young still fight with their
fists, attitudes like this lead to broken hands and broken jaws. In
communities where the young are armed with guns the competition
to be "cock-of-the-walk" has deadly consequences.

A "macho" code of sexual behavior also puts teens at risk for
violence. Teenage males and females tend to accept stereotypical
ideas about masculinity and femininity and to exhibit extreme forms
of masculine and feminine behavior. New to the game, they believe
all the mythic claptrap that says girls (or boys) are objects that can be
won or stolen against their wills. Girlfriends and boyfriends are
treated as possessions or trophies, not as autonomous beings who
freely give their affection and who may freely take it away. Girls may
feel that it is appropriate for them to manipulate people and events.
Boys may feel that it is their right to control the behavior of their
girlfriends and other males whom they see as competition.

Narcissism makes the conflicts between young men and women
dangerous. Narcissistic adolescents have no distance, no perspective
on experience. For them every play is a tragedy, every consequence
is dire, every twist on love's road is momentous. A girlfriend talking
to another guy can feel world-shattering and humiliating, especially
when friends and acquaintances are watching. When this event is
enacted in public a young male may feel that violence is the only way
he can redeem his pride. His friends, titillated by the excitement of a
possible fight, can usually be counted on to encourage his bravura
display.

I am afraid that it is within this stereotypical and aggressive context that much sexual activity occurs between the young. Males sometimes push females into having sexual contact that neither may be

ready to handle. Sometimes, to a degree we are only just beginning to recognize, boys use force. A high school program in the Boston area organized by Emerge, a group that works (often under court order) with men who batter their wives, has discovered a vast sea of unreported sexual coercion and date rape, among the young. It would appear that some young men routinely push, shove, and slap young women into having sexual relations. Even when young women say "yes" freely, they often do so for all the wrong reasons. They may say "yes" because they are eager to please a particular young man, because they are afraid to lose him, or because they do not know that they have the right and power to say "no." When sexual contact does occur, often neither partner knows a great deal about giving sexual pleasure. Both may know the rudimentary facts of conception, but often take no steps to protect themselves from pregnancy or disease. As a parent, physician, and public health educator perhaps I should say here that I do not oppose all sexual expression between adolescents, but I do very much believe in what I could call informed consent. Young women desperately need to be informed about their choices so that they can exercise true, rather than pro forma choice. They need to believe that another future besides early motherhood is open to them. Young males, too, need to believe a bright enough future awaits them to justify postponing parenthood until they are older. Both sexes need to know a great deal more than they do at present about how their bodies work, about contraception, and about sexually transmitted diseases, including AIDS. Just as much as homicide, these are life and death issues.

PREPARING FOR THE FUTURE

FOR MOST SMALL CHILDREN TIME IS VERY SLOW, AND ONE day follows the next in a stream that seems endless. Though they may know better, most children feel and act as though they will be children forever. In adolescence, the child's magical thinking slowly lifts. A sense of time begins to dawn on him. The young teenager begins to understand that the present leads to the future, that present actions have future consequences, and that one day he will be an adult. Comprehension of these concepts take years. Once mastered, teenagers are able to view themselves as life travellers with destinations.

Erik Erikson describes an adolescent as a person who sees himself as possessing a past and a future. Not just any future will do in Erikson's conception. The famed psychoanalyst says teenagers require an *open future* if they are to develop into healthy adults. By this he means a future uncramped by oppressive social, political, and economic conditions; a future in which young people can reasonably look forward to holding decent jobs and supporting themselves and their families.

Having a future gives a teenager reasons for trying and reasons for valuing his life. For the first time, he may be able to see his own actions as significant. Goals and aspirations have more meaning. A 15-year-old who wants to be a draftsman, an engineer, or a tool maker when he finishes school may still procrastinate for hours before settling down to his homework. Still, such a child is more likely to complete his work than a child who believes he is going nowhere.

Attending school is the most important way that young people prepare for their futures. Without a high school diploma, few Americans can hope for a life beyond subsistence. Without a college degree, gaining entry to a middle-class existence, although possible, is increasingly difficult. The future of most children—especially the poor—depends on their academic performance. The children who do well in school—whatever their socio-economic status—generally have confidence that they will be able to shape their own bright destiny. This idea was summed up colorfully by another psychiatrist, Thomas J. Cottle, who grew up in comfortable circumstances near Boston in the late 1950s. "My friends and I," Cottle recalls, "were consumed with the belief that we probably had a damn good chance." Believing in *"a damn good chance"* makes people feel energized and powerful. Believing in no chance makes people angry, passive, ineffectual. It may also make them violent.

Adolescents prepare for the future in another way by participating in "extracurricular activities"—sports, music, art, theater, photography, dance, writing for the high school newspaper, and so forth. Like school work, these activities give young people the opportunity to devote themselves to something outside themselves—a happy antidote to the obsessive self-concern of adolescence. You cannot be a one-man football team or a one-person marching band. Outside interests provide teens with the opportunity to develop cooperative relationships with their peers and adults. Participating in after-school activities is one way they learn how to get along with others, to compromise, and to express what they think.

Developing an interest can also change a young person's self image, providing him or her with a sense of competence; a very important feeling for teenagers to possess. Competence denotes mastery over a portion of experience. The adolescent learns that he is capable of taking charge, of fulfilling a goal that he alone has set. Developing competence in an artistic or athletic pursuit teaches him that all achievement is incremental. Large achievements are the result of a series of small sequential steps. This is an invaluable lesson for adolescents who, like small children, may tend to see achievement as the result of wishing, wanting, or luck. Interests also provide young people with an avenue into a larger world. For example, learning about music by playing the piano or learning about other artists and looking at their work while devoting time to drawing or painting.

By involving themselves in school work and outside interests, teenagers put themselves in the pathway of teachers, coaches, and other concerned adults who may have a great deal to teach them. Adolescents are often better able to take support and guidance from these special older friends than they are from parents. With non-parental adults, no destructive history exists. Both sides can listen. Adolescents can learn without feeling that they have capitulated to their parents.

Non-family members often have the experience and know-how to direct young people in new academic, vocational, and social directions. One person can mean the difference between having a high aspiration for oneself and having no aspirations at all. Alliances with accomplished adults makes it possible for teenagers to re-imagine their futures. An adolescent who is close to a teacher or a doctor or a minister often finds it easy to imagine himself in the favored adult's profession. The leap from "I like you," to "I want to be like you" is one adolescents seem to make quite naturally.

All adolescents need adults very much. They need mentors in whose image they can create themselves. They need models outside their peer group. They need adults to inspire them, to help them interpret life's confusion, and to lead them to an understanding of what goals are worthy. When inspiring adults are missing, a terrible emptiness may exist in the center of a child's life, an emptiness that he or she may fill by doing and becoming precisely what will most hurt himself and others.

Just how important mentors and other non-parental adults can be has been proven by research psychologist Emmy Werner in her longitudinal study of children in Kauai, Hawaii. Since 1955, Werner has followed 700 "high risk" subjects born with multiple difficulties—premature birth, low birth weight, poverty, broken families, parental alcoholism, and parental mental illness. Not surprisingly, two-thirds of her subjects had troubled childhoods in which school failure and adjustment problems were common. By adolescence many boys in the Werner study were getting in trouble with the law and many girls were becoming teenage mothers. The outlook did not look good. Still, the majority of these young people were able to turn their lives around by the age of thirty. A crucial factor in the success of these late bloomers, writes Werner, was the appearance in their lives of mentors and other caring, non-parental adults. Adolescents fortunate enough to come in contact with adults like this were able to envision and take advantage of what Werner calls opportunities for a "second chance." Those youngsters whose lives were untouched by such positive influences continued to flounder well into their thirties.

In the age-segregated society in which we live, many adolescents have little contact with adults, including their parents. I was interested to read some research documenting this. Sociologists interviewed hundreds of students attending an economically and socially diverse mid-western high school. The young people kept detailed logs describing what they did and with whom during a two-week period. The researchers found that their teenage subjects, busy with school, after school jobs that stretch into the dinner hour, and peers often spent as little as one hour a week with their parents. Many families did not eat dinner together. Nor, in general, did the students have other adult friends or advisors.

This lack of adult contact in the lives of adolescents is little short of tragic. As a physician and as a parent, I am always struck by how fervently adolescents hunger for adult guidance and help. In my experience, most teenagers want some close adult to know (most of) what they are doing. Teenagers certainly want adults to know what worries them. They also want to know what adults think, so long as these messages are delivered in a friendly fashion. Many teens, most I would say, are eager for advice about the future, so long as it is presented in an open-ended, non-judgmental, non-dictatorial fashion. The message that is prefaced with the comment, "this is what I think," is much more likely to be received than the message that is prefaced, "this is what you have to do." The message that is spoken in a normal voice will always be heard more clearly than the message that is shouted. Teenagers, however, will not bare their souls on a timetable. Parents can only create time and space for their teens to come to them and then they must wait. Parents who are available and willing to listen, generally find that their teens are eager to talk. Another positive step parents can take is to help orchestrate social situations in which their teenagers have a chance to become acquainted with other adults who can serve as mentors, models and confidants.

FORGING A MORAL VALUE SYSTEM

IF YOU PUT TWO THREE-YEAR-OLDS IN A ROOM WITH ONE toy truck, chances are both children will be crying within minutes. Developmentally, children this age are at an "I want" stage—as in "I want that truck and if you don't give it to me, I will take it and if I can't take it, I will burst into tears." Alone in a room with one truck, two three-year-olds will lunge, grab, hit, and then cry. Few words will be spoken. These children are not naughty or selfish. Their behavior is not bad; it is merely, "age appropriate."

If you put two seven-year-olds in a room with one toy truck, chances are they will find a way to play with the truck. One of the children will take the books down from the book shelf and build a road. The other child will drive the truck. After a while the builder will demand a turn as the driver. The former driver will take all the pillows off the couch and create a cave-garage. The former builder will drive the truck into the garage. This behavior, too, is age appropriate.

What these two short vignettes describe is the moral development of children at two different stages. The three-year-olds exist in a moral universe that is utterly egocentric. I want. I need. I must have. A child this age is largely indifferent to the wants and needs of others. His or her moral and cognitive development precludes the kinds of organized activities that our species requires to survive. The seven-year-olds, on the other hand, live in a far more complex moral environment, one in which an awareness of other people's needs and rights is beginning to dawn, making sharing and play—human interchange—possible.

Developmental psychologists have established that children's morality develops in predictable stages, just as their thinking does. Moral reasoning is the term they use to describe this process, which involves feeling as well as thinking. As a child's capacity to think deepens, so too does his ability to assess the rightness or wrongness of behavior. As the years pass his ability to understand the ramifications of actions—who will be hurt and who will be helped—broadens. By late adolescence he ought to be able to understand that actions can have far-reaching, abstract consequences as well as immediate and concrete ones.

When the capacity to reason morally does not develop along with a child's body, the consequences can be appalling. We learned what this meant when a suspect in the rape of a young jogger in Central Park described the brutal assault as "fun." We learned this lesson again in Glen Ridge, New Jersey when the suspects accused in the gang rape of a young retarded woman justified what happened by commenting that the victim was "flirtatious"—as if flirting could justify thirteen young men violating a young woman.

The developmental psychologist Lawrence Kohlberg of Harvard University created a widely used 5-stage theory* with which to analyze and rate children's moral reasoning. By looking at the first three of these stages (stages four and five describe abstract forms of moral

---

* Kohlberg's theory, in fact, contains six, rather than five stages. Researchers, however, have been unable to document the existence of Stage Six.

reasoning that are beyond our current concern), we can see how the moral thinking of children and teenagers develops and how, under some circumstances, it fails to develop. None of Kohlberg's stages, by the way, describe the egocentric three-year-old who tries to get his way by grabbing and bashing. Kohlberg's work is based on research with children older than three who are capable of more complex styles of interacting.

I call Kohlberg's *Stage One*, which spans the grammar school years and sometimes beyond, the punishment stage. *Stage One* children view relationships, especially relationships with adults, in terms of power and fear of punishment. Actions are motivated by the fear of retaliation. Often this retaliation is more imaginary than real. For example, children in this stage will explain what they see on television news broadcasts by labelling all victims, even the most innocent, as bad and deserving what they got.

By age 10 or earlier, the *Stage One* thinking of most well-adjusted children is mitigated by true concern for others. Adolescent children in trouble with the law, however, seem to be stuck in *Stage One*. One study of youthful offenders highlights this fact dramatically. The juvenile offenders were presented with two scenarios and asked to rate which offense was worse. In Scenario One a boy accidentally breaks fifteen plates. In Scenario Two a boy defies his mother, steals a cookie from the cookie jar and breaks the jar's lid. The delinquents judged the boy who breaks fifteen plates to have committed the worst offense because his act caused the most damage. Non-delinquents of equal intelligence, on the other hand, view this case entirely differently. They are sensitive not only to the extent of the damage, but also to the motivation of the perpetrator. They view the child who intentionally defies his mother as the more serious wrong-doer. Their thinking, unlike that of the delinquents, has moved out of *Stage One* and into *Stage Two*.

I call *Stage Two* the fairness stage. In this stage, which begins in pre-adolescence and sometimes runs through adolescence, young people, as can be deduced from the example above, begin to comprehend and care about justice. Punishments and rewards must be fair. When a child this age believes he has been treated unfairly, he is enraged. In *Stage Two*, young people have the ability to relate in complex ways not merely to individuals, but to a group.

It is my own view that the cognitive and moral shortcomings of adolescents in *Stage Two* explain a great deal about the dynamics of peer groups and also, perhaps more significantly, youth gangs. Moral reasoning at this stage of a young person's development is curiously short-sighted. Their world begins and ends with their own collective, their own group. Furthermore, their desire for fairness can at times be simple-minded. "The guys on D Street bopped (killed) one of us.

We'll bop (kill) one of theirs." In a world in which teenagers have no trouble arming themselves, moral reasoning at this tribal level can, like *Stage One* reasoning, lead a young person into great danger.

I call *Stage Three* moral reasoning the safe zone. In *Stage Three* young people have the cognitive ability to understand the intricacy of the world they live in. They can see beyond themselves and understand their own actions in a moral and legal context. A young person who reaches this stage understands why, for example, individuals need to pay taxes. He knows that taxes provide for the collective needs of the state and nation. Unless we all do our share, he can say, there will be no schools, no good roads, no army, etc.

Young people and adults who reach *Stage Three* in their moral reasoning are less likely to go around "bashing" and "bopping" each other. Their high level of cognitive functioning protects them from their own dangerous impulses. One way to look at Claude Brown's defection from the streets of Harlem is to say that his moral reasoning compelled him to adopt a new kind of life. One of our goals then, when working with adolescents as teachers, counselors, physicians, and clergy must be to help them develop the cognitive capacity and the moral reasoning power to turn away from the dangers on the streets as Claude Brown did. This cognitive approach is being used successfully in a number of programs aimed at reducing the incidence of adolescent violence in schools and communities and among juvenile delinquents.

RISK-TAKING

NO TEENAGER REACHES KOHLBERG'S *STAGE THREE* OF moral reasoning without experimenting a bit with right and wrong. The best of kids do bad things now and then. They may look their parents square in the eye and lie, cheat on a test, or steal a package of cigarettes. No one should condone this behavior, but so long as such breaches do not become habitual, most adults understand that teenagers are experimenting and that this experimentation is fairly normal.

Experimenting and risk-taking are a normal part of adolescence. Teenagers cannot master the developmental tasks required of them without trying out a variety of behaviors. They adopt new styles, new personalities, new opinions, new friendships, new romances, all in an effort to find out what suits them. Some adolescents, of course, are cautious by temperament. They proceed slowly and carefully. Much of their experimentation is confined to non-lethal areas—hair, clothing, taste in music. Other teenagers, the ones we worry about, are temperamentally given to diving first and checking later to see if the pool has water.

Inevitably, there are dangers. Most problems with drug abuse and addiction start with adolescent experimentation. Teenage pregnancy and adolescent violence also can be traced to risk-taking behavior. Most of the time teenagers know at least something about conception, but they often have unprotected sex risking pregnancy (and disease) anyhow. Instead of practicing birth control, they succumb to magic thinking. "I won't get pregnant. Not this time. I'm too young," they tell themselves. A similar kind of magical thinking is at work when a youngster leaves the house carrying a handgun. "I'm cool," he tells himself. "I'm powerful. I'm protected. I can't get hurt."

Abetting adolescent risk-taking are the feelings of immortality and exemption from consequences that most teens experience. These feelings serve a developmental function. They give young people the courage to break away from their parents and stand on their own two feet, but these feelings can be a death sentence. The results of a telephone survey the Massachusetts Department of Public Health conducted with 16- to 19-year-olds reminded me once again just how dangerous it is to be an adolescent. Of the teenagers we contacted, 42 percent revealed that they had been drinking and driving in recent months. Teenagers drink and drive because they believe that they are invincible. This same belief blinds them to the danger when one of them tucks a gun into his waistband and goes down to the playground to "hang out."

Our world is making it increasingly dangerous for adolescents to carry out their risk-taking behavior. Experimenting with crack, which is highly addictive, is different from experimenting with alcohol or even marijuana, drugs to which one grows addicted gradually. Experimenting with sex in the age of AIDS is not the same as sexual experimentation in earlier decades. Experimenting with macho behavior and fighting is different when so many young males are carrying guns. Our dangerous world has removed the margin of error that our children once enjoyed, and we rightly fear for their survival.

5

AN ENDANGERED SPECIES—YOUNG MEN OF COLOR LIVING IN POVERTY

"At Chicago's Henry Horner public housing project, nine-year-old Diante McClain's older brother was fatally shot last spring after an argument with a friend. Two weeks later, amid nearby gunfire, Diante remained glued to a playground swing. His friend pleaded with him to take cover. Instead, Diante continued swinging, repeating over and over again, "I want to die. I want to die.""

Alex Kotlowitz
The Wall Street Journal

An epidemic of violence in the poorest of our poor neighborhoods is decimating a generation of young men of color. The shattering impact of living in an environment saturated with violence and fear is reshaping the lives of poor children. We do not know everything there is to know about the damage that is done to children growing up like this, but we do know that coming of age amidst great violence damages the vital capacity of young people to trust in the goodness of life. Violence robs children of their dreams; it makes them hopeless. We know this, too—that growing up in violence places young people and their communities at terrible jeopardy. For the fact is, those who are the witnesses and victims of violence often become its perpetrators.

THOSE MOST AT RISK

ALL ADOLESCENT MALES ARE AT RISK FOR VIOLENCE. NONE are exempt now, not in the United States. The ready availability of guns; a national ideology that portrays violence as a legitimate way to resolve disputes; a popular culture that glorifies and sexualizes violence; news broadcasts that endlessly reinforce the message that violence is the normal outcome of human conflict—together all these factors promote violence throughout our society. Teenage males are more vulnerable to this message than any other segment of the population.

All young men, however, are not in equal jeopardy. Some are far more at risk than others. While no one is exempt, poverty increases the risk that a young person's life will be marred by violence. Middle-class youths are far less likely to die or be injured during an assault. Those most imperiled are poor, young males growing up in severely impoverished "inner city" neighborhoods. Young men—black, white, and brown—living in such distressed urban areas are the most likely victims and perpetrators of violence. In fact, where a young man lives may be the most significant factor predicting his risk for violence.

Black men are far more likely than whites to be the victims and the perpetrators of violent acts. This racial correlation is not new. Since 1929, when the FBI began keeping racially segregated homicide statistics, black males have run a 6 to 12 times greater risk than whites of dying the victim of a homicide. While blacks are approximately 12 percent of the population, they generally comprise half of all those arrested for murder and non-negligent homicide and half of the homicide victims. For young black men the likelihood of dying in a homicide has been increasing at an alarming rate. Between 1984 and 1988, according to analysts at the CDC, the murder rate of African-American males from 15-to-24 rose by 68 percent. The murder rate of African-American youths from 15-to-19 rose by 100 percent in that same period.

Blame for the deluge of violence in poor inner city neighborhoods is often attributed to drugs and gangs. These twin catastrophes have escalated the violence and the perception of violence in the poorest communities. However, violence was a problem for young men of color long before gangs and crack cocaine started making headlines in the 1980s. Moreover, much gang violence takes places between two people who know each other, who argue, who may have been drinking, at least one of whom has a gun—the same as most non-gang violence. The violence perpetrated by many drug users also fits this model. Drug use clouds judgement and perhaps causes agitation, after which an argument occurs between two people who know each other, at least one of whom is armed and someone is shot, perhaps to death. On the other hand, violence committed by drug dealers to punish or to frighten associates is likely to be criminal behavior well outside the model with which we are most concerned. What must be understood is this: If gangs and drugs disappeared tomorrow from our poorest neighborhoods, our young black men would continue killing each other at grossly unacceptable rates, as they have done throughout this century. Gangs and drugs, which have waned and waxed as negative influences on the poor throughout this century, make violence worse, but they are not the root of the problem.

In some cities, Southeast Asians are at high risk for homicide, but in general those at highest risk are poor, urban young men of color. The term "young men of color" refers to African-Americans and Hispanic-Americans. We know more about African-American homicide, however, than we do about Hispanic. Asked to make an educated guess I would say that in many Hispanic communities the assault and homicide rates are probably just as catastrophic as in inner city black communities. The data to prove this assertion, however, is limited. In the city of Los Angeles from 1970 to 1979 data exists showing that the homicide rate of Hispanic males increased nearly 300 percent from 9.1 per 100,000 population to 32.6 per 100,000 population. This figure was lower than the black rate, but significantly higher than the white rate and was increasing more rapidly than the others. Nationally, we do not know the homicide rate for Hispanic males. FBI crime statistics classify Americans as black, white, or other. Hispanic Americans may be listed in any one of these categories. No aggregate Hispanic homicide statistic is kept. Nor is federal census data broken down to specifically describe the circumstances of Hispanic-American communities. Even when data does exist, deciphering it is a problem. The umbrella term "Hispanic" encompasses many different groups of markedly different socio-economic characteristics. What is true for impoverished Puerto Ricans living in New York City may not be true for middle-class Cuban-Americans living in Miami. These differences make generalizations difficult, but they should not blind us to the fact that the lives of many young Hispanic males are being twisted and distorted by the high level of violence in their neighborhoods.

The Waltons

12-year-old Lafayette Walton lives in a war zone. His skills are a survivor's skills. He knows how to fling himself to the ground at the sound of gunfire. He knows how to crawl on his belly through the dirt to safety. He knows how to distinguish a .357 caliber Magnum from a .45 caliber revolver. He knows how to stay clear of the armed thugs who control the building where he lives at Chicago's Henry Horner Homes housing project. He knows how to keep quiet about what he sees.

There is no one to protect Lafayette or his five siblings from violence. To live in the project is to live outside a protected circle. Inside the circle are middle-class people, middle-class neighborhoods, middle-class institutions. Outside are the very poor, the very powerless. When Lafayette and his siblings leave their first floor apartment, their mother does not know if they will return. She cannot take their safety for granted. The police move in and out of the project every day, confiscating weapons and drugs, answering calls, making arrests, but they will not or cannot make the shooting stop.

During the summer, someone is shot, stabbed, or beaten every three days at Henry Horner Homes. That bald statistic fails to capture the heart-pounding terror of Lafayette's brother, 9-year-old Pharaoh Walton, who finds himself in the middle of a drug-gang gunfight on his way home from school. One of the combatants has a submachine gun. Just a few yards from the safety of his home, shots blaze and career around Pharaoh, tearing up the earth, smashing into walls. The boy bangs and then kicks his own front door, begging to be allowed entry. The roar of battle drowns out his pleas. No one can hear him, no one opens the door. Eventually, Pharaoh does make it to safety, gaining entrance to a different apartment.

12-year-old Lafayette has seen a number of young gang members who were involved in the drug trade get shot and die. A few weeks after Pharaoh's narrow escape, one bled to death just yards from the Walton's apartment, but other kinds of shootings, beatings, stabbings, and rapes occur more frequently. Weapons are ubiquitous, and family disputes often end in violence. Women as well as men resort to physical force, and project residents are often the victims of crime. Just a few months earlier, knife-wielding muggers slashed the hand of LaJoe Walton, the children's mother, permanently paralyzing two of her fingers.*

THE PSYCHOLOGICAL IMPACT OF VIOLENCE

THE STORY OF THE WALTON FAMILY'S STRUGGLE TO SURVIVE at the Henry Horner Homes was the subject of a memorable profile published in the *Wall Street Journal* in October 1987. Staff reporter Alex Kotlowitz followed family members and friends for many months, chronicling the full sweep of violence in their lives. Kotlowitz probed the appalling psychological impact of living in a war zone, seeking to understand what living in a world without safety means to children and to adults.

Kotlowitz is not the only observer to compare the circumstances of inner city children to growing up in a war zone. Many psychotherapists think that children exposed to violence develop the same symp-

---

* Based on the reporting of Alex Kotlowitz in *The Wall Street Journal*, Oct. 27, 1987.

toms as "shellshocked" soldiers in wartime. Psychiatrists first began using the diagnosis post traumatic stress syndrome to describe the circumstances of Vietnam veterans who were unable to adjust when they returned home. Afflicted veterans were depressed, passive, hopeless—unable to rouse themselves and actively pursue the making of new lives. They abused alcohol and drugs. Many suffered from headaches, nightmares, and "flashbacks" during which they would relive in terrible detail the violence they had experienced overseas. Frightened and vulnerable, they often carried weapons. Some committed more violence when they returned to the United States.

Children trapped in violent circumstances may also exhibit the symptoms of post traumatic stress syndrome. Like Diante McClain, the little boy who would not run away to escape the bullets, they may become depressed and passive. They may regress dramatically, exhibiting the behaviors of much younger children—sucking their thumbs, wetting the bed, sometimes refusing to speak. Even those whose outward symptoms are not dramatic are likely to have little energy for school work or other activities that would allow them to prepare for an independent future.

In recent years, mental health providers have begun to see signs of post traumatic stress syndrome in crime victims, in the victims of terrorist attacks, and in children chronically exposed to violence in their homes and communities. In many parts of the country therapists have begun reaching out to the victims of violence. In Roxbury, Massachusetts, where I live, the health center has organized a "Living After Murder" program that counsels adults and children who have experienced the murder of a close friend or relative. Counselors in this program also offer help to children who have not yet lost a loved one to murder, but who are struggling with the stress of living in a violent environment.

The director of the "Living After Murder" program, psychologist Mohamed Seedat, says that feelings of helplessness and depression are common among children in violence-plagued neighborhoods like Roxbury. Children trapped in urban terror, he says, turn to the adults in their lives for reassurance of safety. They want adults to give them the feeling that they are "contained," meaning held and protected. When adults cannot or do not provide reassurance, children tend to become very angry and lash out, Seedat says. They are shouting to us, "I am vulnerable," he says. The society, however, seems not to be listening. When parents and others are not powerful enough to provide a safe environment, children are emotionally devastated— desolated. They feel themselves abandoned in a dangerous universe, which they are. Aggression is all they have with which to fight back. Ultimately, Seedat says, the kids turn on each other violently. He blames escalating gang violence in Boston on the rage of children whose basic need for protection and safety—a need that every child possesses—has not been met.

Seedat, who is from South Africa, says the situation for many black children in the United States is remarkably similar to the situation of young blacks in South Africa. Poor black children in these two distant lands are both born into circumstances saturated with violence, in which black-on-black violence and violence in general shapes their daily experience. However, living in the United States, Seedat says, is in many respects worse than living in South Africa. In South Africa blacks are filled with the hope and expectation that the political struggle to which so many are dedicated will give birth to a fairer and more peaceful life. Here, he says, since the end of the civil rights movement, many poor blacks have lost their faith and hope in improving their lives.

My friend and colleague, Carl Bell M.D., director of Chicago's Community Mental Health Council, has used a variety of means in the attempt to quantify the amount of violence to which inner city kids are exposed. He conducted surveys of 1,035 youngsters at four high schools and three grammar schools in a high crime area of Chicago's South Side. By the age of 11, four out of five of the children in the survey had seen someone beaten up either at home or in the street. One out of three had seen a shooting or stabbing. One quarter had seen a killing. By looking at police accounts of homicides, Dr. Bell has documented that hundreds of children in Chicago, Detroit, and other urban areas witness murders each year. According to his figures, in Los Angeles County alone, hundreds of children each year witness the murder of a *parent*. Extrapolating from Carl Bell's figures, we can begin to sense the dimension of the problem. All across the nation hundreds of thousands—perhaps millions—of inner city youngsters are daily exposed to what can only be called toxic levels of violence. Harm—great harm—is being done. This is tragically obvious.

THE UNDERCLASS

SOCIOLOGISTS DESCRIBE THE WALTON FAMILY AND THEIR neighbors as members of "the underclass." This phrase refers to profoundly impoverished Americans, many of whom are black and brown-skinned, who live in urban neighborhoods where nearly everyone else is poor, where few men work, where most families are headed by women, many of whom are on welfare, and where violence is prevalent. For example, at the Robert Taylor Homes housing project in Chicago, 93 percent of the families were headed by a single parent—almost always a woman—in 1980. Of the non-elderly families, 83 percent received welfare. 20,000 people lived at the Robert Taylor homes that year. That's one half of one percent (0.5%) of Chicago's population. Still, 11 percent of the city's murders occurred at the Robert Taylor Homes—that's more than 20 times the rate one would expect based on population. Scholars looking at underclass neighborhoods like this express concern that an entire generation of children is growing up immersed in violence, cut off from non-violent standards and values. Children like this may never know anyone who handles emotional crises and difficulties without violence. Very often most of what they know about the world outside their neighborhood is provided by the violence-saturated medium of television.

Up until the 1980s, few sociologists believed that an underclass existed in the United States. Focusing special attention on the waves of white immigrants who arrived here in the late 19th and early 20th centuries, they argued that in America, extreme poverty was almost always a temporary phenomena. Families experiencing want were expected to rise out of poverty as a result of their own hard work. Even when extreme poverty lasted an entire lifetime, the children of the poor were believed able to achieve a better life. The American idea that one's children will do better than oneself was seen as applying to all classes of Americans, including the most impoverished. To a large extent these assumptions were true for white immigrants and for many brown-skinned immigrants from the Caribbean, but they have proven false for a significant portion of native-born African-Americans.

Looking at information from the 1970s and 1980s, many experts have begun to conclude that the poorest of the poor, of whom a disproportionate number are black, are becoming a permanently isolated underclass, far removed from the economic mainstream. Scholars have reached this conclusion after studying conditions in neighborhoods like that surrounding the Henry Horner and the Robert Taylor housing projects. In these neighborhoods, chronic poverty, passed from generation to generation like a genetic disease, is the rule. The young are not doing better than their elders. Grandmother, daughter, and granddaughter may all be single mothers, dependent on welfare for support. Grandfather, father, and son may all be out of work and maintain little closeness with their offspring. Like the Waltons who talk incessantly of leaving the Henry Horner Homes but have no realistic way to escape, few born into underclass neighborhoods are able to move up and out. Like the Waltons, they are left behind to cope with the misery endemic to an underclass neighborhood. Their escape is no more likely than that of the lowest born in a formal caste system.

One of the most influential scholars looking at the emergence of the black underclass is a sociologist from the University of Chicago,

William Julius Wilson. Professor Wilson sees the origins of the black underclass in the convergence of two more or less unrelated trends. The first of these was economic: Between 1960 and 1980 the American economy was remade. Manufacturing ceased to be the nation's economic base. Foreign competitors, particularly from Asia, began to produce manufactured goods at a lower cost and more efficiently than domestic companies. American steel, automobiles, electronics, textiles, and clothing no longer dominated domestic or foreign markets. Millions of relatively well paid manufacturing jobs that required little education and few skills disappeared from downtown manufacturing centers in the Northeast and Mid-west.

In New York, Chicago, Philadelphia, and Detroit, 1 million manufacturing, retail, and wholesale jobs were lost between 1967 and 1976. As a result, hundreds of thousands of blue collar workers were forced out of the labor market. Whole industries were closed down. Men who had worked all their adult lives no longer had jobs or access to jobs. There simply were no buyers for the skills these workers were selling. Nationally, lost blue collar jobs were at least partially replaced by white collar jobs in banking, finance, and other service industries. The new jobs, however, required high levels of education and skills. Few of the newly unemployed lower-class men and few of their offspring were qualified for these new jobs.

The impact of this economic displacement reverberated throughout the inner city. Hundreds of thousands of black working men no longer had a place in the legitimate economy. Moreover, sons and nephews who had expected to follow their male relatives onto the assembly line or factory floor were left in the lurch. In good times, those who were employed knew about job openings in their factories and in their fields. They passed this information on, helping relatives and friends find employment, but when entire industries shut down, one person could no longer help another. The destabilizing effect of these economic changes was multiplied by huge demographic shifts occurring in black inner city communities.

This takes us to Wilson's second point about the emergence of the black underclass: Until the late 1960s the vast majority of non-rural black Americans lived in urban neighborhoods that were "vertically integrated." This term means that rich and poor and in-between lived together. The laborer and the judge and the junkie might all have lived on the same street. They did so because racial segregation limited the housing choices of those who were better off. Expanded legal rights won in the 1960s, however, made it possible for middle-class blacks to leave the inner city to live in less densely populated urban and suburban neighborhoods. Millions of relatively prosperous working class and middle-class blacks left ghetto areas in the 1970s. Wilson surmises that when the most affluent residents left, inner city neighborhoods lost a crucial anchor. Departing in droves were the strong, the skilled, and the ambitious. The adults remaining in the inner city tended to be more troubled, less educated, less ambitious, and less able to encourage their children in positive directions. Children remaining in the ghetto no longer had the example of fellow blacks who were working hard and achieving success. They no longer had role models to emulate on their own block, in their own neighborhood.

It is in the convergence of these two major trends that Wilson sees the making of a tragedy. Inner city neighborhoods lost their white collar residents at the very moment that many blue collar residents lost their jobs. Entire neighborhoods were depopulated of laboring men—blue collar and white collar—who earned enough to support their families. From this tree grew a crop of bitter fruit. Wilson notes that in 1965, 25 percent of black children had been born out of wedlock. By 1982, 57 percent of black children were born to single mothers, and in a "rustbelt" city like Chicago where blacks had been devastated by the collapse of heavy manufacturing, 75 percent of black births in 1983 were out of wedlock. In the same year, 95 percent of teenage black births in Chicago occurred outside of marriage. When men could not work, they lost the respect and the status associated with providing for a family. Poor black women turned away from permanent alliances with unemployed black men. Alone, women could (meagerly) support their children on welfare. Marriage to unemployed men offered no such guarantee. Black men, demeaned by the economic conditions that made them economically superfluous, withdrew from the family scene. Men and women alike were deeply wounded by this breach.

These wounds cut deeply into the flesh of the black community. Research indicates that the drastic increase in the numbers of very poor black families headed by women was the most significant factor leading to rising rates of crime and violence in the poorest black communities in the 1970s and 1980s. Robert J. Sampson, an associate of Wilson's at the University of Chicago, examined data related to robbery and homicide in more than 150 American cities. He found that the scarcity of employed men in poor black communities set in motion a train of destructive events. Male joblessness led to female-headed families. The increase in female-headed families, in turn, is associated with significant rises in the homicide and murder rate. These effects, to use the terminology of sociology, were found to be "independent of" race, age, income, welfare, region, neighborhood density, and so on. What this means in non-academic terms is simple: Regardless of the race or class of individuals, when large numbers of men are out of work and large numbers of families are headed by women the rate of crime and violence in that community rises sharply. This fact is as true for whites as for blacks. White communities with chronic male unemployment and high rates of female-headed households are as troubled by violence and crime as underclass black neighborhoods, but there are fewer such neighborhoods—unemployment hit black communities much harder than white ones. Even the worst white inner city neighborhoods, Sampson has written, tend to have more employed males and more wealth than similarly situated black communities. This data regarding single-parent families should not be interpreted as derogatory to single mothers. What the numbers highlight is not the inadequacy of women, single or otherwise, as parents, but the terrible stress under which impoverished single-parent families live. Under the best of circumstances, raising children is a difficult job, but when families are poor; social supports are absent; schools fail to teach; job prospects are missing; the streets are alluring and dangerous; non-violent males are not available to help with discipline and provide an example—the job of raising children can become nearly impossible.

The significance of these developments cannot be overstated. Throughout the 1970s and 1980s hundreds of functioning, stable black inner city neighborhoods slid downward. During a period when the population of the nation's fifty largest cities declined, the number of poor people in these cities, a disproportionate number of whom were black, increased. The number of people living in extremely poor areas increased even more. These increases and decreases were not subtle. For example, between 1970 and 1980, the combined population of New York, Chicago, Los Angeles, Philadelphia, and Detroit decreased by 9 percent. The number of poor people in these cities— again, a disproportionate number of whom were black—increased by 22 percent. What is truly astounding, the number of people living in extremely poor areas in these cities increased by 161 percent. This is the underclass. High blue collar unemployment, in conjunction with middle-class flight, transformed poor neighborhoods into underclass slums in just ten years. The human impact of these numbers cannot be clearer. According to my friend Glen Pierce, Director for the Center of Applied Social Research at Northeastern University, between 1973 and 1986 the income of young black males without high school diplomas declined nationally by 40 percent. In that 13-year span the wealth of young black males was cut in half. That decline, representing a gross decline in employment, will reverberate throughout black communities for many years. Research data show conclusively that successful adult employment is part of a cumulative process. The young need to work and earn wages, not only for the immediate benefit wages bestow, but for the future. Those who do not establish a work history in their teenage years are much less likely to work continuously as adults.

THE SHORT LIFE OF A FORMER FOSTER CHILD

For a brief time two years ago, Reggie Brown, known as Gizmo to his friends, emerged from the ranks of the anonymous young homeless to enjoy an unlikely celebrity. His tragic odyssey through the foster-care system had cast him as a plaintiff in a lawsuit that held out the promise for sweeping changes in what happens to children after they become too old for foster care.

The fleeting attention did not alter the course of Mr. Brown's harsh life, which led from nights spent sleeping on the subways and in abandoned buildings, to Rikers Island (prison), and back again.

His gift for survival ran out on the streets of Harlem when, three months shy of his 22nd birthday, he was fatally shot in the back. Those who knew him said he seemed doomed by his past and his homelessness, and they were saddened, but not all that surprised, to learn that he had been killed . . .

"All Gizmo's life was a statistic, and damned if he didn't end up a statistic," said one of his friends, Darryl Wood . . .

—Sara Rimer
The New York Times,
Nov. 11, 1987

Reggie Brown's friend, Darryl Wood, was right. It is easy to think of Reggie Brown as a statistic. His death illustrates the statistic that homicide is the leading cause of death for young black men, from 18 until they reach middle age. Other tragic statistics apply to him as well. Such as the one that describes the increasing number of black children—close to 60 percent—growing up in families headed by women. Or the one that says at least 50 percent of all young black men in New York City drop out of school prior to graduation. And then there is the new statistic that documents a significant relationship between homelessness and homicide.

But to me Reggie Brown is not a number. He is a face with a smile so broad, so full of warmth and life, that it can shine through a newspaper clipping that is beginning to turn brown. "Gizmo had a smile you wouldn't believe," said a priest who ministers to the homeless.

Every inequity that can befall a life seems to have befallen Reggie Brown. He was born poor and diabetic. When he was 13, a male friend of Reggie's mother threw him out of a second-story window. His spinal cord was injured. After that, Reggie did not live with his mother anymore. Nor did he ever again have a permanent address. Emotionally needy and disruptive, he entered the foster care system. He was moved around a lot. His school record was spotty. He dropped out.

When Reggie turned 18, he was discharged from foster care by officials of the City of New York. He had a ninth-grade education and no skills. A welfare worker gave him cab fare and the address of the men's shelter on the Bowery. Later, he became one of the plaintiffs in a successful suit brought by an organization representing the homeless. The courts ruled that foster children must be prepared for independent living before being released from supervision. Advocates in New York City say it remains to be seen if this new rule will be enforced.

For nearly four years after turning 18, Reggie supported himself doing small-time hustles. His skills as a thief and hustler were laughably inept. He stole a car worth 250 dollars and was arrested at the toll booth before he could cross the Hudson into New Jersey. He was in and out of prison. He was killed when a 19-dollar drug deal went bad.

People who knew him say all Reggie wanted out of life was a room of his own. A room that was his. Where in two months or three, he could not be turned out. He never got it.

COMMUNITY COLLAPSE

POVERTY ALONE DID NOT KILL REGGIE BROWN.

Poverty alone does not destroy a child. A poor child growing up in a stable family has a fighting chance in life. So does a child from a troubled family who grows up in a stable community. However, when schools no longer believe that children can learn, when vital city services are only meagerly apportioned, when there are few local businesses to employ the young, when churches have less influence or have packed up and moved to the suburbs, when there are few recreational facilities to occupy children, few agencies offering hope and opportunity, and when violence becomes the norm, the outlook for children is dismal. These are precisely the circumstances of the underclass, the circumstances into which Reggie and hundreds of thousands of other young black males in the inner city have been born.

Being born into a poor troubled family in a neighborhood overwhelmed by a deluge of poor troubled families is what killed Reggie Brown. In underclass neighborhoods like the one in which he was born and the one in which he died, the necessary balance between those who are self-sufficient and those who need help has been disturbed. When everyone needs help, no one is available to do the helping. When very few are employed, there is no stable economic base. The local institutions that people turn to in times of trouble are not capable of handling the quantity of people needing service. Many collapse under the weight of need surrounding them. Over time the poorest neighborhoods are depopulated of helping people and helping organizations.

One might expect government services to take up the slack in the poorest neighborhoods, but this does not happen. City resources tend to go to affluent neighborhoods, neighborhoods in which people have the power to demand attention. Garbage-collection and fire-fighting are notoriously deficient in many poor neighborhoods. Nor do police resources always go where they are most needed. Emergency medical and ambulance services are notoriously unsatisfactory in very poor neighborhoods. This is not a trivial matter. Slow response time can turn even routine assaults into homicides. Victims who could be saved die of their injuries because medical help does not come quickly enough.

The destructive impact of a poor troubled family in a neighborhood lacking effective governmental, charitable, and civic organizations cannot be overstated. Like arteries transporting blood throughout the body, these organizations are lifelines that save many, many children. Governmental agencies, churches, schools, after-school programs, Y's, boys and girls clubs, chambers of commerce, service clubs, health centers, etc. offer adults and children support, solace, refuge, and resources. When these institutions cease to function effectively, communities are delivered what is often a mortal blow.

There is another facet to all of this. Functioning institutions, along with functioning families, are central to a community's capacity to uphold a certain code of non-violent behavior. Individual citizens cannot successfully demand of each other and their children behavior that is legal and morally acceptable. Non-violence must be a community standard, supported and reinforced by institutions and groups within the society. In the absence of an enforced community standard condemning violence and lawlessness, the police are unable to staunch the violence and mayhem. In fact, in such circumstances the police often become part of the problem, adding to the sum total of violence within an underclass community.

When individuals and institutions cease to regulate the behavior of residents, a vicious cycle is set in motion. People look at the lawlessness surrounding them and they feel powerless to change the conditions under which they are living. The more powerless people feel, the less effectively they demand observance of standards of behavior. The more the rules are breached, the more degraded everyday experiences become. The more pathology people see, the more people feel uninhibited about succumbing. After a while it seems as if everyone takes drugs or drinks or acts out violently. At a certain point a critical mass is reached. When people look around they do not see any evidence that any other kind of life can be lived except one of violence and despair. At that point the pathology in the community multiplies unimpeded. It was into communities like this that Reggie Brown and Lafayette Walton were born; it was in such a community that Reggie Brown died.

CHILDREN

THE ECONOMIC AND SOCIAL CHANGES THAT OCCURRED IN the poorest black communities in the 1970s and 1980s hurt children in particular. Growing up in a household headed by a woman, especially a young woman, often means growing up poor. This is true of almost all children in all communities, but it is especially true for black children. In 1982 in central city areas throughout the nation, 60 percent of all poor families were headed by women, 78 percent of all poor black families were female-headed.

Federal guidelines classify a family of three with an income of less than $745 a month as poor. That's a combined family income of less than $9,000. Using this yardstick, the Children's Defense Fund estimates that in 1989 nearly one in five American children were poor. Nearly one in three families headed by young adults were poor, and nearly one in two—half—of all black children were poor. During the 1980s, while the number of poor families with children was rapidly rising, 40 billion dollars was cut from programs for poor children and families.

Often the women who head poor families are children themselves—15, 16, 17 years old when they give birth. Many of these young mothers are poorly equipped to rear healthy, competent children with the resources and personal strengths to burst free from the bonds of multi-generational poverty. Often girls have babies because they want someone to love *them*. Indulging in the magic thinking that is typical of adolescents, they romanticize the emotional paybacks of parenthood, while not focusing on the expense and the sheer physical drudgery that caring for a small child entails.

Some interesting points have been raised about the competing developmental imperatives of adolescence and motherhood. Becoming a teenager and becoming a mother are events that travel in opposite directions psychologically. Young adolescents are by necessity, self-absorbed, self-obsessed, narcissistic, egocentric. These traits help teens separate from their families and develop their own identity. The traits new mothers need in order to manage the demanding job of rearing a small child are in direct conflict with these. New mothers need empathy, the ability to put themselves in their squalling babies' place, to understand what their babies feel and to accurately imagine what they need in order to be safe and comfortable. Empathy is derailed by the adolescent's age-appropriate narcissism. During my years practicing adolescent medicine, I got to see precisely what this conflict means when a 14-year-old pregnant girl for whom I cared refused to eat properly and gain the weight that is necessary to produce a healthy child. The girl starved herself and her child because she was to perform in a fashion show at her school and she did not want to look fat. Her "normal" adolescent narcissism was jeopardizing her own health and the physical well-being of her unborn child.

The developmental incompatibility of young moms and their offspring can result in a lose-lose psychological outcome. The young mother's psychological and cognitive development may be short-circuited by premature motherhood. She may never have the chance to finish high school or go to college. She may never have the opportunity to resolve and relinquish her adolescent emotions and beliefs and become an independent person. Needing her own mother to help care for the baby, she may never successfully become independent of her family. With so much maturing left undone, her relationships with men are unlikely to be very satisfying.

Just as a young woman's development is often thwarted by early parenthood, so is her child's. A child's cognitive and emotional development is predicated on his parents' development. The world to which they introduce him is his world. If their world is cramped and limited, so will his be. Unless older adults and family members provide her with additional resources and support, the young, single mother's *underdevelopment* is likely to be repeated by her child. The end result is a tragic circle in which the mother's failure to thrive leads to the child's failure. Generation after generation may never come close to reaching their emotional or intellectual potential.

BOYS WITHOUT FATHERS

AS A BLACK WOMAN AND AS A MOTHER, I HAVE COME TO believe that one of the most precious gifts my husband Charles and I give our children is our healthy marriage. The majority of black children in America today are growing up without such an example. They do not have the opportunity to live with and learn from two parents who are balancing the ups and downs of love and anger, who are handling responsibility, earning a living, struggling with the commitment to stay together. This is a profound disadvantage for children of both sexes, especially those—half of all black children—who are growing up poor.

I do not mean to say that women raising children alone are doomed to failure. Many single women rear healthy, upstanding daughters and sons—my husband Charles is one such man, reared by his mother who was divorced. Financially and emotionally, however, women who lack a mate with whom to share the burdens of parenthood are at a disadvantage. Moreover, and perhaps most importantly, those who are poor and live in a family without a father are subject to a kind of double jeopardy. Poverty itself is an assault on children's self esteem. Destructive too is the psychological impoverishment of having only one parent. Many poor children living in these circumstances sense their mother's underlying disappointment and anger toward the men in their lives. Watching their mothers struggling to raise a family alone, girls learn to expect little from men, financially or emotionally. Boys learn that their maleness is, at best, an ambivalent quality.

One psychoanalyst has called the loneliness of boys for male intimacy and a male figure after whom to model themselves, "father hunger." I find this phrase particularly poignant and particularly accurate. As the mother of an 11-year-old son I am amazed and touched to see how eager my child is for the company of his father and for other adult males. I have watched him watching his father and his father's male friends. He observes everything. The way these grown men talk, how they think, what makes them laugh. Their gestures, their attitudes, the way they hold their bodies. In their presence he is a rapt student learning how to be a man.

Boys suffer from the absence of non-violent male role models at home. Many have a hard time establishing who they are supposed to be. All the research indicates that boys in father-absent homes have great difficulty with sex roles and what's called gender identification; that is, the establishment of a satisfying identity as a male if you are male or a satisfying identity as a female if you are female. Moreover, the research indicates clearly that boys without fathers at home have a more difficult time managing their aggression than boys who do. Often these boys have a shorter attention span. They are distracted. They have more difficulty than other boys with school performance and they have a difficult time adjusting socially. Some of these problems, no doubt, are related to poverty, but there is a significant body of evidence indicating that even middle-class children who are missing a father have a disadvantage in life.

Yet when fathers, stepfathers, and boyfriends are on the scene, the relationship is often fraught with tension. The lessons adult males teach children can be negative ones—drinking, drugs, illegal activities, and domestic violence. Sons may see fathers and stepfathers treating women as objects, manipulating them, or otherwise using them to their advantage. Men and maleness are diminished in their own eyes. Young black males in the impoverished underclass setting usually grow to manhood in an environment where very few feel good about their manliness. The phrase, "you're no good," said by mothers and grandmothers to sons, sometimes in affection, sometimes in anger, reverberates throughout poor black communities predicting the behavior of young black men, robbing them of their pride and self-esteem.

6

WHAT THE KIDS SAY

I find trying to survive in this world very hard, but when there's violence on the streets, it makes survival even harder. I think about how many innocent people get killed every day. I think about kids getting killed at young ages. I think about the elderly people, who have no one to do things for them. I think about the fear that they have each time they come out of their homes. I think about how some old people have to stay locked up in their own homes, because they are afraid to stay inside, and they are even more afraid to come out. I don't think that life should be this way.

I think about all these different gangs that are out on the streets, trying to take over different turfs, which don't even belong to any of them. Every day we hear that someone has been shot or stabbed. Why can't these young kids understand that they also are a part of this human race? Each day when I come home from school I stay in the house until the next morning, when it's time to go to school again. It's getting so it's not even safe to stay inside of your own home. When I leave school in the afternoon, I try to find a safer way to walk home. But there's no safe way to come. No matter which way you come, you always have that fear inside. I wish that everybody could stick together, as brothers and sisters. I wish that the day would come when people could walk the streets without fear of being shot, stabbed, robbed, or just plain molested.

Tomorrow is another day. And I wonder what it will bring. But deep down inside I already know that it will be another day of trying to find a safe route home from school, seeing the kids on the streets trying to be bad, seeing some old person walking in fear, seeing the police cars, with their lights flashing, and their sirens on, seeing the ambulance coming and going, and seeing the youth of America being shot down, and killed, before they even had a chance to live.

Prize-winning Essay
Mukiya Adams, 17 years old
Jeremiah E. Burke High School
Boston

In the fall of 1989 my co-author Michaele Weissman and I spent quite a bit of time at the Jeremiah E. Burke High School in Boston's Dorchester neighborhood observing and talking with students about violence. For me, these meetings were a homecoming. I knew the Burke very well. The school had been a learning place for me, and the students, teachers, and administrators there had been my friends. For three years (from 1983 to 1985), I had taught my 10-week violence prevention curriculum at the Burke as part of the sophomore health program. Teaching those tenth graders had helped me to understand the way teenagers think about fighting and about violence, and had helped me to refine the curriculum.

The experts say that the best schools are small and have strong principals. The Burke meets both of these requirements. The school has only 900 students, most of whom are African-Americans, some of whom are the children of immigrants from Haiti, Cape Verde, Jamaica. (There are also Hispanic students and a smattering of Asians and whites.) The Burke's principal, Albert Holland, a tall, athletic-looking black man in his forties is a strong, sure advocate for his students, his school. Mr. Holland patrols the halls before school and between classes, greeting students by name. He is known to be fair and the students and the teachers trust him. He has helped to make the Burke, once a dreaded assignment for students and teachers, a school both groups are proud of, a school where many students learn, graduate, and go on for more education.

The Burke is an oasis of safety in what many call Boston's most dangerous neighborhood. Drugs and gangs and poverty flourish, as does little else, in the streets surrounding the school. Castlegate Avenue, from which one of the city's most visible gangs gets its name, begins at the front door. Getting to and from the Burke can be like an infantry march through guerrilla infested territory.

The gang scene in Boston is not as organized or as vast as it is in some other cities. Many gangs are groups of kids who grew up together; their home block becomes their turf. Though there are an estimated 30 to 40 street gangs in Boston's poor neighborhoods, only a handful of them are thought to be ruthless drug-dealing gangs operating as profit-driven, organized crime units. Still, you don't have to be the mafia to commit crimes and hurt people.

While only a few of the gangs are thought to be major players in the drug business, members of many gangs deal drugs on a low level, earning enough to provide themselves with nice clothes, jewelry, and weapons, while guaranteeing their own supply of illicit substances. Some gangs diversify into other areas of crime—car theft, mugging, robbery, burglary, and so forth. All gang members in Boston seem to have ready access to guns; some have sophisticated arsenals.

A backdrop to our visits at the Burke was a storm of shootings in

Boston's poor black neighborhoods that occurred in the fall of 1989. Police in Area B, which includes the three contiguous areas of Roxbury, Dorchester, and Mattapan, reported that 101 people had been wounded in 170 shooting incidents between September 6 and October 16. Four people were killed. Young black males between 16 and 24, many of them gang-affiliated, were implicated in more than half of the attacks. Residents of Area B said that the actual number of shootings during the five-week period was much higher than 170. Bursts of gunfire had become so common that the police were not even notified unless someone was injured.

We did more than talk to students at the Burke about violence. We asked them to write about how it feels to live in a violent environment. As an inducement, we offered $50 in cash as a prize for the best essay on the topic "Surviving in a Violent World." The winner was 17-year-old Mukiya Adams, a student in the Burke's special drop-out prevention program. Her composition was also published in the school newspaper, *The Burke Informer.*

Thirty-three students from grades nine through twelve submitted entries. The work of these young authors was not always polished, but it was remarkably frank—so frank that in order to protect the writers, we have not used their names. The students' willingness to disclose their concerns about violence and, in some cases, their concerns about their own violent and dangerous behavior is a testament to the adults at the Burke, who have created an environment where kids feel physically and psychologically safe.

Even I was surprised by the depth of emotion abounding in the essays. Fear, despair, and feelings of powerlessness poured off the pages. Student after student expressed the idea that their situation is inevitable, that they cannot escape it. Few suggested ways to mobilize their community against violence. These young people seemed defeated by the violence and all the other social ills) surrounding them. Fatalism was their main defense. Many wrote about the victims of violence *"being at the wrong place at the wrong time."* One college-bound student, a young woman who gives the appearance of being vigorously in charge of her own life, wrote,

> No one knows for sure when they will be a victim of violence. It could be innocent you who always minds your business. Bullets have no name nor eyes. That's why there is no strategy for surviving in a violent world. You can protect yourself as best as you possibly can, but when the time comes for you to be hit with violence, you won't be missed.

All the students, male and female, wrote about being afraid. One young woman wrote:

Surviving in the streets of Boston has been real rough. You don't know what's going to happen today or tomorrow. You don't know if you'll ever see the people that you love, when you walk out that door.

Another young woman wrote,

You cannot walk out of your house without looking behind you every step of the way.

Then she added, "I cannot sleep at night, because I'm scared the gunshots that I hear may come through my bedroom window.

Her fear, like the fear of all these students, is grounded in reality. In Boston and elsewhere in recent years scores of urban Americans have died when random bullets screamed through their windows and doors. In New York City, in a two-week period during the summer of 1990, four children—one a 9-month-old standing in his walker—were shot to death by bullets fired outside their apartment walls, windows, and doors.

Many of the teenagers write about knowing kids who have been shot and kids who have been killed. A ninth grader wrote,

Surviving in a violent world is almost impossible. The reason why I say (this) is because every summer three or four of my friends or people I know die or get hurt badly. I am surprised I am still living in this violent world. I have come very close to dying a lot of times, but I guess I am just lucky.

They all felt their futures were jeopardized.

We are told that we are the future, yet being a teenager growing up in the inner city part of Boston. I find it difficult to believe. How can you see a future when there is a black teen shot or killed every day? Out of every three people that are killed, two of them are black. . . . It (is) easy for some to say, 'keep hope alive' when they're not dealing with the problems that we the people who live in the inner city have to deal with.

Another girl, a senior, also referred despairingly to Jessie Jackson's well known exhortation:

Reverend Jackson always says to 'keep hope alive,' but I wonder if he expects parents who are informed that their son/daughter was just assaulted, or that your wife/husband has been murdered to keep the hope alive?

This writer continued, describing the incertitude that violence had introduced into all relationships in the inner city:

> It's sad to see my aunt sitting up at night wondering if her son will make it home or will she get a phone call from a stranger telling her that he's dead. It's getting so bad that a lot people are scared to send their little ones to school because a bullet may fly through a window and kill them. You never know what could happen. Sometimes I sit and think. 'Am I going to be next, will I live to get married and have children?'

Many referred bitterly to the ease with which guns can be obtained in their neighborhood. One young woman wrote,

> Young men and grown men, even children get guns like they buy cigarettes in the store or bubble gum.

Another, also a female, talked about why kids carry guns:

> They think by carrying guns, that they will be protected from dying.

A number of kids referred to the death of 9-year-old Tiffany Moore who was sitting on a mailbox talking to friends when felled in a drive-by shooting. The students, especially the girls, identified with this young victim. One wrote,

> It is not safe to sit in front of your house anymore.

A ninth grader recalled the exact date of Tiffany's death:

> Take young Tiffany Moore. She was sitting on a mailbox on August 19, 1988 when some irresponsible person passed by in a car shooting and struck her. She died, everybody know that, but nobody knows what she had planned for her life, what her dreams were in life.

The kids blamed gangs and drugs for the death and calamity in their community, although some seemed to comprehend that the problem of violence was larger, even, than its most visible manifestations. One male wrote,

> One of the most important things teenagers face in our day is violence. Not gang-violence, (or) drug-related violence. I am not saying that they are not a problem, but the real problem is just plain old violence. . . .

A girl wrote about the disputes that trigger so many violent interactions among adolescents:

> Teens are killing each other for some stupid things like chains, drugs, money, girlfriend or boyfriend or for just a stupid argument,

she wrote. Nobody suggested that more effective ways were needed to deal with conflict, but one young woman did ask rhetorically

> What ever happened to apologies like 'I'm sorry,' 'excuse me,' or if you want to be hip about it, 'my bag?' "

Many of the kids, especially the boys, wrote about disputes over sneakers and hats. Getting caught wearing the wrong brand of either on alien turf is considered a fighting and sometimes a shooting offense by some of the gangs. Survival requires that even kids with no gang affiliation observe gang rules concerning dress when they travel through or spend time in that gang's turf. At the Burke, there is one brand of sneakers and hats to wear; this code to use the students phrase, "rules." While a few kids wear brands that are considered neutral, most go along with the dress code and wear the ones favored by gang members. To wear a brand associated with a competing gang is to court an attack. At other schools in other neighborhoods, the rules are different. The problem for kids arises outside of school. The clothes that are safe to wear at school may be interpreted as an act of aggression in another neighborhood. A young male wrote,

> You can't walk down the street without worrying should I be wearing this particular hat in the neighborhood where I live because the 'Homeboys' (gang members) in the 'hood' wear different hats.

Another student wrote,

> A guy around my house got shot just because of a hat. Just because you have a black and red Adidas hat you can't walk in certain places.

A young woman wrote,

> I was on my way to fifth period class in school when one boy accidentally stepped on another boy's newly bought Adidas. He was stabbed. Just over a $70.00 pair of sneakers.

One writer who identified himself as a gang member and seemed to be extremely divided on the question of gangs, wrote,

They are taking brothers lives over, 'Yo, you stepped on my sneakers,' or 'You tried to talk to my girl and did not respect her when she
didn't say anything.' "

In his essay this young male veered back and forth between horror at
what is going on in the streets:

It seems like everyone has just gone mad,

to a rational defense of the gangs.

I am down with a gang and its not what everyone seems to think,
especially the news reporters. All the gangs are violent, but people
let's be real.

(I am not sure if he means to say here that the violence is less sensational than the way journalists report it, or if he means as everyone
is violent why make such a big deal about *this* violence.)
This young gang-affiliated male blamed inadequate patrols by Boston police for the violence on the street:

Recently those shootings that took place has everyone talking . . .
about how they are scared and what kind of protection they need.
First of all the police put on big fronts on television, but they are not
even trying (to stop the violence). Because if there (had been) more
security on the street there would not have been many shootings the
other weekend.

(This opinion is not so far-fetched. Police Area B where all the shoot-
ings occurred is the scene of nearly 70 percent of the homicides in
Boston, but commands only 25% of the assigned police.)
From the police, his attention turned to drug dealing:

Drugs play a big part in gang violence. While gangs are standing on
street corners, they are getting the money too. Because if you are
down (involved with a gang) and you want to stay looking fresh you
got to get the green paper.

He concluded his essay by sharing with readers information about
what drugs were currently hip.

Words up! crack, cocaine and the new jack ice (a combination of
heroin, chrystal methodine, and cocaine) is the top money making
products.

Not all the kids want more police protection. A senior at the Burke wrote a searing essay in which he blamed the police for much of the violence in the inner city.

The police are like vicious dogs at times. The police come into black neighborhoods and snatch on kids, beat kids, cus you out, your mother and anybody else. How would you feel to get beaten or thrown in jail for nothing? That causes anger and frustrations which leads to violence. Who are black people going to let their frustrations out on? White people? No! Police? No! They let their frustrations out on each other, and it is accepted. It is accepted in a way that not much happens if a black person shoots a black. Let a black shoot a white; it's a big situation.

He continued bitterly that, the black

community backs up police instead of helping us and we are their children. The police will even stick a gun in my face or tell me that such and such said this and that about me, (alleging that he is a gang member). Believe that, because it is true.

The media also earned this young writer's ire:

The media hypes everything. They can ask me and my friends something on T.V. and call us a gang. How did gangs get into having your same friends that you had years ago when there was nothing to say about gangs? Two years ago I was hanging with my friends who I hang with now. Nobody called us a gang until a year ago. Why?

One young man formerly connected to the gangs wrote about his struggle to get his life back on track:

The world today is very violent and it is hard trying to survive. I picture the world as a big tree, and everyone starts at the bottom and when you are at the top you have survived. On your way to the top are many branches, twigs and leaves. I try to move to the top very fast, but carefully.

I made a lot of mistakes. On the way I have shot at people. I have gotten into gangs. I have stabbed people, and have fought people. As I moved deeper down the branches, (they) get thinner and thinner and at the end that is where I fall and die. What I tried to do is leave the branch. Put myself in reverse and move on.

I moved back a little. I go to school and I don't sell drugs yet, hopefully, I won't. Hopefully, I'll just move the right way, move towards a positive branch.

This young writer does not know if he will be able to withstand the pressure to sell drugs, whether or not he will find the strength to

move towards a positive branch.

As if trying to bolster his belief in himself, he writes plaintively in the last line of his composition,

A negative person belongs on a negative branch, and I am a positive person.

Beneath the surface of his words, we can feel how fragile his hold is on that positive view of himself, how close he feels to the place that he describes as the branch,

where I fall and die.

What is revealed in many of the essays is the loneliness of their authors, especially the males. All too often parents are portrayed as people who are unable to provide financially or emotionally for their kids. The young are left to fend for themselves in an indifferent world. The writer of the following composition describes how family abandonment encourages young males to turn to what he derisively calls *"the wonder drugs"* for solace and for a livelihood. He vividly shows how adults in the drug trade take advantage of teenagers, with results that are calamitous. In the world this young man presents there are no benign adults and there are no happy endings:

The place is Dorchester and the year is 1989. Everything is crazy! Young kids are selling dope and drugs, family members become 'based.'* And for the kids, it is hard to comprehend the drugs and gang murders and close friends dying. With no one to turn to they try to stay strong, and all they see is death and all they think about is survival.

Some kids have to steal and do undercover crimes, meaning white collar crimes because their mothers and sisters and fathers are on crack! . . . some kids they turn the wrong direction, searching for shelter and food. They turn to the dope man! And he teaches them how to survive on the streets, hipping (encouraging) them to sell the wonder drugs.

And most kids sell and become users, and drop out of school with no hope for the future. . . . All kids are different, some start off with "weed" (marijuana) pills, crack, and even heroin. But most kids start with "weed" and get the high of some kind of relaxation, to kill time they can clock on the block (hang out on the street), or sometimes

* "based," meaning free-based, a potent way to smoke cocaine.

they start with that crack which is mostly used to keep them awake, so they can make that dope man's money. And that's a shame when low income families turn out to be lawbreakers. But if you look at it this way, it's not the kids' fault how they turned out. It's the parents fault! The kids were doing whatever it takes to survive, and they learned from those so called grown-ups!

Drugs and also drug-selling is the Slow Death Syndrome, and even in some cases fast death. . . . When kids are exposed to the street, they become victims and the drug dealers take advantage of their fresh minds and souls to make them rotten and ruthless. So by the time they hit high school, some kids start shooting heroin and when that happens, Satan has won half the battle.

I remember a kid named Joel. Joel was a great kid, but started with the wrong friends and his so-called friends showed him how to shoot heroin, and how to share needles. So he went on shooting himself with that wonder drug, and he came down one day with the Slow Death Syndrome. But at first he did not know what was wrong until he went to the doctor. And the doctor told him he had a very very bad illness that could not be cured. . . AIDS, which is also called the Slow Death Syndrome.

The kids who are not alone, who have parents who are able to exert a positive influence over their lives, have a significant advantage. One ninth grade girl who had dabbled in drug dealing used her mother (and her boyfriend) as a sort of moral barometer, helping her to make the break from the drug trade:

I'm going to tell you something. I used to sell drugs. It wasn't fun at all. Maybe the money (was fun), but my boyfriend didn't like neither the money or the selling. Anyway, these people who used drugs were terrible. They wanted it for $10 and all that. I couldn't do it (for that price), so I just stop because if my mother ever hear I did something so bad she would destroy me. It was terrible how they feened coming (the drug fiends came) to my bedroom window knocking, begging for just one hit.

Another girl credited her mother for helping her to get back on course after a suicide attempt:

I do remember when times were rough, when I felt that there was no use to go on with life, with even the result of attempting suicide, I just could not live with the pressure of my time, hard times. . . .

I have known friends that have been killed, stabbed, shot and even raped, all because of living in this violent world. I have learned to escape it all partly through my mother's love and encouragement, and by using common sense. It is hard trying to survive in this society where you don't know if you might be the next innocent bystander shot by rival gangs feuding over materialistic nonsense.

In their essays, students groped for explanations of the disorder surrounding them. Many, particularly the young women who are more likely to be observers rather than participants in gang and drug activities, seemed to understand the powerful role that peer pressure was playing in triggering violence. One young woman wrote,

> The guys out there are always trying to show each other that they are somebody.

Another girl used slang to express the fact that drug dealers and other bad guys had become role models in her community. She wrote,

> These days, it seems as if babies are born and programmed to be little hoods and gangsters. All the young ones want to be like the older guys clocking dollars and looking fly (making money and looking cool).

Isolating themselves from the dangers of the street was the only form of protection most of the kids could imagine. Go home. Stay home. Don't hang out.

> I just mind my business, get an education, come home to where it's usually safe,

wrote one girl. In the inner city, however, most adolescent social life takes place on the street. Not hanging out removes adolescents from danger, but it also removes them from the company of their peers. One young man advocating isolation as a form of self-protection described just how difficult this choice is to make:

> Young people have to learn to bear pressure, take insults and withstand humiliation. The majority of teenagers today crack at this point.

That young people must chose between survival and their developmentally-compelled need for age-mates strikes me as tragic. Teenagers must form relationships independent of their families. They must leave home and experiment with new relationships, new forms of behavior, new social identities. Compelled to choose between isolation and the streets, most, understandably, choose the streets. One young male explained this decision, writing:

> It is safe in the house, but you got to come out because there is more happening on the streets—girls or your homeboys and all that. You just can't hide from it. There aren't really a lot of places to go in this city. I go outside people are hanging on the corners selling narcotics making thousands of dollars a week. No one is doing anything about it.

The only young person who wrote confidently about avoiding the violence on the street was a young athlete.

> Why should I get involved in violence when there are other things out there in the world?

he asked.

> The way I get over in a violent world is by getting involved in sports. I play basketball, football and I also run track. Staying out of trouble is really very easy if you get involved in many of the city's recreational clubs.

Sports occupied this young man, constructively consuming his energy and limiting the amount of time he had to get in trouble. Because he practiced after school, he did not leave the school building when most of the other students, including the troublemakers, departed. That in itself provided him with a form of protection. Kids who are not near trouble, tend not to get in trouble. Moreover, being in training provided him with a socially acceptable excuse for avoiding dangerous activities, including using drugs. No doubt his athletic pursuits helped protect this young man from trouble in other less tangible ways, too. Having an interest outside of himself that required discipline and dedication, an interest in which his own needs and desires were subservient to the needs of the group, seems to have been a vehicle through which he was able to mature. Though only a ninth grader, his essay exhibited unusual self-confidence and composure—qualities that can be nurtured on the playing field.

Present in this young athlete's essay is a generous portion of self-esteem. He seems to like the person he is. He is fortunate to feel this way. Many African-American teenagers growing up in poverty have a difficult time liking themselves. The messages they receive from the dominant society about what it means to be poor and black interferes with their capacity to approve of themselves. In her essay, one young woman revealed her awareness of the world's harsh judgement of her community:

> I'm a sixteen-year-old black female who lives in Dorchester. Violence is around me almost everyday. I've seen young teenagers like myself getting shot up over two dollars over an argument. I've seen gang members shooting at other gang members. Why? Because they want to prove to themselves that they are tougher and badder than others. They wear specific colors to signify who they are and what gang they are down with. And what races are doing these things? Blacks. It hurts me to know that we've had so many black leaders, who have

helped us along the way to prove that black people are not as bad as they've lead us to believe.

What this young writer seems to be saying is that she is hurt that young members of her own race, with their history of protest and their history of strong black leadership, are joining gangs and committing violence. She is contrasting the lessons black leaders have taught all Americans—that black people are "not as bad as (white people) have lead us to believe"—with the "lessons" she fears white and black America will infer from the violence perpetrated by young black males.

Another young woman expressed despair and a tragically low level of self-esteem when she spoke about the crime and violence within the black community. She wrote,

> For blacks, life is even worse. Mostly all of society is blaming us for the violence. Why? Cause we are poor. We have almost no type of communication in the home.
> Blacks have gone way down on the map. That's why we feel if we sell drugs we can be above the whites. I'd just like to say that whites are ahead of us cause they have brains, not because of money.

The psychologist Hussein Bulhan, Ph.D. has written extensively on the psychology of oppression. Bulhan says it is common for the members of oppressed groups to feel that they are responsible not only for themselves, but for the actions of all the members of their group. When some blacks behave in illegal or immoral ways, other black people feel ashamed, as if they were personally responsible.

In psychological terms, Bulhan explains, every oppressed person is really twice oppressed. First they are oppressed by external forces. There is another oppressor, however, which Bulhan calls the internalized oppressor. This is when the oppressed person believes that what "they" write about him, what "they" say about him is true. If what "they" say about him is bad, then he feels that he is bad. All groups struggling to liberate themselves—ethnic minorities, women, homosexuals—carry on a two-way struggle, needing to free themselves both from the external and the internal oppressor. The young woman's comments about the relative intelligence of blacks and whites seems to me to come straight from her internal oppressor. As a black person she seems to believe her fellow blacks (and by extension herself) are less smart and less worthy than whites. Feelings like this are in their own way as violent and as destructive as guns and knives.

One important antidote to internalized oppression is ethnic pride. The young male who angrily denounced the Boston police as "vicious dogs," wrote perceptively about this issue:

The community should start trying to help the children, offer them things that may give them a sense of value like love and respect. I think these children need to learn their racial background before 430 years ago when we were Africans. I think the community should push for that kind of information in public schools from the people who held it back from us so long. And let it be taught to the black children in public and private schools so we won't look at each other with hatred. We need to be taught to love and respect each other as brothers and sisters. If we don't have that, then we are lost.

I quite agree with this young man that young blacks need to know about their African and their African-American heritage. Pride in one's ethnic origins is an important component of identity; it is difficult for a person to know and like himself without knowledge of his ancestry. But young blacks, especially young black males, need more than a book-learning relationship with their origins. They also need intimate contact with others who are like themselves. Adult friends and mentors of their own race and sex play an important role in helping young people of color achieve a positive self image. Ron Ferguson, Ph.D. an Associate Professor of Public Policy at the Kennedy School of Government has done some very interesting work in this area. He feels that having successful older African-American males available as mentors and models can mean the difference between young males of color who can function in the academic, social and economic system and young males who cannot. Mentors are essential, Ferguson says, because they help young blacks understand the extremely complicated social context into which they have been born.

Ferguson has conducted surveys that highlight just how confusing the world can appear to young black males. Interviewing high and low-achieving young males of color he found that both groups often felt feared and scorned. Graduate school-bound college students and high school dropouts in a parenting group reported receiving very similar messages from both adults, black as well as white. When surveyed, they reported that strangers "sometimes" or "always" thought they were dangerous; storekeepers "sometimes" or "always" expected them to steal and teachers "sometimes" or "always" expected them to be stupid. Black females and male and female Hispanics were far more likely to answer these questions "almost never," "never," or in the case of the teacher question, "sometimes."

Though both groups of young men reported experiencing the same degree of rejection from strangers, store-keepers and teachers, their interpretation of these daily rebuffs were startlingly different. All of the young men who were bound for graduate school mentioned race when asked to explain the reaction they inspired. Somehow, they understood that they themselves were not to blame, what they experienced was part of a much larger sociological problem. Only one of the members of the young parents group, on the other hand, mentioned race. The rest explained the response they elicited by saying, "I don't know," or, "It must be the way I look or carry myself." Ferguson believes this response indicates that these young men blame themselves for the negative reaction of others.

Ferguson comments on his findings by noting how important it is for impoverished and low achieving young men to have mentors and guides that can help them first interpret the world around them and then when they have achieved more insight, help them move their lives forward. Young men who lack this support, he believes are much more susceptible to the daily bombardment of negative input from the society at large. Ferguson believes the implications of his findings apply equally strongly to young white males from blue collar backgrounds, who also have a hard time liking themselves and finding a positive place in the economic and social life of our society. Class, as well as race, he notes, can be a destructive stigma.

In their essays on surviving in a violent world, seven of the Burke students, all female, wrote about the violence in their environment as auguring the end of the world. Daily shootings and murders make kids (and adults) feel as if the world is veering toward a cataclysm. One girl wrote,

> I think it is time for God to make a new life form. They are bringing the world to an end everyday and don't realize it.

Another wrote,

> I believe if God had known how the world would turn out, he would have destroyed us all when it rained 40 days and 40 nights.

A third wrote in the same desperate vein,

> It is going to be the violence that is going to kill all of us, not only in Boston, but in the whole world. It is not going to be nuclear war or World War II or IV that is going to kill all of us. It is going to be the violence—the drugs, the gangs, and the guns.

Yet another young woman summed up the tone of all these essays with a tragic conciseness. She wrote,

> As for the future, I see a bunch of bodies lying on the street.

7

GANGS

"Cool, articulate, savvy and dead at 21." That's how the *Boston Globe* described Tony Johnson's short life when he died in the summer of 1988.

According to police, Tony Johnson was the boss of one of Boston's most criminal youth gangs, the Corbets, also known as the Corbet Crew. Named after a street in Dorchester, the Corbets, who surfaced in the early 1980s, was the city's first, big-time, drug dealing teenage gang.

The Corbets were not a bunch of kids fighting to control a bit of urban "turf." They were a machine for making money, big money. In the early days, Corbets in expensive clothing and lots of gold dealt drugs from the windows of new black Cadillacs. Over the years the cars changed, but the mission of the organization remained the same.

Tony Johnson came up as a junior Corbet. Junior Corbets were young kids, apprentices, who earned their stripes by stealing goosedown coats and sneakers from other kids. Police say some of the junior Corbets graduated to killing for the gang.

When he was 16, Tony Johnson was charged with murder. He was a minor. Authorities sought permission to keep him in custody until he was 20. They were foiled on a technicality of the law and Tony walked after three months in a youth services facility.

That was the last time the police were able to pin anything on Tony Johnson. Though Johnson kept his own hands clean, authorities say he directed the drug business. Insiders say Tony Johnson had a genius for organizing criminal activity. In 1987 he is said to have structured Boston's warring drug gang into a loose confederation designed to keep New York dealers from taking over.

Tony Johnson's mother says it is all a lie. Her son was a college student not a gang leader. She accuses the police of harassing Tony, following him, stopping him several times a night to search for drugs or weapons.

It's true that Tony Johnson was a student. He graduated from the Burke High School and attended Hudson Valley Community College in Troy, New York for one year. His mother says he was packing his car to return to school when he was killed.

The night he died Tony Johnson went into the alley beside his family's Dorchester house to move his Audi to make room for his new Volvo. He was shot in the face by an assailant. Authorities believe the attack was an act of retaliation for an incident in which Tony Johnson had slapped a rival's girlfriend.

His basketball coach at the Burke remembers Tony Johnson as a gent. "He was one of the nicest kids; mannerly, generous." Not all the teachers at the Burke agree. A history teacher there says Tony Johnson was a "cold-hearted tough and a drug trafficker."

After Tony Johnson died, the peace he allegedly forged among rival teenage drug gangs collapsed. Police blame much of the violence that has since erupted in Boston on the resumption of teenage gang rivalries. "After he got killed," says one cop, "all hell broke loose."*

YOUTH GANGS

YOUTH GANGS LIKE THE CORBET CREW ARE NOT NEW. Teenagers, especially males, have been banding together in gangs and cliques and paramilitary groupings probably as long as organized society has existed. Even a superficial familiarity with anthropology, world history, and literature presents scores of examples of youth gangs in every historical era. Juliet's Romeo and his Capulet-hating pals were certainly a kind of youth gang. So were the Sons of Liberty who fomented our own American Revolution here in Massachusetts. Small cells of Khmer Rouge rebels in Cambodia. The militant Black Panther party active in the United States twenty years ago. They were all youth gangs set in their own unique times and places.

Gangs satisfy a whole range of normal adolescent needs. The most significant of these is the adolescent hunger for peer approval and acceptance. *But violent gangs are not normal.* When young people feel that their lives are knit into the fabric of the society at large and when they face the future knowing that a fair share awaits them, they do not form or join violent gangs, although they do form social clubs, fraternities, sororities, and other age-mate groups. Violent gangs arise

---

* Based on the reporting of Sally Jacobs and Kevin Cullen in *The Boston Globe*, Sunday, March 26, 1989.

when young people face a future of limited opportunity and despair, when for military, political, social, or economic reasons the life that awaits a young person has been stripped of meaning and validity.

From a developmental perspective, however, anti-social groups such as youth gangs and pro-social groups such as fraternities have a great deal in common. Both kinds of associations exist to provide members with an interim emotional base, one that gives substance to the ambiquity the adolescent feels when he is between the dependency of childhood and the independence of adulthood. Pro-social and anti-social, they satisfy the adolescent need to belong to a group, separate from one's family. Pro-social and anti-social, they provide young people with goals and objectives, a world view, and a place where they are valued. Group membership gives some purpose to life. The more adrift a young person feels, the more powerful the attraction of the peer group, but even well-adjusted young people need what groups offer.

Rituals are one way anti- and pro-social groups satisfy the developmental needs of adolescents. Interestingly, these rituals tend to be similar, whether adopted by adolescents operating inside or outside of the law. The secrecy typical of youth gangs and of many sororities and fraternities suits teenagers trying to carve out areas in which they can be separate and distinct from their parents and siblings. The idea of wearing special clothing, "colors" that identify members, provides young adults with an outlet for their narcissism. In high school I belonged to a sorority called the Charmettes. Our colors were pink and white. On the day we met we all wore pink and white uniforms. There was not much difference between the Charmette "colors" and the "colors" sported by Los Angeles's infamous warring gangs, the Crips and Bloods. Initiation rituals, common to adolescent groups the world over, speaks directly to the adolescent need to prove oneself. Usually prospective group members, be they sorority "pledges" or youth gang "wannabees," must undergo some sort of trial to prove their loyalty to the group. That's what pledge week, initiation rites, and hazing are all about. Once they pass, new members are allowed into the inner sanctum, where the affection and loyalty of other insiders is guaranteed.

What differentiates pro-social groups from anti-social ones is violence. All gangs are violent or potentially violent. In some highly organized gangs, violence may be controlled by a strong leader who determines whether and when force will be used. In less organized gangs, violence may be haphazardly enacted. Police say that gangs without strong leaders are sometimes the most brutal because they can be dominated by their most aberrant members. The internal organization of gangs varies, but the psychological dynamic remains the same: When young males come together as a gang, the group exerts a powerful influence that is capable of eliciting violent, illegal, and anti-social acts from individual members that they would not necessarily commit if acting alone. In the context of the gang, vile acts may be executed by adolescents who in themselves appear to be rather ordinary.

In the cause of repression and even genocide, wicked regimes throughout history have found ways to create gangs and control their violence. Gangs of Hitler youth in pre-World War II Germany beat and murdered Jews; Mao Tse Dung's Red Guards in China beat and murdered intellectuals; the bloody Renamo insurgency of young thugs in Mozambique are but a few examples of youth gangs used by political dictators to further their own destructive ends. It could be argued that major drug lords use gangs of American teens in similar ways. I point this out to put the youth gang violence in our own culture in a larger context. For good and for evil, history is often forged by gangs of young males. Ablaze with a nearly boundless energy, untethered from their birth families, not yet connected to families of their own making, young males in every culture are a highly combustible resource.

THE RESEARCH

HISTORIANS SAYS YOUTH GANGS HAVE BEEN PRESENT IN the United States throughout our history. In this century beginning in the 1920s, bands of poor, urban, adolescent males have fought each other, usually over the control of small strips of urban territory—"turf." Up until the 1960s, most of the publicized gang activity involved white ethnics—young males of Irish, Italian, Polish, and Jewish descent. Usually, gang allegiance was short-lived and relatively harmless. While some gang members graduated to prison and a life of crime, the majority eventually left their gangs and found permanent employment. High school graduates and high school dropouts were able to find jobs in heavy industry and manufacturing when they outgrew the gangs.

In recent decades, gangs have come to be associated with the entrenched poverty of inner city neighborhoods that have been denuded of manufacturing and other non-service jobs. Though some white gangs persist, and in some areas of the East and West coasts violent Asian gangs are common, the gangs that predominate are gangs of black- and brown-skinned males. Because there are few legitimate job opportunities for former gang members, many young people now stay in the gangs throughout their twenties and thirties. An estimated 10 percent of all gangs are female. Most female gangs are the less violent auxiliaries of male gangs, although some experts have noted the increased aggression of some girl gangs. In "hardcore" areas of Los Angeles, the city most afflicted by gang activity and gang violence, gang membership can be a family tradition, with two or even three generations of male and female participation in the gangs.

Newspaper and television accounts of gang activities tend to present a picture of a national gang monolith made up of hundreds of thousands of teenage drug dealers in expensive foreign cars. This picture is very much distorted. While many gang members do sell drugs, researchers believe that the majority of gang members do not. Moreover, most of the gang kids who sell drugs are not the big time dealers in BMWs that are the staple of daily reportage. Most are small time dealers who use drugs and sell drugs to help provide themselves with a subsistence income. Carl S. Taylor Ph.D., a sociologist in Detroit, conducted a major five-year study of the gangs in his city and came to the conclusion that there are three very distinct kinds. Taylor's definitions, confirmed by the work of other scholars, makes it easier to understand the gang scene in Detroit, Los Angeles, and Chicago, and also in cities like Boston where the gang problem, though certainly serious, is seen as somewhat less than in these other locations.

Taylor himself is an interesting figure, both businessman and scholar. His interest in the gangs originated back in 1980 when he was running his own security company in Detroit. One of his clients was the Joe Louis Arena, for which he provided security. In his book, *Dangerous Society*, Taylor recounts his first exposure to the new breed of youth gangs at the arena on the evening of a major concert. "While standing at the ground level backstage entrance, I noticed a caravan of luxury late model limousines. . . . I mistakenly thought that the stars of the main act had arrived for the concert. To my surprise, a group of youngsters wearing fire-engine red sweatsuits and high-top, white leather, unlaced gym shoes poured out of the limousines. They appeared to be some sort of club—the identical sweatsuits made them almost look like a high school track team—except for their expensive, gaudy gold jewelry; the cables of gold were incredible."

Taylor's curiosity about these well-heeled teenagers who peeled one hundred dollar bills off fat wads to pay concessionaires led him back into academia and the area of sociological research. He designed a study that involved a survey of the gang scene and in-depth interviews with gang members. He concluded that Detroit police had their facts wrong; that gangs had not disappeared from Detroit, but were in fact flourishing. Taylor determined that the gang scene in Detroit was made up of three types of organizations, all of which commit crimes, all of which are violent some of the time, and all of which are likely to be armed. In other ways these three kinds of gangs differed significantly from one another.

Scavenger Gangs: Scavenger gangs are the least organized and the least "successful" gangs. Leadership of these groups can change daily or weekly. Scavengers do not have any pre-planned goals. Their crimes are spontaneous, as is their method of banding together. Taylor says that the members of this kind of gang are likely to be low-achievers and drop-outs who are prone to erratic behavior. Scavenger gangs are looked down upon by other more organized gangs. After an initial period of disorganization, some scavenger gangs, like tropical storms that get upgraded to hurricane status, retool themselves into *territorial* gangs.

Territorial Gangs: These are the turf-loyal organizations we all tend to think of when we think of gangs in Los Angeles. *Territorial* gangs which are also known as *fighting* gangs, are highly organized and highly elaborated with formal initiation rites for entering members and many other ceremonies, tradition's, and practices that separate members from non-members. Often gang members wear particular clothing; sneakers, scarves, etc.; in recent years, however, police harassment has prompted many gang members to trade in their "colors" for less noticeable clothing. The members of *territorial* gangs are young people who have usually done very poorly in school. Often they have troubled family lives. Many speak little English. The gangs provide them with the sense of being *someone* and they are proud to be identified as members.

A major activity of *territorial* gangs is fighting. The whole point of marking off your own territory is to keep somebody else out. Fighting provides gang members with an opportunity to prove themselves, sometimes by exhibiting extreme or even foolhardy degrees of bravery. The Chicano gangs in Los Angeles call this kind of courage "locura," which means cultivating an attitude of wildness or "quasi-controlled insanity." Among other things, "locura" is an effective weapon of psychological warfare. Opponents are likely to tread carefully when facing an opponent whose courage hovers on the side of madness. Moreover, by adopting an attitude of "locura" a young male may have an easier time controlling his own fear and anxiety about fighting.

These days the turf boundaries that *territorial* gangs protect from incursion may be merged with the boundaries of a gang's drug-selling territory, but this is not always the case. *Territorial* gangs sometimes sell drugs and sometimes do not. The primary purpose of these gangs, however, is social, not economic. Drug selling is a vehicle for survival, not the reason these gangs exist.

Corporate Gangs: The red-suited gangs Carl Taylor saw at the Joe Louis Arena in 1980 were members of a *corporate* gang. These groups are also known as *crews*. In Boston, Tony Johnson's Corbet "crew" was a *corporate* gang. These days members of gangs this sophisticated would not wear clothing that would draw attention to themselves. Though made up of teens sometimes as young as 14, *corporate* gangs are really highly structured criminal conspiracies organized to sell drugs. *Corporate* gangs can best be compared to the "Mafia" gangs that sold alcoholic beverages during prohibition. Members of *corporate* gangs are gangsters in the traditional sense of the word. Discipline, secrecy, and strict codes of behavior are required of every member. Punishments can be severe. Taylor says in Detroit corporate gangs are structured so that individual members have little knowledge of the organization as a whole. The organization exists to do business, usually by selling narcotics for maximum profit. Turf, colors, and other romantic notions are irrelevant to its central mission. Members of *corporate* gangs, though not necessarily schooled, are often highly intelligent. Leaders must be capable of sophisticated strategic planning, personnel management, and money management.

Terry Williams, Ph.D., is a sociologist and "urban ethnographer" associated with the City University of New York who spent nearly five years tracking the comings and goings of a *corporate* drug gang or crew located in upper Manhattan's Washington Heights neighborhood. From 1982 to 1986, Dr. Williams spent two hours a day, 3 days a week with the eight members of a teenage cocaine ring. "The Cocaine Kids" were young teens—14, 15, and 16—when he met them. Hanging out with these youngsters in cocaine bars, after-hour clubs, discos, restaurants, crack houses, on street corners, in their homes, and with their families, Williams was able to document some of the facts concerning the role of adolescents in the cocaine and crack trades.

Retail distribution and sales of cocaine in New York City, Williams says, is controlled by Latino and African-American teenagers under 18 years of age. The "Cocaine Kids" were sophisticated cocaine distributors who sold their products wholesale to other dealers, and retail to users large and small. The crew received their supplies from a Colombian source referred to as "the connect," or connection. Only Max, the crew leader, knew the identity of or had contact with "the connect."

Members of the gang did their selling at an "office," an apartment, really, rented for that purpose, and at the clubs and bars they frequented. Most were too successful to deal on the streets, although they would occasionally. Washington Heights, where the "office" was located, is one of New York City's major drug markets. Cocaine sales there are dominated by dealers from the Dominican Republic. Seven of the eight gang members were Dominican.

The ability to speak Spanish, as well as his immersion in a Hispanic culture helped Max cement relations with "the connect," a Spanish-speaking Colombian. Each week Max received between 3 and 5 kilos of pure cocaine from the "connect" on consignment; he did not pay for the cocaine he received until it was sold. Max adulterated the drugs, cooking up batches of crack, and preparing packets of no-longer-pure-"pure"-cocaine. He then apportioned the drugs to his crew who may or may not have adulterated the "pure" cocaine again. Max decided how much each crew member received based on his past performance. In 1985, the 3 to 5 kilos of cocaine Max received each week had a street value of between $180,000 and $350,000, Williams says. That means that in one year the crew could have sold as much as 15 million dollars worth of drugs. Williams notes that the value of cocaine fluctuates widely and that most dollar estimates related to its sale are untrustworthy. Still, we can say with certainty that great sums of money were being generated by Max's crew.

Terry Williams met Max when the ambitious young dealer was only 14. In the course of their friendship, Max managed to put together a functioning crew and to "get behind the scale;" to deal in significant quantities of cocaine and interact directly with a major distributor. Williams says "to get behind the scale" a kid must be able to handle huge amounts of money, control his own use of cocaine, interact successfully with drug buyers, and be able to handle a weapon—traits one would not expect many 14-year-olds to possess. The kids who make it into this position are smart, self-controlled, and resourceful. In other circumstances, they would certainly be expected to make significant contributions to our society. The fact that Max, with all his brain-power and precocious business acumen, could barely read and write English says a great deal about what is happening in our poor neighborhoods.

The other seven members of Max's gang were more typical adolescents. All, by the way, including Max, were routinely armed with firearms. None of the others had Max's cool detachment, his judgement, or his self-control. Many had the tendency to overindulge in their own product and then lie to themselves about how much they were using. The crew viewed crack as a dangerous, low-class drug to be avoided, but they loved snorting pure cocaine. One of the crew members said cocaine gave him the courage to face the unpredictable streets. Another member of the gang, Max's older brother Hector, had been a major cocaine dealer at the age of 16, but was no longer considered reliable because of his raging cocaine addiction. Another one of Max's crew was a female dealer named Kitty, who was married to a male dealer, Splib. Kitty and Splib were the parents of a small child, whose care, like the care of children in many two-career families, was the subject of numerous arguments. Masterrap, another crew member, was designated the second man "behind the scale." When Max was absent, Masterrap would weigh and package the drugs for the other dealers and for sale at the "office." Chillie, the most successful dealer in the gang, also ran the office. It was he who hired the son of the building superintendent as a "stash catcher." During a raid, the gang arranged to throw their stash out the window to be retrieved by the "catcher." For this the young "catcher" was paid a weekly fee. Charlie, the only African-American in the gang, worked as a bodyguard and dealer. He was in charge of the office arsenal, including a 9-millimeter semi-automatic weapon and a machete.

Members of *scavenger* and *territorial* gangs look up to *corporate* gangs like Max's crew the way the owner of a neighborhood *bodega* looks up to a self-made supermarket magnate. Sometimes members of *corporate* gangs are recruited from *territorial* gangs. In general, however, many academic researchers believe that there is not a great deal of interchange among these gangs. They say *territorial* gangs tend to remain as territorial gangs; they do not usually evolve into *corporate* gangs. This view is at odds with the belief of local police officials in heavily gang-infested cities like Los Angeles, and it is at odds with the impression usually given in the mass media. Some police officers and many reporters erroneously convey the idea that the members of *territorial* gangs are all on their way to becoming millionaires selling crack and other drugs.

The failure of the mass media to accurately describe gang activities has been an important topic in the research about gangs for decades. Writing in the 1970s, the respected criminologist Walter B. Miller suggested that the ebb and flow of reporters' and editors' interest in youth gangs has created entirely erroneous public assumptions about gangs. The public believes, says Miller, that periods of intense and violent gang activity have, in recent decades, been punctuated by periods of gang inactivity. The truth is, Miller wrote, gang activity has remained constant over the decades. What has waxed and waned is the interest of journalists.

In the 1980s it is not clear if gang activity has increased or not. It does appear that the rate of gang violence has increased. This may be attributed to the fact that youth violence in general has increased, and that among the impoverished males who make up the gang population gun carrying has become the norm.

The most destructive aspect of media discussion concerning gang violence is the failure to differentiate among the kinds of gangs. The discussion of turf or *territorial* gangs is routinely merged with the discussion of *corporate* gangs. The net effect is to create the idea that most gang members are cold-blooded professional drug dealers of the *corporate* type who use violence to maximize their business profits. This is not true. Most gang members who deal in illicit substances are users and low-level sellers who belong to *scavenger* or *territorial* gangs. They are not getting rich from dealing drugs or committing other crimes. They are not living well at all. The research indicates without question that most gang members are impoverished school drop-outs with a history of violent victimization at home and in their communities, who commit crimes to get by, and whose affiliation with their gang may be the only reason they have for liking themselves and feeling proud.

Looking at the gang scene in Los Angeles County is instructive. Los Angeles has more gang activity and more gang violence than any other city in the nation, followed by Chicago. In Los Angeles itself and in the 70 satellite cities that comprise L.A. County, law enforcement authorities estimate that some 70,000 young people are affiliated with 700 gang "sets." This figure includes "wannabees," as well as hard-core gang members. (Throughout Los Angeles County, 90 to 95 percent of young people are *not* in gangs. Even in the most heavily gang-infested neighborhoods, the majority of young people are *not* gang-affiliated.)

The L.A. gang scene is ethnically-dominated. Mexican-American gangs and African-American gangs predominate. The Mexican-American gangs are *territorial*. Members are not major figures in the trafficking of illicit drugs. Youth workers say so far as violence is concerned, Latino gang members pose a greater threat to each other than to the society at large. Rarely are they accused of murdering non-gang members. In general, it is African-American gangs, not Mexican-American gangs, that have been associated with drug dealing and drive-by shootings. All of the black gangs are affiliated with either the Crips or the Bloods. These super-gangs operate through Los Angeles County, as well as in other parts of California and in other states.

Most African-American gangs in Los Angeles are *territorial*, like the Mexican-American gangs. The heavy involvement of some of the black gangs in interstate drug dealing has led observers of the L.A. gang scene to believe that some *territorial* gangs have evolved into *corporate* gangs. Experts cited in a recent federal survey of gang activity believe that as some gang members in Los Angeles have aged they have lost interest in the social aspect of gang affiliation. Selling drugs and making money is what seems to concern them now. Although it appears, that some Los Angeles *territorial* gangs have evolved into *corporate* gangs, it is important not to overemphasize this fact as this is not the normal growth pattern of gangs in general.

Sorting out the exact relationship between the black gangs and the drug trade is extremely difficult. Law enforcement authorities estimate that no more than 10,000 of the county's gang members are involved in the drug trade—that means one in seven gang members are involved in drugs and six out of seven are not involved in drugs. Clearly, most gang members are not significantly involved in the drug trade. Nor can we blame most of the gang violence on drugs. In 1989, 570 people died in gang-related violence in Los Angeles County. Police confirm that the majority of gang deaths are related to arguments over turf, arguments over sneakers, arguments over jewelry, arguments over wounded adolescent pride—the same trivial issues over which most adolescents argue, fight, and sometimes die. In 1988 in one L.A. district, under the jurisdiction of the sheriff's department, there were 96 gang-related deaths. Seven of these were related to drugs. In other districts, the number of gang/drug deaths is higher. Still, this statistic shows the danger of making assumptions about the gang/drug/violence connection.

WHY KIDS JOIN GANGS

BURIED IN THE RESEARCH ABOUT GANGS ARE CLUES TO THE origins of gang violence and perhaps clues to future interventions. Ethnographic research conducted in Philadelphia and elsewhere with gang members and gang leaders has established a profile of gang attitudes toward violence. Many of the gang leaders interviewed in depth in the Philadelphia study were desensitized to violence as the result of their own victimization. As children they had seen and been the objects of violence in their homes and in their communities. Their experiences had shaped the attitudes of these young males toward perpetrating violence. They accepted violence as the normal and appropriate way to resolve minor and major disputes. They could imagine no response to criticism or any form of rebuke, except violence. They had no strategies, no methods of dealing with conflict, except violence. They simply had not been taught any. They believed that a quick, almost unconscious violent response to almost any offense is a part of human nature; gangs reinforced what the environment taught by encouraging and praising members' willingness to fight.

THE DEVELOPMENTAL MEANING OF GANGS

GANGS ARE THE DOMAIN OF POOR URBAN MALES. ALL gangs provide inner city kids with a sense of community, a sense of belonging. A Los Angeles school teacher, Pat Rice, who works at a gang-besieged junior high school in Watts described the attraction of the gangs for the children at her school to Tom Brokaw on the NBC News Special *Gangs, Cops and Drugs,* aired in August, 1989:

> "It's a very insecure way of life that they come from and children at this age need a lot of security. They need rules and guidelines. Many of them come with very, very poor academic skills from elementary school. They can't read. They're very poor in their math skills. And . . . they're just prime for something positive.
>
> The gangs have a structure that they gravitate towards because there are rules, there are colors, there are guidelines. And this is what all kids need.
>
> Gang activity manifests itself on a day to day basis. For example, I'll come in, in the morning and my classroom will have been vandalized. And the gang graffiti will be all over the posters and the walls. And the kids see it as a positive way to make a statement. I've been here. I was here . . . I was part of something."

"I've been here. I was here. I was part of something." This haunting statement sums up what the gangs offer to kids. Gang membership is an antidote to the terrible feeling of "being no one," and of being unimportant that is bred in poverty and social dislocation. School failure, unemployment, and family dysfunction tear at the shreds of a young person's self-esteem. Gang membership balms these wounds. In the gang, each member is somebody who is valued, someone, in fact, who is worth dying for. Sneaky, a 19-year-old gang member and convicted felon from Los Angeles explained his commitment to the gang, saying, "This is our own little family . . . I love these guys with all my heart."

Up and down the line, the gangs speak loudly and clearly to the developmental issues of adolescents. Kids who are successful—academically, athletically, or in other ways—are able to ignore the gangs' message because their developmentally-shaped needs are being fulfilled elsewhere. Kids whose needs are not being nourished by the environment may have little armor against the gangs' attractions.

The gangs give poor kids a feeling of recognition. Adolescents want to be noticed. They want to be special, and like all children they prefer negative attention to no attention at all. Or, as one gang member in Boston said, explaining the appeal of the gangs: "They just want people to know their name."

The more attention peers, adults, and reporters give gang activity in their area, the more gratified gang members feel. During my many visits to the Jeremiah E. Burke School in Dorchester I saw this phenomena at work. School officials, security guards, and teachers cannot help paying special attention to the gang members in their midst.

Flashy displays of gang colors, hats in particular, are not allowed at the Burke. Gold jewelry must be tucked inside clothing or removed. Still, everyone in the school and the neighborhood knows who the gang members are. School officials separate members of rival gangs whenever possible. Areas where gangs congregate—in the lunchroom and elsewhere—are well patrolled. Adults go to great lengths to be informed about gang activities and to let gang members know that they will be dealt with fairly, but firmly. I am convinced that attention to gangs is what makes the Burke a safe school, but it is hard to deny that even at a fine school like the Burke, where youngsters' positive achievements are recognized and praised, that the steps adults take to neutralize possible gang trouble is itself a kind of salute and even, to the kids, a kind of tribute to the gang presence. This is true in all urban schools where gangs maintain a high profile.

The publicity that gang violence generates in the press is another way the gangs satisfy the adolescent hunger for recognition. One gang member told a reporter that every time a crime is committed on a gang's turf, the gang feels proud, even if members had nothing to do with it. Like out-of-work actors, gang members carry their press clippings to prove they are big shots. Another gang member told the *Boston Globe*, "kids like to have their names in the paper, even if someone is killed or something." Filled with images from T.V. the gang members fancy themselves romantic outlaws—"public enemy number one," is the way one violent young "gangster" described himself.

The media colludes with gang members to present an image of inner city adolescents that is completely distorted. In Boston, it sometimes feels that the *only* way a kid in the inner city can get any recognition is by joining a gang and doing something criminal. I spoke about this subject after school one afternoon with members of the football team at the Burke. The students told me with great bitterness that neither of the city's two daily papers regularly covers their teams or any other inner city sports teams. One young athlete told of running an 80-yard touchdown to win an important game. That event was not seen as meriting newspaper coverage. That same Saturday the *Boston Globe* and the *Boston Herald* covered a high school football game in an affluent, predominantly-white suburban city. The young football player at the Burke added that if a gang member from his school had shot someone that day his picture would have been plastered on the front page of the papers.

It is not just the media that nourishes gang members' grandiose fantasies. Many of the institutions of our society unwittingly gratify kids' hunger to appear powerful, dangerous, and exempt from consequences. This is certainly true of the criminal justice system. Because of their age, kids who commit violent crimes, including murder, do not go to jail where they would be brutalized. In Massachusetts, which has a more benign system for juvenile offenders than many other states, they are sent to detention facilities to be protected and rehabilitated. Protection is necessary, and of course I applaud the notion of rehabilitation, especially when the subjects to be rehabilitated are as young as 13 or 14. Still, the way society cares for youthful offenders sometimes takes the form of "too much too late."

During my tenure as Massachusetts Commissioner of Health I visited one juvenile detention facility that spent $65,000 a year on each of its young charges. Every inmate had a room of his own. The teacher-student ratio was 1 to 4. Adults in this facility were very invested in the young males in their care. Adults saw their job as "re-parenting;" inmates called their counselors "Dad." The recidivism rate in this model program was reduced, but I cannot help wondering why such fortunes were lavished on kids who had already committed serious offenses, when so very, very little is spent on kids at risk for violence who have not yet committed major crimes. Where are the adults paid to "re-parent" adolescents from troubled families who have not committed a major felony? Spending state money on prevention makes much more sense. How much more effective it would be to provide 15 or 20 young males at risk with therapeutic interventions before a major homicide or assault occurs. Given current fiscal realities, I find it difficult to justify spending $65,000 on just one child. Even if dollars were not an issue, I am not sure that any punishment should occur in a country club setting. Punishment where it is deemed necessary ought to be fair and absolutely nonviolent, but it ought to be recognizable as punishment. Otherwise we are rewarding our young offenders for committing anti-social acts. Our children need to know that they are living in a society with limits and rules and even, as a last resort, punishments. I am afraid today we do a very poor job of constructing a society in which the rules make sense.

None of the developmental issues associated with adolescence are more urgent than those related to sexual identity. How do I become a man? How do I prove myself? How must I behave? Kids, especially poor kids whose environment may contain few positive role models, desperately want answers to these questions. Gangs provide them.

Gang ideology defines a man as someone who is loyal to his friends and ruthless to his enemies, regardless of the consequences. These simple ideas make manhood accessible to many young men who cannot live up to mainstream definitions; those that associate manhood with the capacity to make money. In the gang context you need not be employed or employable, you need not support your wife and children to feel that you are adequate. You only need to be willing to fight.

The willingness of gang members to fight and even to kill makes a certain developmental sense. While adults struggle with ambivalences and ambiguities, most teenagers still reside in an all-or-nothing universe. One side is good, the other side is bad. This concrete and absolute way of thinking represents a stage of cognitive development, and, as Kohlberg has pointed out, a stage in moral development. Gangs embody the adolescent us-against-them perspective to an extreme. Every gang must have a rival, an adversary, or an enemy; without a "them" to hate, gangs are not gangs.

Members of the *territorial* and *corporate* gangs live by a moral code that is the embodiment of this tribal level of cognitive and moral development. Their capacity to empathize is limited by the boundaries of their group. Violence may rightfully be committed against those outside their group. One 14-year-old gang member in Los Angeles, accused of committing a drive-by shooting when he was 12, told a reporter that he shot his rival, "Cuz he was an enemy." He didn't feel any other justification for his act was necessary. When questioned, he added: "I wasn't going to cry about it, because he was an enemy and I wasn't going to feel sorry for him." When pressed to tell if he had felt any remorse, the young man mumbled, "For a while I got drunk to hide my feelings." (When reading this young man's words I cannot help thinking about all the superhero television programs he probably watched in which enemies were portrayed as utterly vicious non-humans with whom no compromise was possible and for whom no pity was necessary. Certainly little in our mass media helps poor, inner city kids like this move to more sophisticated levels of moral and cognitive reasoning.)

Fighting presents kids with an alternative to the boredom and the feelings of depression that are endemic in the poorest neighborhoods. Giving oneself over to the group, surrendering to "locura," mitigates fear, mitigates anxiety. The adrenaline flows. Facing death, a kid in a gang may feel very alive. Without fighting, there is no way of proving manliness. Going to prison can serve a similar function. Gang kids are proud to do time in "the joint." Going to prison is a gang member's way to show that he is "tough enough to take it." One ethnographer who followed gang kids in Milwaukee for several years goes so far as to call prison a kind of ritual sacrifice that gang members seek out as a way to display their commitment to their set.

Gang members' overdeveloped sense of personal pride is a reflection of the impoverishment of their environment—they have little to feel proud of except their reputation—and it is a reflection of their age-appropriate narcissism. When deference is withheld, when someone "disrespects" or "disses" these kids, the consequences can be fatal. For example, in Boston kids at the Burke spoke so about what can happen when one kid steps on another's sneaker or when one guy talks what is considered out of line to someone else's girl, and in New York the member of one drug gang was shot to death after he refused to "give five" to a rival. Billy Stewart, a Boston probation officer who knows the street scene well, comments, "If you don't show 'em 'spect they get it by shooting or stabbing."

The insanity of killing over minor points of etiquette is fed by the inability of teenagers to grasp the permanence of death—theirs or anyone else's. Kids talk about dying in glamourized and unreal ways. They do not believe that they will ever die. One member of the Crips told a *Harpers Magazine* forum, "The highest honor you can give for your set is death. When you die, when you go out in a blaze of Glory, you are respected. When you kill for your set, you earn your stripes. You put your work in."

Some kids even believe themselves exempt from serious injury. One young male injured in a shootout astonished the emergency room personnel at Boston City Hospital by saying that he had no idea getting shot would *hurt*. He was surprised that he was in pain! That's a detail somebody left out of the T.V. script. This incident highlights the television-fueled capacity of adolescents to believe themselves exempt from consequences. Youth workers say when the patina of presumed immortality begins to wear off, young people can best be lured out of their gangs. When somebody close to a gang member is killed or the gang member himself is seriously injured, his gang allegiance may be thrown into question. Confronted by the brutal facts, gang members begin to understand that the consequences of violence are shot bodies, crippling injuries, and the endless sorrow of families and friends. Once they know this, they can no longer cling to their delusions of immortality. Absorbing the tragic reality of violence, their behavior begins to change.

8

DRUGS, GANGS, GUNS, AND COPS

DEATH OF A DRUG DEALER

"The life and death of Preston (Little Man) Simmons, a 14-year-old marijuana peddler who was shot and killed last Thursday, is a story that has become dismally familiar in his part of the world.

When he was executed in the courtyard of his housing project in the Bronx, he became one of almost 140 homicide victims aged 18 or under in New York City this year . . . many of them killed in drug-related incidents . . .

That the case of Preston Simmons is so commonplace is what gives it special weight. His existence at the Castle Hill Houses, a sprawling public housing complex in the East Bronx, was typical of life in the underclass. And the legacy of despair he left behind provides little hope of a better life for the next generation.

Like Preston's mother and grandmother, his girlfriend will become a teen-age mother next month when she is due to deliver his child. The girlfriend, 17-year-old Denise Butler, doubts that her child's life will be much different from that of Preston, a personable youngster who made his spending money by selling $5 bags of marijuana.

"If he is still living around here," Miss Butler said of her expected child, "I guess he will be selling drugs, will be forced to sell drugs, or will have a lot of bad habits."

Preston was killed . . . while walking from his girlfriend's apartment . . . to his family's apartment . . . He . . . was approached by a group of at least four men.

One of them pulled a 9-millimeter automatic pistol from his waist and shot Preston twice . . . and then shot him nine more times as he fell in the snow . . .

—Kevin Sack
The New York Times,
Nov. 29, 1989

As the story describing Preston Simmons' brief life makes clear, 14-year-old "Little Man" Simmons did not get rich selling marijuana. His profit on a "nickle bag" (five dollars worth) of marijuana was $1.50. It appears the most the young dealer earned in a day was $30 to $45, with which he bought food, designer sweatsuits and gifts for his girlfriend. His ambition to move up in the drug trade apparently motivated his murder.

One can imagine what having cash in his pocket must have meant to Preston Simmons, whose mother had been receiving welfare since the birth of her first child and whose father was an abusive drug user who was driven from the family by court order. At the time of Preston's death, the total income of the eight-member Simmons family amounted to less than $850 a month. This sum, derived from welfare and disability benefits, meagerly supported Preston's mother, and her seven children, who ranged in age from fifteen months to eighteen years, including one son who was mentally handicapped.

Preston's family lacked the resources to help him grow up. Here was a child whose family described as self-reliant from a very young age who could see no path in the legitimate economy that would lead to an independent future. Nor did the community into which he was born provide the institutional wealth, the direction or the support that his family could not offer. School might have been expected to serve this function, but like many young men of color who come of age in the underclass, Preston operated outside the academic mainstream. Diagnosed as hyperactive, he was enrolled in a Special Education class where his teacher described him to reporter Kevin Sack as a polite young man who performed adequately. In the Special Education classroom, "adequate" has more to do with behavior than with the capacity to read, write and do math at a grade level that would make a child eligible for legitimate, well-paying employment. For young men like Preston, all too often schools are experienced as a hostile environment where they are unwanted.

Preston lived surrounded by poverty, struggle, and defeat. Virtually everyone he knew was poor. The average yearly income for the 2,000 families living in the Castle Hill Houses was $11,000 a year. Most of these poor families—three-quarters of them—were working poor. One quarter, like the Simmonses, had no working adult and survived fully on welfare. The feeling in the project that law-abiding folks had already lost the fight was as destructive as the poverty that lurked there. In recent years, the Castle Hill projects had been overrun by crack dealers who had sucked the sense of safety and security from the daily existence of project residents. Gunfire had become common at the project. Just six weeks prior to Preston's death, a 17-year-old was shot to death at the project in what police called a territorial drug dispute.

Preston's death was an ordinary event in the "drug war" that viciously scarred the face of urban America in the 1980s. No child is too small, no grandparent too old to be exempt from the drug-induced terror. The booming traffic in illicit drugs, most especially cocaine and its derivatives, has introduced near anarchy into hundreds of poor urban areas all over the country. In these beleaguered neighborhoods drug dealers have cowed and silenced the majority of poor and working people who reap no benefit from their trade. Frightened families are caught in a drug-induced nightmare. The simplest assumptions of civilized life—that parent and child will be able to walk down the street unmolested, that a child will return home safely from school— are denied them. Their reality is automatic weapons fire, shootouts, crossfires, and the fear of stray bullets. Each evening ordinary parents in these areas lay their children down to sleep far from the windows, not knowing if they will rise safely in the morning.

Neighborhood is a compelling element in the drug story. Preston Simmons' decision to become a drug dealer and his subsequent death can be comprehended only within the context of the neighborhood where he grew to manhood. We are each the beneficiaries or the victims of our own place and time. The drug trade (not to mention the surcease that drugs offer) is most attractive to those who have few realistic options. Looked at most broadly, the drug problem that is decimating our inner city neighborhoods is much more than a drug problem. It is also a job problem. A housing problem. A family problem. A problem of hope and hopelessness. We are mistaken when we look at the bullet-pierced body of 14-year-old Preston Simmons and see the enemy.

Would this child have made other, constructive choices if he had been given a chance in life, a real chance? Of course we will never know an unequivocal answer to this question, but I, as a physician and a public health educator, must answer "yes." Yes, of course, he would. Children are not born drug dealers or drug users. They are born wanting to "fit in," to do their share, to have a place, to participate, and to be recognized and valued for what they contribute. It seems to me a society that thwarts the desire of so many young people to have a place in its legitimate economic life is tragically in need of reform.

CRACK: THE DRUG OF CHOICE

A GREAT MANY AMERICANS DIE OF HEROIN OVERDOSES each year. In big cities, according to federal data, nearly as many people die from heroin overdoses as from cocaine overdoses. Moreover, a great many Americans, like Preston Simmons, stand on street corners selling a cornucopia of illicit drugs—marijuana, amphetamines, LSD, PCP, ICE, quaaludes (barbituates). Still, when we think of drugs we do not think of heroin or these other drugs, we think of cocaine and its cheap, smokable derivative—crack. Cocaine-based drugs indelibly altered the urban drug scene, enlarging its scope and making what was always violent, searingly so.

Cocaine-based drugs were the drugs of choice, especially among young people, throughout the 1980s. Most recently the use of cocaine and cocaine-derivatives appears to be declining a little among the young. New users have heard the message that cocaine kills and are turning to other drugs, including heroin, which is making a comeback, especially in its smokable form, and ICE, a particularly nasty combination of chrystal methadone, cocaine and heroin. The number of already-addicted cocaine and crack users, however, remains high.

Like many of the product choices Americans make, the popularity of crack resulted from smart marketing. In the early 1980s, a glut of cocaine from South America flooded the United States and caused drug prices to decline. To get rid of their excess supplies, drug wholesalers needed a new product; one with more mass market appeal than pure cocaine, which costs a great deal and had an up-scale, not-for-the masses reputation.

Crack was the answer. Crack is cheap to produce and can be sold very profitably for as little as three or five dollars a "hit." When smoked, crack gives a powerful high that dissipates quickly, leaving the user starving for more. Moreover, no hypodermic needle is required to get high on crack. Many users, particularly women, are squeamish about injecting substances into their veins, and they fear using needles that they know can transmit the AIDS virus. The only equipment crack smokers need is a pipe. For this reason and others, crack is a non-sexist addiction. As many women as men are users.

It ought to be noted that some experimentation with drugs, including alcohol, is generally viewed as normal adolescent behavior. Drugs and alcohol appeal to the risk-taking, break-the-rules, live-intensely spirit common to adolescents. Research indicates that when young people dabble with drugs their reasons may be no more complicated than simple curiosity, the desire to get "high" and feel good, and the desire to act grown up. They may also be responding to peer pressure. So long as they are able to stop before their drug use becomes habitual, such experimenting may be relatively harmless. Unfortunately, many young people can not stop. For them, using alcohol, marijuana and tobacco leads to more dangerous and addictive substances, such as cocaine and its derivatives.

Crack is produced by cooking cocaine with various adulterants such as baking soda. After cooking, solid, flaky, white rocks of crack cocaine are left. Dealers shave or chip small portions off the rock, package them in small vials or in tinfoil and sell them on the street, in bars, and in crack "houses"—rooms where crack is sold and smoked, where crack smokers socialize, and where young girls often sell sex in exchange for crack.

For drug sellers crack was a dream product. The drug's initial low cost attracted a new generation of young users who naively thought crack was a cheap, safe high. They were wrong. Crack has a unique biochemistry and is very addictive. According to Dr. Jack Henningfield, chief of the clinical pharmacology branch at the Addiction Research Center in Baltimore, crack is more addictive than any other substance humans consume excepting cigarettes. Dr. Henningfield's research indicates that one in six people who try crack will become addicted. Nine out of ten who start smoking cigarettes become hooked, although an addiction to cigarettes is far more forgiving than an addiction to crack. Cigarette smokers can live with their "habit" for years before their health is harmed, but after only a few exposures to crack, users have a destructive, craving, gnawing in their bellies. To satisfy their crack hunger, users do not buy one vial or ten—they buy hundreds of vials of crack a week, investing huge sums of money in this "cheap" drug.

Like a hit song that sweeps across the nation, the taste for crack swept through urban neighborhoods in the 1980s. Hundreds of thousands of young Americans were soon addicted, and it did not take long for the addiction to begin destroying lives. Addiction to other drugs is a gradual process. Users can often function for extended periods of time before their lives fall apart. The onset of the disease of alcoholism, for example, may take years to develop fully. In the intervening years, incipient alcoholics can muddle through, working and raising their families, but the process of crack addiction is like a tape run at double or triple speed. Within weeks the hunger for crack is insatiable. Addicts are soon devoting their days and nights to the use and pursuit of crack. They do not eat adequately and they do not sleep; physically they decline very quickly. Because of the high number of female users of child-bearing age, crack put millions of children at risk for neglect and abuse.

THE CRACK TRADE

KIDS USE CRACK AND KIDS SELL CRACK. IN CITIES ALL OVER the nation the drug trade has become a major employer of the young. In New York City, the employment of children by adult traffickers is a twenty-year tradition. Children first entered the drug trade in the early 1970s following the passage of the "Rockefeller Laws." These stern additions to the criminal code mandated lengthy prison sentences for those convicted of possessing even small amounts of illicit substances, particularly heroin. Because those under 18 are not subject to adult law, drug dealers eager to avoid convictions for narcotics possession began to employ children to hold and transport their drug supplies. Over the years the roles those under 18 play in the drug business have expanded significantly.

The practice of hiring under-age drug operatives, begun in New York, was quickly adopted by drug traffickers in other cities. The younger children are, the more innocent they look, the less likely police are to search them. For $20, $50, or $100 a day, children as young as 8 and 9 are hired by older dealers, some still teenagers themselves, to do an assortment of drug related jobs. Kids work as "lawaway"— holding drugs. They work as lookouts, warning dealers that the police have been spotted. They work as "stash" guards, guarding stored-away drugs, and they work as "touts," extolling the virtues of one particular dealer's brand of drugs and directing buyers to him.

Kids also deal. In cities all over the country small children have been arrested while selling crack cocaine. In Boston an 8-year-old was apprehended with 30 vials of crack in his coat. What draws these youngsters into the drug trade is the chance to earn money. In the poorest communities dealers are often the only visibly "successful" adults that children see. The cash-rich drug traffickers play their role to the hilt, dispensing free samples, flashing large amounts of cash, wearing expensive clothing, putting on a show. Of course, kids and their parents are impressed by the dealers' displays of conspicuous consumption. They are no different from the rest of us, whose heads turn at the sight of a gorgeously dressed celebrity alighting from a stretch limousine. While adults and children in more advantaged circumstances have numerous models of success, in the poorest neighborhoods dealers may be the only people "making it." All the rest are struggling to survive, often working at the most menial jobs, jobs that do not provide them a living wage.

For the youngest children in the drug trade the money to be earned fulfills their every dream. Children this age comprehend money in concrete terms. They do not think about owning a house, or being able to afford health insurance. They think about tennis shoes, sweatsuits, television sets—desirable objects that are otherwise unobtainable, that make a tangible difference in their day to day lives.

Money is not the only lure that attracts young people into the drug trade. More often than not drug sellers are drug users. At the bottom of the drug trade, users and dealers are more or less interchangeable. This assertion was confirmed by a National Institute of Justice 1989 study in Detroit. Researchers followed 97 crack users and found that two-thirds categorized themselves as "user-dealers." These young people sold crack on the street to support their own crack-smoking habits which, on average, cost them about $250 a week.

According to law enforcement officials, the penetration by corporate, organized-crime-style, teenage drug gangs or "crews" into the crack trade has been surprisingly deep. In many parts of the country, says United States Attorney Roy Hayes of the Eastern District of Michigan, "teenagers have come to dominate all aspects of the crack business." They are being used by the international drug bosses, who oversee the importation of cocaine into the United States to process, package, cut, distribute, and sell coke, and even enforce discipline in the ranks. Another expert notes that high level distributors like to use adolescents because adolescents are willing to take chances adults would not. Their reckless, risk-taking attitude suits the needs of adult drug bosses at the very top of the drug dealing hierarchy.

In recent years many teenage drug dealers have begun to do business outside their own neighborhoods and even outside their own states. Highly professional, corporate-style drug crews from Detroit, for example, have expanded into smaller cities all over the Midwest. In 1989 police in Columbus, Akron, Toledo, Cincinnati, Wheeling, Charleston West Virginia, Richmond, and Indianapolis all reported that crack, imported by corporate gangs from Detroit and elsewhere, had arrived in their cities. These teenage interstate drug sellers flooded the market with a glut of cheap drugs, which had the effect of generating lots of new business while driving local dealers, who could not compete on price, out of the drug trade. In Columbus, Ohio alone, in a space of a few months police arrested fifteen young drug couriers at the airport coming in on flights from New York, carrying cocaine they estimated had a wholesale worth of $700,000. Turned into crack and sold on the street, this supply would have been worth much more.

On the West Coast, many of the gang members colonizing new drug markets are associated with the Crips and Bloods. Gang members fleeing "the heat" (the police) in Los Angeles, travelled to Seattle, Portland, and Anchorage to "chill out." (Stay away until it is safer to return). They quickly realized that there was money to be made selling crack and cocaine in these new markets. Using the established network back home to provide them with product, gang members went to work creating distribution systems. Corporate-style Crips and Bloods do not wear their colors when they arrive in a new city. They are looking for market share; old disputes are irrelevant to their mission. In some places, Crips and Bloods even work together.

GUNS AND DRUGS

GUNS PLUS DRUGS EQUAL HOMICIDE. IN THE 1990s, THIS new equation dominates big city police work. In Washington, D.C., the homicide rate doubled between 1980 and 1988. As the number of homicides soared, so did the number of victims found to have ingested cocaine. The Medical Examiner in the District of Columbia reported in 1989 that 80 percent of the bodies of the 438 homicide victims in that city contained residues of cocaine. That means that eight out of ten homicide victims ingested cocaine or one of it's derivatives within twelve hours of being found dead. (Cocaine is not detectable unless tissue samples are taken within that time period.) A large proportion of these victims had also consumed alcohol. Coke users drink heavily to counteract the drug's unpleasant side effects, which include jumpiness when under its influence and depression when the drug wears off.

No other city has as high a correlation between homicide and cocaine-ingestion as Washington, D.C., but in most cities, cocaine is showing up in the bodies of a significant portion of homicide victims. In Detroit, for example, the medical examiner reports that 50 percent of the 740 homicide victims in 1988 were found to have residues of drugs, usually cocaine, in their bodies. In New York City, the medical examiner reports that in 1989, 40 percent of 1,905 homicide victims were found to have ingested cocaine in the hours before death. Nearly 40 percent also showed significant traces of alcohol in their blood.

Gathering data on homicides is a tricky and inexact business. If bodies are not discovered immediately, if victims live for several days after an injury, if post-mortems are not carried out punctiliously, if data is not reported and recorded accurately, the results may not be accurate. It is best to look at this kind of information as an approximation. Even so, from the statistics related above I think one has to conclude that in our nation's cities, cocaine is a major risk factor associated with homicide.

The correlation between cocaine and violence has at least three different sources:

First, criminals like to use cocaine before committing crimes because it makes them feel brave, confident, and in command. High on cocaine during the commission of a crime, adrenaline pumping through their bloodstreams, criminal offenders are likely to be buffeted by waves of aggressive impulses. That violence would occur in these circumstances is hardly surprising.

Second, cocaine's psychopharmacology predisposes users to commit violent acts. Cocaine is not a calming opiate like heroin. Heroin addicts desperate for "a fix" will commit violence to get money to buy drugs, but when they are high—and the heroin high lasts for 3 to 4 hours—heroin addicts pose little threat to anyone. Cocaine is different. Cocaine is a stimulant. It increases motor activity, and makes users jumpy, irritable, and in some cases paranoid. People who are high on coke see threats where none exist. Moreover, the alcohol that coke users consume may further distort their thinking and push them in the direction of violent action.

Third, within the drug trade, violence is universally recognized as a legitimate tactic for protecting one's turf and expanding one's holdings. To use a bit of business school lingo, "the culture" of the cocaine trade is inherently violent. Cocaine is sold on the retail level by thousands of independent entrepreneurs like Max and his crew. There are few "Godfathers" to carve up territory, apportion markets, settle disputes, and maintain discipline. Instead, dealers function more or less independently. With no centralized power asserting control over most retail distribution, anarchy reigns. Those who want to stay in the game must be willing to meet, match, and surpass the violence of their adversaries.

The violence that surrounds the sale and distribution of illicit drugs is notably different from the other forms of violence discussed in this book. Drug trafficking violence does not originate with the inability to handle anger and other emotions. It may be unrelated or only tangentially related to the model describing a "typical" homicide—two people who know each other, who have been drinking, who argue, one of whom has a gun. This form of drug violence is calculated, rather than spontaneous, and premeditated.

Reporter Leon Dash from the *Washington Post* has closely observed and written about the teenage drug scene in Washington, D.C. Dash says what is driving up the homicide rate in his city is the street-level murders of one young, small-time drug dealing teenager by another. More often than not these homicides are caused by drug deals that go bad and by drug thievery.

The life of young street-level dealers, many of whom are crack users, is a desperate and sordid affair. On the street, each person must look out for himself, each person is a predator. "Stick up boys" steal the drug supplies of other dealers. Sometimes dealers smoke up their supply of crack and say they have been robbed. Either way, dealers are always afraid, always running from someone. In Washington, D.C., suppliers punish dealers who do not pay up by beating them with baseball bats. One 20-year-old dealer, convicted of a murder when he was 17, whom Dash interviewed in prison says he told the dealers who worked for him that he would take his baseball bat not to their bodies, but to their heads if they did not pay when they were supposed to.

Dash says if a dealer lets himself be "ripped off" in any way, he risks looking weak and being made completely vulnerable. Once crossed, he has to kill, otherwise word will spread on the street that he is a "mark." Sometimes the drugs in question are only worth 5, 10, or 15 dollars. On the street, no one can afford to be known as a person who did not exact retribution when crossed. If people "mess" with your money, Dash explains, they have to be hurt. As a defensive measure, the code of the street says everyone associated with the drug trade must routinely "exert maximum force." That means shoot to kill no matter what the provocation.

Children as young as 12, 13, and 14 are routinely drawn into this vicious world. Leon Dash believes that a crucial moment occurs when young males arrive at junior high school and realize that the education they have received has not prepared them to do junior high work. It is then, Dash says, that these youngsters opt for what the reporter calls "the parallel value system." The kids make a conscious decision to enter the illegal economy—dealing drugs and committing other crimes in order to "get theirs" now. They see "the parallel value system" as their only realistic choice, their only way to obtain what they want. This is the same moment when girls "decide" to become teenage mothers.

If the boys are successful as drug dealers, Dash says, they shower the mothers of their children with material goods and cash—imitating the male providers they see on T.V. They give their girlfriends and their children all the luxuries; expensive designer this and expensive designer that. Boys walk around school with big rolls of bills in their pockets. Their money has to be seen, has to be spent. Girls go wild for them. They are heroes. It is the American dream, Dash says, played out according to the way adolescents see the world.

THE GRANDIOSITY OF A KID WITH A GUN

TEENAGERS NEED TO SWAGGER A BIT AND BE GRANDIOSE— such posturing is part of their narcissism. They need to overestimate their own talents, and underestimate the risks that await them. Grandiosity helps teenagers make the leap out of the nest toward independence. Without their inflated self-confidence, false though it may be, few teenagers would have the nerve to strike out on their own.

Grandiosity, however, is not risk-free. Rehabilitation wards are full of young people in wheelchairs who overestimated their own skill and behaved recklessly when driving, diving, swimming, climbing, or fooling around. Often the worst of these so-called "accidents" happen when young people have been drinking. Alcohol increases a drinker's grandiose regard for his or her own capacity to control events, machinery, and circumstances.

Guns, too, make a person grandiose. Carrying a weapon makes

most people feel important and strong, maybe even invincible. The more vulnerable a person feels, the more seductive the attractions of a firearm hidden in the dresser drawer, in the glove compartment, or carried on one's person. This is true of adults and of adolescents. When an adult carries a gun, we hope that his or her judgement will mitigate against the grandiose feelings the weapon is likely to instill. This is our expectation, for example, with police officers who are generally armed both on- and off-duty. As we have seen time after time when police officers shoot unarmed assailants, the judgement of grown men and women, especially when they operate in dangerous circumstances, can be lethally flawed. With adolescents, there is even less reason to expect good judgement to prevail.

When a teenager carries a gun, we have everything to fear. A roster of developmental traits conspire to put him and us at risk. An adolescent with a gun is a person who feels invincible, a person who believes he will never die, a person who is likely to have little judgement about the use of alcohol and other addictive drugs. Time after time, all these points intersect with deadly consequences. Simply put, armed teenagers lack restraint. This is precisely why drug dealers like to employ adolescent gunmen. As one prosecutor in the Dallas, Texas, district attorney's office put it, "Adolescent gunmen have itchier trigger fingers. . . . You put a gun in a kid's hand, and they are more dangerous than adults." The comments of "George," a young gang member in Boston, who describing his own gang activities (which began when he was 12), selling drugs, and carrying a gun, illustrates the dream world in which some armed and dangerous young people operate. "I was carrying the gun just to be carrying it," he said. "I wanted to be someone big. To me a gun changes a person. It makes 'em brave. Sometimes, I would go on the roof and shoot in the air. I felt like 'let 'em come up on me, I'd be like Hercules.' I even said, 'let a cop come. I'll get 'em.' "

GANGS, KIDS, AND COPS

ALL THE GEORGES ON THE STREET, IMITATING BEING BAD, strike terror in the hearts of urban police forces. The police know the murderous capacity of the arsenal these "children" carry. Fantasies may fire the imagination of George on the roof. However, there is nothing make-believe about the threat posed by a child carrying a 9-millimeter gun. The unpredictability of these young assailants is one of the reasons police officers in many of our nation's cities routinely wear bullet-proof vests.

When 12-year-olds carry concealed weapons, police have a difficult time telling the good guys from the bad. Gangs and drugs have complicated their jobs. The most innocent-looking youth may be armed with deadly force and willing, even eager, to use that force. To protect themselves, the police feel they must treat every kid in every inner city neighborhood as a potential killer. This belief has caused relations between police and communities of color, never good to begin with, to deteriorate.

In Long Beach, California, in early 1989, a black police officer from a nearby community was stopped for a traffic violation. The black officer alleges that the white officers who pulled him over, believing he was a criminal assailant, beat him and threw him through a plate glass window. This incident, which is in litigation, says a great deal about the relationship that exists between black males and police officers. Police all over the nation have been accused of routinely using excessive force when dealing with black suspects.

On both coasts residents of the black community are beginning to speak out about the violent interaction between young males of color and the armed officers charged with protecting the public safety. In Boston this issue received national attention following the murder of a pregnant white woman, Carol Stuart, in the predominantly black Mission Hill neighborhood. Charles Stuart, who was the real assailant, claimed that he and his wife had been shot by a black male, a would-be robber. That allegation led to an invasion of the Mission Hill neighborhood by 100 police officers, who questioned and searched black males, apparently with no regard to the description of the alleged assailant. Many of the suspects were ordered to strip from the waist down before being searched—a procedure that is unconstitutional.

The "invasion" of Mission Hill by Boston police was not unusual, nor were the indiscriminant searches. For many months Boston police had been carrying out a controversial "search on sight" policy in areas with a high concentration of gang activity. Young men were routinely stopped, searched, and questioned by officers who had no apparent reason to suspect them of committing any crime—except the tone of their skin. "Search on sight" was applauded by some in the black community, but many others expressed outrage at a policy that singled out suspects solely on the grounds of race, apparently in defiance of the fourth amendment to the constitution that requires police to have "probable cause" for suspecting a crime has been committed before they search a suspect.

Boston is not the only city where such controversial police practices are common. In Philadelphia, similar tactics have been used repeatedly and have been repeatedly knocked down in court. As a result of a 1985 police anti-drug offensive called "Operation Cold Turkey," Philadelphia was required to pay half a million dollars in damages to 1,444 suspects, most of them young black males, who were stopped and searched without sufficient legal justification.

In Los Angeles, where civilian suits against the police have sky-rocketed as a result of alleged strong-arm tactics, a recent high profile attempt to suppress gangs and gang violence was called "Operation Hammer"—the name tells a lot about the tactics of the operation. Thousands of young males of color were stopped and searched. Thousands were arrested and later released without being charged. The inability of police to make these arrests stick tells a great deal about the effectiveness of such operations. These sweeps do not represent high quality police work. They terrorize, do not get criminals off the street, and engender terrible, and ultimately terribly destructive, resentment in minority communities.

A number of Mexican-American gang members from the gang-ridden Aliso-Pico district of Los Angeles described to novelist Earl Shorris their interactions with the Los Angeles Police Department:

"They (the police) stopped us at the park . . . I was walking away. He (an officer) seen me; he was passing by. He jumped over the fence. He hit me here in my face. He picked me up. He grabbed my chains, threw them in the trash. He got me by my balls, started squeezing my balls and threw me on the ground. . . .

". . . They stopped, just like that, and started beating us up. They hit my homeboy in the head. Cut him up. . . . Came after me. Boom! Hit me in the stomach. . . .

"I was in the station all day, until the night (brought in as a murder suspect; someone else was later arrested and charged in the crime.) They were saying, "We got people saying it was you." And I was like, "if you got so much proof take me in." They started beating me up when I said that. . . .

"Once we were coming back from the store . . . and this cop and a lady cop stopped us. They hit my homeboy; they were beating him down. He had a beanie. This cop took out his gum from his mouth and picked up the beanie and put the gum on my homeboy's head and smashed it down with the beanie.

"If you say you want a lawyer, they'll kick ass. "What did you say? You want to press charges against me?" They'll take you somewhere, they'll take you to the factories and beat the shit out of you. Everybody's scared of the factories. . . ."*

The police, of course, have their own version of all these events, and I have no way of assessing the truth or falsehood of these particular allegations of police brutality. Yet, it is clear that the general context of the interaction between young black- and brown-skinned males and the authorities is troubled and hate-filled. The essence of this relationship so far as the gang members are concerned was summed up by another Mexican-American "gangster" in Aliso-Pico

* From "Sanctuary for L.A. Homeboys," by Earl Shorris, *The Nation*, Dec. 18, 1989.

who cursed the L.A. Housing Authority police whom he said had stuck a gun into the mouth of his "homeboy." "They're just a gang," said the young gang member, referring to the police, "but they're legal."

Philippe Bourgois, an anthropologist from San Francisco State College, who has been doing fieldwork on the street/drug culture in East Harlem in New York City for the past five years, confirms what the young "gangsters" in Los Angeles say—that police routinely treat males in inner city neighborhoods in vicious and humiliating ways. Describing one incident in which a police officer pushed him across an ice cream counter, "spreading my legs and poking me around the groin," Bourgois wrote: "That night in the bodega I did what I had learned to do when being frisked—stare at the ground, avoid eye contact and mumble obsequiously, "Yes sir," whenever appropriate. Failure to behave subserviently in the face of unjustified police action, Bourgois implies, would certainly have violent repercussions. Bourgois is a white professional.

The fact, I think, simply cannot be denied that the police introduce some of the violence into poor communities. The kids say the violence of the police is a catalyst for their violence. The police say the violence of young gangsters and drug dealers is a catalyst for their use of necessary force. Either way violence begets more violence. I believe that police officers all over the nation, including minority police officers, fail to understand the terrible rage that they trigger when they treat black- and brown-skinned males with so little regard for their dignity. Most of the time this rage remains invisible. When it surfaces, the police are surprised and hurt. They feel betrayed by the very community they say they are trying to protect. So it was in Boston, following the shooting death of Carol Stuart. So it was all over the country after the notorious black rap group, NWA, recorded a rap song complete with police sirens wailing, in which the singers exhort other blacks to commit mayhem (the verb was less polite than this) against the police. I in no way condone NWA or their song, but I hear in it an outrage that I sense will not go away and that I very much fear is adding to the already unbearable violence in poor minority communities.

FAMILIES

NOT ALL INJURIES INFLICTED ON POOR NEIGHBORHOODS by crack and other drugs are visible. Some of the most life-threatening wounds cannot be seen. These are the invisible injuries sustained in "the drug war" by poor families—families that poverty and social dislocation had imperiled even before drugs become a factor in their lives.

Imagine the life of a working mother, the head of a single-parent household that includes herself and three children. The four live in a public housing project. The woman earns six dollars an hour as an aide in a nursing home. That's $240 a week—about $1000 a month. From this she must pay $275 a month for rent, she must feed and clothe herself and her children, she must pay for electricity, a telephone, diapers, carfare. Life is an endless struggle to make ends meet, punctuated by visits to the phone company and the power company billing offices pleading with them to restore her service. To earn extra money, the woman works overtime, but then she is not home in the evening to supervise her children. This worries her. She knows what is happening in the streets, but feels powerless to protect her children from it. Then one Friday evening, the woman's 15-year-old son hands her $200 in cash and says this is for Christmas presents, or Easter outfits, or help with the bills. What does this exhausted woman do? Does she question her son and give back the money, telling him she wants no droppings from the obscene trade in drugs? Or does she quietly tuck the money in her purse?

When parents are poor and struggling, many find it impossible to say "no" to an infusion of drug-generated cash. Saying "yes" has unexpected consequences, however. When children become providers parents can no longer exert control over their behavior. Terry Williams, the East Harlem anthropologist who studied Max's drug gang, explains what happens when parents begin to accept and even to rely upon the drug-generated cash from their children. "The child in essence becomes the parent. Then you can't tell them what to do. The balance of power has been shifted. Suddenly, as a parent, you turn the other way. You are reaping the benefits of the drug trade. This is altering the whole structure of the family," says Terry Williams.

When parents' economic position is compromised by poverty, the power of their authority is undone. Children lose the single most important source of restraint in their lives—the restraint on behavior that follows a firm, non-ambivalent parent, "No. No, you may not. No, I will not allow it." The very children who are most at risk, who most need to know that their parents stand for upright, pro-social values are abandoned to their own adolescent grandiosity. No parental voice of caution is available to temper the adolescent's get-rich-quick nobody-can-harm-me fantasies. Moreover, as a breadwinner, often in a family lacking any other male provider, the drug-dealing child becomes a kind of role model, teaching younger siblings the quick and dirty way to line one's pockets.

Involvement with crack is by no means confined to the younger generation. Many parents are also users and sellers of crack. One of the attributes that differentiates crack from other drugs is the number of women, many of them young mothers, who are users. In New York City, in Washington, D.C., in Kansas City, in Portland, Oregon (and presumably in many other cities) arrest data gathered by the Justice Department indicates that at least as many women as men are using crack. In fact, many believe that more women than men are crack abusers. The impact on children of having a crack-addicted mother is crushing. How can young mothers chasing the short-lived crack high provide children with even minimally acceptable standards of care—adequate food, an orderly life, cleanliness, a safe environment? Often they can not, a fact attested to by the skyrocketing number of reported cases of child abuse. In Massachusetts, between 1980 and 1989 reports of neglect and abuse increased nearly 500 percent from 15,000 cases annually to 70,000. In 1990, the figure jumped another 17 percent. Rising rates of drug and alcohol use are blamed.

Crack is the final blow, the blow that shatters families previously damaged and demoralized by conditions in the underclass. The conditions for women in poverty have grown so much worse in the past decade, the possibility of escape from poverty has grown that much more remote. Many women have simply relinquished themselves to a life with only one remaining goal—to satisfy their addiction.

I despair to think of a generation of underclass children coming of age whose mothers are addicted to crack and other drugs. How violent will our cities be when the sons of addicted mothers enter adolescence? One national study estimated that 375,000 babies a year—11 percent of all babies born in our country—are exposed to alcohol and illicit drugs while in utero. This prediction is only an estimate, an estimate that some experts in the field believe seriously overstates the problem. As all women are not tested during pregnancy and all babies are not tested at birth, we cannot know for sure how many fetuses are poisoned in utero by dangerous substances. We do know that some of the offspring of maternal drug users are born addicted and some are not, but we do not know why. Similarly, there is a great deal of debate, but no firm answer, about how much alcohol is dangerous during pregnancy. However, all physicians agree that the less a pregnant woman drinks the better.

Another subject for debate is the ethnic and socio-economic characteristics of pregnant substance abusers. Most of the research on this subject has been done in inner city hospitals where the patients are predominantly black and brown-skinned. Researchers assumed, erroneously, that most pregnant substance abusers were minority members, but a study published in the *New England Journal of Medicine* in 1990 has poked a hole in that idea. The researcher looked at substance abuse among pregnant women in Pinellas County, Florida. In this study, 10 to 11 percent of pregnant women were abusing drugs. This figure held up across racial lines. What differed was the drug of choice. Black women tended to use cocaine and crack; white women tended to use marijuana.

No one knows what smoking marijuana does to the unborn, but there is reason to believe that crack-addicted infants can sustain serious neurological damage, more serious than infants whose mothers smoke pure cocaine. Infants born addicted to crack are extremely irritable and uncomfortable. Their addiction makes them twitch and jerk. They are likely to be premature and suffer from low birth weight—placing them at risk for many serious complications, including respiratory trouble and retardation. Physicians and nurses who care for these addicted infants have begun to speak out about a generation of "crack babies." They are describing infants who do not make eye contact, who do not form attachments to other human beings, who do not play with toys in an organized and meaningful way and who appear to have serious and persistent emotional and cognitive difficulties. How common, how permanent, and how costly these impairments will prove to be will not be known for years to come, but it does not require four years at Harvard Medical School to predict how bleak the outlook is for seriously impaired children born to poor mothers who are drug addicted, in neighborhoods decimated by drugs.

I fear for these children and their parents. I fear for our communities, and I fear for our society that seems so blindly oblivious to the dire circumstances into which so many of our future citizens are being born. While the federal government pours billions of dollars into drug interdiction, relatively little goes to prevention and treatment. Much, much more is needed. Just as AIDS was ignored until the rate of infection soared to the point where the epidemic threatens to deplete our financial and medical resources, so do I fear the ignored arrival of these addicted infants will haunt and harm us later. This view, I might add, is shared by Robert M. Stutman, the former chief of New York City's 500-agent office of the Federal Drug Enforcement Administration. During his federal tenure Stutman was viewed as one of the nation's most effective drug fighters. Since leaving federal service, Stutman has loudly proclaimed the importance of improving education, prevention, and treatment programs. "Agents knocking down doors and aircraft carriers off the coast of Colombia," he says, will not solve the drug problem in this country. "We are counting on drug agents to solve a problem that they alone are unable to solve. We still don't have places to put the bad guys, we don't have meaningful prevention programs, and we don't have a treatment system that begins to deal with a communicable disease."

As a physician and public health educator I have no doubts whatsoever that "meaningful" prevention and treatment programs could make a major impact on the nation's drug problems. I would begin with free, universal, prenatal services. I believe every pregnant woman in our society ought and must be eligible to receive nonpunitive pre-natal care, including food supplements where necessary. Drug-using women must be made to feel welcome—that's the only way we will be able to get them into treatment. So far as drug treatment is concerned, every man and especially every woman who seeks treatment ought to be immediately served by an appropriate program that meets their long and their short term needs. No questions asked. No waiting lists. Our society will soon be pouring tens of millions of dollars into treating "crack babies"—babies who may never become full functioning, contributing members of society. Treating impaired infants is a laudable endeavor, but we can save these dollars and we can save an endless abundance of human suffering if we act to ensure the birth of healthy children. Our society is angry at people who use drugs—especially women who use drugs. I understand that anger, although I also understand that most who are drug addicted started using between the ages of 10 and 15 years old. As a society we have to go beyond our desire to punish the "bad women," the "bad mothers" who use drugs. Simple self-interest tells us that we must provide treatment and care for these young women, to prevent their offspring, or more of their offspring, from being born addicted to brain-destroying drugs. Any other course is madness.

DRUG MONEY: NOT WHAT IT'S CRACKED UP TO BE

THE DREAM OF WEALTH THAT LURES POOR KIDS INTO THE drug trade usually turns out to be an illusion. Not many poor kids are getting rich, really rich, selling drugs. At most they may have some of the trappings of wealth—gold jewelry, a fancy car. They may have some cash in their pockets, if their drug habits have not gotten out of hand, but they are not making enough money or the right kind of money to get "ahead of the game." Rarely does a kid use the drug business to burst free from poverty.

In four years of heavy dealing, working six days a week, twelve hours a day or more, none of "the cocaine kids," except Max, managed to sock away any money. Cool, calculating, and able to control his own drug habit, Max beat the system, acquiring a fortune large enough to underwrite his entry into a legitimate business in a new location. The rest of the gang had little to show for four years of sweat, four years of danger, four years of making the Colombian "connect" a very rich man. One member of the gang was "on the skids"—pathetically addicted to cocaine; one was dead, two worked in menial jobs, two were still working in the drug business and one, about whom we can feel hopeful, was a student.

Using drugs, sharing drugs, going to clubs and restaurants required the constant outlay of a great deal of cash. That's where "the cocaine kids' " money went and why they had nothing left to show for their efforts. Lower down the ladder, on the level of street dealer, stash carrier, runner, guard, and tout, kids are making a lot less money than Max and his pals. The fabled $500 a week, or $1000 a week pay just to hold a packet of drugs turns out to be just that—a fable. The drug business is a giant pyramid. Big time dealers and distributors make sure that the profits flow upward—toward them. Moreover, with such an abundance of labor available, those controlling the trade feel no pressure to pay high wages. Everyone lies to everyone else about all the money they are making. Somehow, a few seem to really strike it rich. For most, drug dealing is just another dead end job.

Even under the most lucrative of circumstances what teenagers in the drug trade make is a kind of television wealth. That's wealth without substance, wealth for show. They buy cars with cash, but do not possess a drivers licence, or have insurance. When they get in an accident, they walk away from a brand new vehicle. Dealers have no health insurance. They have no social security number. They have no work experience to list on a resume. Years spent in the drug trade are just blanks that remove drug industry operatives even further from the mainstream.

The lucky kids stay alive long enough to realize that dealing drugs is a trap. They see their friends and associates maimed, murdered, and in jail, and some of them have the insight to see that they are headed for the same destinations. They realize that they are not exempt from the consequences, and that's when the smart ones get out. One former drug dealer who exchanged his grandiose profession for a job in a car wash paying $4.50 an hour, told a *New York Times* reporter. "I just grew out of it, man. I just grew up. There comes a point where you know it ain't gonna last."

9

THE PUBLIC HEALTH
APPROACH

THE REAL BLACK NORM: NON-VIOLENCE

I GREW UP IN A NON-VIOLENT FAMILY.

My father, who died of a heart attack when I was in medical school, was a calm, morally persuasive man with a strong social conscience. He had high standards of conduct and self-control. When my father was angry, I knew it, but I never saw him explode or hit anyone, including my sister and me. Nor did my father speak badly of other people. He would forcefully argue a political point, but his defense of his opinions never degenerated into a personal attack.

Both my parents were skilled at controlling their anger. When my sister and I misbehaved, they punished us by taking away special privileges. They yelled sometimes, but they did not hit. Nor did I ever hear my parents argue, although as an adult I learned that they used to go down into the basement to "disagree." Upstairs, they presented a composed and united front.

Like many people of our generation my husband Charles and I are somewhat less restrained than our parents were when it comes to showing all of our emotions, including anger. Up until our children were the age of three or four, we did give them an occasional swat on the bottom when they were naughty, but perhaps because of my parents' example, I always felt bad when I resorted to spanking. I knew there was a better way to discipline. We do not spank our children now, but we do let them know when we are angry at them and at each other. Like my parents, Charles and I wait until we are alone to *really* argue.

I believe children benefit from seeing their parents manage their feelings, especially anger. By seeing adults express anger *without los-*

ing control, kids learn that anger is not too dangerous or too over-whelming to face, to feel, and to let go of. Developmentally, these are lessons that help children mature emotionally.

Teaching youngsters how to express their feelings without being crushed by them is an important part of what we give our children, and it is not just parents who can do the instructing. Some years back, the assistant minister at our church, using three balloons, gave a wonderful demonstration during the children's sermon of how anger could harm or benefit an individual. The preacher, a black male, blew up the first balloon and then let it go. The balloon careened wildly around the room. The minister said this balloon illustrated how un-predictable and destructive anger released without control could be. Next he blew up a balloon until it was very large. What would hap-pen, the minister asked, if he kept blowing without releasing any of the air? The children all knew that the balloon would pop. This, he said, was an example of anger denied and unexpressed; anger like this, when allowed to build up for a long time, can hurt the person who feels it. The third balloon was blown up and let go in a controlled way in front of a pinwheel. As the air was released, energy in the form of a breeze was directed at the pinwheel, making it twirl around. This third example, the minister said, showed how anger recognized and harnessed could energize its possessor, leading to constructive action.

Back in the days when my parents were raising my sister and me, nobody talked about "managing your anger constructively." I think my parents' social activism was one effective way they handled their anger, but they did not verbalize what they were feeling. Probably they reined in their emotions more than was healthy. Today we are more direct. We express our feelings to one another. Still, I cannot help appreciating my parents' restraint. As a doctor, I have seen so many lives ruined by domestic violence that is passed from one gen-eration to the next. How grateful I am to my mother and father for providing me with a loving, secure, and non-violent environment in which to grow up. How grateful I am to them for providing me with a model of a loving, committed, and non-violent marriage.

Because of the kind of family in which I was raised, non-violence to me is an African-American norm. I do not think black Americans or any group of Americans are innately violent. Because of my relation-ship with my father and my husband I have always assumed that black men are strong, compassionate, and committed to their fami-lies. I have never doubted that when black males or any males behave aggressively they do so as a result of what they have been taught, not as a result of race, or any genetic factor.

If I had been brought up in a different kind of family, I might not have responded as I did when I arrived at the emergency room in my third year of medical school and learned how blase most medical practitioners are about the violence committed by and against young black males. Because of my family background, I was not prepared to accept as fact that violence was inevitable in minority communities. What I had learned at home and in the all-black neighborhoods of Atlanta where I grew up, had inoculated me against the "that's the way it is" school of thinking. I knew too many non-violent black men to believe "that's the way it is."

As a physician, I did not agree that the medical community was powerless to prevent young black males or members of any group from hurting one another. I believed that physicians and other medical personnel could help reduce homicide and other forms of violence; what was needed was the will to define the injury and death associated with homicide and assault as a medical issue. Other forms of "intentional injury"—suicide, spouse abuse, child abuse—were now defined as medical problems. I wanted the assaults and homicides that occurred between acquaintances added to the list.

I believed that the lack of outrage doctors expressed in the face of so much mayhem, represented, in a sense, society's acquiescence. So long as "they" were killing each other, nobody seemed to mind. By not condemning violence or seeking to prevent it, physicians were delivering the message to the young minority males whom they treated for stab wounds and gunshot wounds that black-on-black violence was routine and even acceptable. By not expressing outrage, physicians reinforced the violence. Without meaning to, they were telling young minority males that their injuries and even their deaths were not worthy of outcry. I found the delivery of this kind of message intolerable. I had become a doctor because I was attracted to the physician's ability to take action. That's what I wanted to do. Take action. I wanted to begin to take action to reduce the terrible toll of violence on all Americans, but most especially upon the young. I found it hard to believe that every physician did not feel as I did.

THE ATTRACTION OF PUBLIC HEALTH

IF I HAD BEEN A SURGEON I MIGHT HAVE DEVOTED MYSELF to research on ways to improve trauma care. If I had been a psychiatrist, I might have poured my energy into creating therapeutic interventions for families victimized by violence, but my goal as a physician had always been to bring about the greatest good for the greatest number. For that reason, the public health approach to medicine *with its emphasis on prevention* had always attracted me. Preventing disease had always seemed to me to be the physician's highest calling. In addition to violence, the kinds of medical problems that interest me the most—teenage pregnancy, for example—are questions that make the most sense from the perspective of prevention. Even my decision to specialize in adolescent medicine after I completed my residency in internal medicine was an expression of my interest in prevention. Much of the physician's job when caring for teenage patients is preventive: we use an array of prevention strategies to help teenagers lay the foundations for long and healthy lives.

Not surprisingly, when I began to think about violence in a medical context, I saw this problem not as one that, say, required better surgical techniques, but one that required the creation of public health strategies such as health education in the classroom; health education via the mass media; community awareness; hospital-based screening for risk determination. I was impressed by the way these strategies were being used to combat smoking, heart disease, lead poisoning, child abuse, and other menaces to the public health. I wanted these same strategies to be applied and evaluated to reduce adolescent violence as well.

I was especially interested in using the emergency room as a point of outreach. Patients who had been stabbed or shot seemed so vulnerable and receptive to me. Their injury tore open their defenses. They did not feel immortal or immune. Most of them were frightened and wanted a way to save themselves from future injury and pain. I believed that this emotional receptivity created an opportunity we could seize to teach them about violence. I wanted every young male to understand that violence represented a serious risk to his longevity. Once they understood this, I believed we could lure them into counseling and help them change their behavior.

It took me a while to get going. During my last year in medical school, I had produced the first version of my high school violence prevention curriculum. That was the same year that our son, Percy, was born. After Percy's birth, I continued to think about violence and talk about violence, but I did not do much. Struggling to meet the dual demands of motherhood and medicine during three difficult years of internship and residency, I had little time or energy for crusading. In the last year of my residency at Boston City Hospital, I was pregnant again and nauseous—nauseous, as is my style when pregnant, for nine whole months. Our daughter Mimi was born shortly after I took the medical boards that led to my certification as a legitimate practitioner of internal medicine.

The years following Mimi's birth were easier. I was finally through with my training. No more 36 hours on-duty, 24 hours off-duty. No more nights on call. Settled, with a dual appointment as an internist at Boston City Hospital and at the Harvard Street Health Clinic in Roxbury, I could again begin thinking about violence. My concern was far from academic. I was hired at Harvard Street to care for inner city adolescents. My patients were at high risk for violence, both as potential victims and potential perpetrators.

Driving me on was a vision of all the young males who had been stitched up and sent back out onto the streets to kill or be killed. I have always been appalled that our society finds the lives of young males, especially young black males, so little worth saving. To me these young men have always been beautiful—misguided sometimes, but beautiful nonetheless, full of energy, full of life. I suppose more than most people, I like adolescents. I do not find adolescent males frightening. If anything, I identify with their headstrong, plunge-into-life style. I can see in them the children they were just a year or two before, children who are often left to bring themselves up in a world that has no use for them. In so much that they do I hear these kids asking, "Where is my place in the world?" Instead of answering this question, many in our society have chosen to hate—hate and fear young black- and brown-skinned males. When we see them coming, we clutch our pocketbooks and cross to the other side of the street. We never ask ourselves why the only power we can imagine our young possessing is the power to hurt themselves, each other, and us.

I renewed my efforts to prevent adolescent violence where I had left off with the violence prevention curriculum. I knew the curriculum needed work if it was ever going to become a usable document for students and teachers. To this end, I forged alliances with two inner city high schools where the administrators were committed to reducing student fighting. The schools to which I offered my services were Cathedral High, a private, Catholic school located on the edge of Roxbury and the Jeremiah E. Burke High School in Dorchester, which is public. For several years I was in and out of both schools, teaching, talking, videotaping students as they dramatized the kinds of situations in their lives that lead to fights and violence. The more contact I had with students, the more convinced I was of the curriculum's importance. Adolescents were eager to talk about violence and they were eager, desperate really, for adult insight and solutions. Moreover, the insight the curriculum provided students about their own anger and the understanding it gave them of how fights happen seemed to be among the factors that helped administrators at both schools reduce fights and restore a sense of safety and security to their buildings.

Meantime, I was casting about, looking for allies, talking to other physicians about the role health care professionals could play in helping to reduce adolescent violence. Many of my colleagues, though respectful, though I was misguided. They saw violence as a regrettable inevitability of human life, like taxes or old age. I was told again and again that as violence was not a disease, medicine could not cure it. This statement always surprised me. Doctors were playing an increasingly active role in many areas related to health that had little to do with disease in the old-fashioned sense. My colleagues were fighting in favor of laws requiring children to ride in special car safety seats. They were campaigning in favor of mandatory seat belts. They were involved in efforts to curb smoking and impede drunk driving. They were screening patients in hospitals for battery and child abuse. Physicians were broadening their base, defining the pursuit of good health in new and imaginative ways. To my mind, violence prevention fit right in with all these other forms of "health promotion"— that's the public health term used to describe efforts to market good health—and I could not understand the resistance of many physicians.

"PREMATURE MORTALITY"

MY EARLY BELIEF THAT VIOLENCE POSED A SIGNIFICANT threat to the health of our nation's young was empirical. The "data" I looked at were the mass of young trauma patients flooding the emergency rooms at Boston's teaching hospitals. While I was in the emergency room patching up the wounded, public health officials in Atlanta at the Centers for Disease Control and in Washington, D.C. in various federal offices were looking at statistics related to "morbidity and mortality" (injury and death) and coming to some startling conclusions concerning the prevalence of violence in our nation. Trained to look at health problems quantitatively, epidemiologists discovered that many of the old threats to the nation's longevity had been replaced by a new set of problems that had little to do with air-born germs and infection.

Antibiotics, inoculations, and other advances in modern medicine had wiped out infectious diseases as the primary threat to health in this country. Americans in great numbers were no longer dying of influenza, measles, polio, pneumonia, typhoid, or tuberculosis. In the early part of the 20th century epidemics of these ailments had swept across the country, killing millions of Americans; many of them young and healthy. In the second half of the 20th century heart disease, cancer, and stroke were the most common killers of Americans. These were ailments that primarily effected people who were middle-aged or older; children, adolescents, and young adults were not often affected.

The statistics showed clearly that injury, not illness was the most significant threat to the health of young Americans in the latter part of the century. Suicide, accidents—especially auto accidents—and homicide were the most common causes of death among young people under the age of 25. While other health threats decreased, the threat of these three to the young increased. As a result, adolescents were the only age group in the latter half of the 20th century to register an increase in "age adjusted" mortality. That means that more adolescents than ever before were dying as a result of the rising number of adolescent suicides, accidents, and homicides.

From an epidemiological perspective, suicide's, accidents, and homicides have much in common. All three are violent. All three are likely to involve alcohol abuse, and perhaps drug abuse. The victims of all three are often depressed. Some public health experts go so far as to say that like suicide, many or even most of these deaths are "intentional." They explain by noting that many fatal auto "accidents" are not "accidental," at all, they result from deliberately reckless, "intentional" behavior, such as speeding and drinking and driving. Homicide, they say, can be intentional in two ways. Perpetrators "intentionally" assault their victims, while victims may "intentionally" seek out their own victimization. The experts call this kind of homicide "victim precipitated," meaning that depressed young victims "intentionally" trigger the fights in which they die, in order to die. While impossible to prove, this theory certainly bears consideration. What cannot be disputed is that all these forms of "premature mortality" rob many productive years from young, healthy individuals. For that reason these deaths are of great concern to public health officials.

The statistics impelled forward-looking public health officials to redefine the mission of public health and redirect their efforts. A major goal of the federal public health community became an effort to reduce "premature mortality" among otherwise healthy young people. Federal funds flowed in this direction. Suicide prevention efforts, particularly those aimed at adolescents and young adults, were increased. New campaigns to educate young people about the dangers of drinking and driving were undertaken, and the public health community committed itself, for the very first time, to reducing interpersonal violence.

In 1979, public health took the plunge into the uncharted waters of violence prevention. That year, the Surgeon General of the U.S. published his first national agenda for health promotion and disease prevention. The agenda outlined 15 priority areas related to health requiring national attention; among them, the reduction of interpersonal violence. Reducing violence, the Surgeon General said, would save lives, prevent injuries, reduce pain and suffering, and improve the quality of life for millions of Americans.

The Center for Disease Control, (CDC) which had been instrumental in encouraging the Surgeon General to include violence as one of his health priorities, established a violence epidemiology branch to track the incidence of interpersonal violence, just as other "epidemics" were tracked. Mark Rosenberg, M.D., M.P.P. was head of the CDC branch. His vision and his dedication shaped the federal violence prevention effort throughout the 1980s.

CDC grouped assault and homicide along with other "intentional" injuries—child abuse, spouse abuse, and rape. By studying these violent events together, public health investigators revealed a common thread among them. Most violence, it was discovered, occurs not between strangers, but between people who know each other, or who are related to each other, at least one of whom is unable to tolerate frustration or resolve conflict. When relationships explode, terrible injury or death is often the result. Long before the most extreme expressions of violence occur, a history of hitting, beating, fighting, and abusing often exists. Underlying each of these violent acts is a human failure. One or perhaps both persons caught in a violent relationship cannot relate non-violently. A history of family violence is often to blame for this inability.

By designating violence reduction as a national goal, the Surgeon General set the agenda and helped provide funds for the fledgling public health effort to combat violence. A small number of far-sighted African-American physicians, psychiatrists, psychologists, and academics realized immediately that the federal interest in violence reduction was of profound importance. They believed that the time had arrived to begin addressing the problem of violence within black communities. In 1980 the first symposium exploring homicide among black males was organized by the Federal Alcohol, Drug Abuse and Mental Health Administration. Some black Americans and some black leaders were leery, however. They feared that opening the issue of violence among blacks for public discussion would provide the dominant society with fuel for its racist beliefs and attitudes. Even today, this remains a sensitive issue for many black Americans.

Mark Rosenberg's interest in my violence prevention curriculum helped to promote my work nationally. Mark shared my belief in education as a technique for reducing adolescent violence and homicide. He was enthusiastic about my work at Cathedral High and at the Burke where I had developed high energy, hands-on techniques for engaging teenagers in the discussion of violence, and he was interested in what I was learning. The students had taught me that every fight had a history. Usually fights developed slowly, in stages, during which a chorus of "friends" and on-lookers carried stories from one side to another, acting as catalysts to violence. What the students were teaching me was confirmed by the research on violence.

Mark encouraged me to continue working on the curriculum, which he thought would eventually turn out to be a significant teaching tool. Later he invited me to give a talk about my work at a very prestigious forum, the 1985 Surgeon General's Conference on Violence as a Public Health Problem. This important conference brought together some of the most influential and creative people in the new field of violence prevention. I had the chance to meet and mingle with these smart, receptive, and challenging colleagues. Among them was David Nee of the Burden Foundation who later played a major role in supporting and underwriting the publication of the curriculum.

The 1985 conference put the Surgeon-General-Koop-stamp-of-approval on the public health approach to violence. The Surgeon General was widely respected as a leader in health. What he thought worth pursuing was taken very seriously. His support gave legitimacy to the effort to define violence as a public health problem and to reduce violence by using public health interventions. As a result of my participation in the 1985 conference, I came to be known nationally as someone who was striving to reduce adolescent violence. My work stood out because few others in public health were designing interventions to reduce violence. Most of the effort thus far had gone into data collection.

THE STRENGTHS AND WEAKNESSES OF THE PUBLIC HEALTH APPROACH

PUBLIC HEALTH EXPERTS SEE THEIR MISSION AS TAKING place in four separate stages. Before the problem of violence can be addressed, they rightly say, the nature of the problem must be known. So *Stage one* requires the development of "surveillance systems for morbidity and mortality associated with interpersonal violence." Translated, that means sophisticated systems for collecting information about whom is being hurt and under what circumstances must be designed and implemented. *Stage two* mandates the "identification of those who are at risk for non-fatal events." This means data collected must be studied to determine who is at risk for being injured. *Stage three* demands the "application of case control methods to the exploration of modifiable risk factors for victims and perpetrators." This means that using rigorous research techniques trial interventions aimed at modifying the risky behavior that research has revealed leads to injury must be devised. *Stage four* states that trial programs must be "rigorously evaluated." That is find out if the intervention worked. With public funds in such very, very short supply, this is an extremely important step. However, I find it disappointing that there is no *Stage five* exhorting public health officials to fight like hell to see that successful strategies are widely implemented.

What public health lacks is a sense of urgency. Scientists trained to analyze data carefully and dispassionately are not the best advocates for changing the world. That is why, although I am completely committed to the public health approach to analyzing, understanding, and reducing violence, I have always been something of an outsider in the public health establishment. I see myself as a friendly goad, standing inside the field cheering my colleagues on to greater feats of daring. I suppose by nature I am more of an activist and less of an analyst than others in this field. That does not mean, however, that I do not recognize and value public health's considerable strengths.

Long before public policy people had even dreamed up the term, public health was an interdisciplinary field. In the public health universe problems are defined widely and their solutions are seen as resulting from the collaboration of diverse specialists. I learned during my years as Commissioner at the Massachusetts Department of Health that there are few social problems, including violence, that belong exclusively to one government department or another. So far as I am concerned the only hope for solving social problems is for specialists from "opposing" camps to join together. I have no doubt, for example, that reducing violence requires the creative collaboration of the criminal justice establishment, the health establishment, the mental health establishment, the social service establishment, and the education establishment. I am not talking about a few top bosses holding "summit" meetings. I am talking about the troops, the mass of cops, probation officers, doctors, nurses, therapists, counselors, social workers, and truant officers working together every single day. When a kid enters the emergency room with a gunshot wound to his thigh after having been shot in a dispute over a jacket, I want him to be as well treated for the "disease" of violence as he is for the traumatic injury he has sustained. When that young man is blanketed in therapeutic interventions that involve his parents, his pregnant girlfriend, the probation officer assigned to him on a previous case, the kid who shot him with whom perhaps he has had a long-standing feud, his school, which is about to expel him, and perhaps even his younger brother who has just started to act out violently—that's when we will start to make a difference. All this might sound like pie in the sky, but collaboration does not in fact cost a lot of money, not when the agencies doing all the jobs I have just described are already using up taxpayers' dollars as they attempt and fail to address one by one this young man's problems. Just think of the tens of millions of public dollars we can save each year if we can keep some of our young minority males out of prison!

Public health gained its insights about collaboration not after years of trying to go it alone, but at the time of its inception. Public health officials have always depended on the cooperation of many bureaucracies to protect the lives of the nation's citizens. Public health departments routinely rely on the help of the public schools to see that children are inoculated against communicable diseases. They rely on the media to deliver important health messages. They rely on the police and the courts in all sorts of ways. When public health inspectors, for example, identify filthy conditions in a restaurant, they have the power and resources of the police and the courts to help close it down, and in the most extreme cases, to keep it closed.

Public health doctrine asserts that large national problems require multiple solutions. Multi-tiered strategies that address different segments of the population are used routinely. These interventions, known as primary, secondary, and tertiary prevention strategies, speak to the needs of specific groups of citizens:

Primary prevention strategies are designed to reduce health problems in the general population. This form of prevention involves educational and public information campaigns aimed at teaching the mass of American citizens about risk factors. Primary prevention strategies to combat heart disease, for example, include programs that raise the consciousness of the general public to the dangers of eating fatty foods, or smoking, or having a high cholesterol count.

Secondary prevention strategies are interventions aimed at people who are at risk. For heart disease secondary prevention includes efforts targeted to those who are at risk for developing heart disease because they smoke, have high blood pressure or high cholesterol, or have a family history of the disease.

Tertiary prevention encompasses all the strategies designed to prevent those who are already ill with heart disease from becoming sicker. Tertiary strategies are more intimate than the others. They usually involve some form of one-on-one, group, or self-help counseling.

When public health experts get together, their discussions of prevention strategies can get to splitting hairs. Are programs that help smokers stop secondary or tertiary prevention? The debates can rage for hours. So far as I am concerned, however, the details are not so important. What counts is the overall public health model and the understanding that one form of intervention is not capable of changing behavior. Some old-fashioned public health advocates, it ought to be noted, dislike all interventions that rely on changing behavior. These conservatives prefer "instrumental" interventions like inoculation programs and programs to put safety latches on guns. In general, however, the field has been steadily moving in the direction of using the full range of interventions to change attitudes and behavior related to health.

I find the public health approach to changing behavior intrinsically sophisticated. Few in public health, for example, would attempt to combat drugs by exhorting kids to "just say no." Public health people understand that behavior is difficult to alter and that change comes not as a result of a quick fix, but following a steady barrage of interventions that erode destructive attitudes and behavior over time. As a result of continuous public health agitation, in the 25 years since the first Surgeon General's report condemning smoking, the incidence of smoking has declined by 30 percent nationwide. This improvement was brought about by an array of primary, secondary, and tertiary public health strategies targeted to every segment of our population. An amazing list of institutions has taken part in the effort to prevent people from smoking: Local, state, and federal health departments have undertaken campaigns against smoking. The mass media has produced and broadcast public service messages condemning smoking. The media has also lessened the practice of glamorizing cigarettes by showing actors and actresses smoking in films and television programs. Private physicians have exhorted their patients to quit smoking. Schools have urged their students not to start smoking. The American Heart Association and the American Cancer Association have campaigned mightily, even launching an annual national quit smoking day. Private employers have underwritten programs to help smokers quit. Airlines, public buildings, private offices, restaurants, and in some cases even bars have banned smoking in public. The list goes on and on. There is virtually no institution in our nation that has not been enlisted in the effort to induce Americans not to smoke.

The public health campaign against cigarettes represents public health at its best. Looking closely at this effort, we can also see some of the weaknesses in the public health approach, however. The greatest of these is the inability of public health experts, despite 25 years of effort, to convince blue collar and poor Americans to quit smoking as often as more affluent Americans have. Anti-smoking efforts, like many public health campaigns, have been more successful in tapping into the hopes and the fears of upper-income people than those of poor or blue collar Americans. For whatever reasons, the consequences of smoking as articulated by the health establishment are more likely to encourage affluent people to quit. Some blame this class-based difference on the fatalism of the poor. Poorer Americans, it is said, do not believe that they can control their own destinies, and so do not act to quit smoking and protect their health. Others say poorer Americans are more oriented toward immediate, rather than delayed gratification and so have a more difficult time quitting smoking. Whatever the reason, the public health establishment has not been able to convince large numbers of those in our society with less money and social standing to stop smoking. This has to be seen as a significant problem, although one I feel confident can be resolved.

For those of us who wish to use public health strategies to prevent violence, this socio-economic skewing of the smoking issue is highly instructive. Public health strategies to reduce violence will be useless unless they speak directly to the needs of poor, brown-skinned peoples whose lives are most often misshapen by violence. Preaching is ineffective, and so are messages that make no sense in poor communities. For example, it would not be productive to tell a working mother earning $5 an hour that her children should watch less violence-saturated television. That T.V. may be the *only* child-care that mother can afford, and at least so long as her children are watching television, she knows they are not out on the streets. I believe what we need to do is open up the local public school in the afternoon, provide tutorial help to students, and implement recreation programs so that all the kids of working mothers have some place to go where they can learn and play and be safe. That's what I call a meaningful violence prevention intervention for that woman, her family, and her community.

We need programs that are culturally specific, age-appropriate, and that involve the target population in the decision-making process. We are not going to reduce violence if our time and our dollars are spent talking *at* teenagers, for example. We are going to have to talk *with* our teens and then design violence prevention strategies based on our conversation with them. Those at risk for violence and other poverty-related social problems are not unreachable, but we will not reach them sitting in our offices.

There is another important lesson to be learned from the anti-smoking crusade. When we look closely at this struggle, it is clear that public health people have rarely been out in front leading the anti-smoking bandwagon. Public health physicians and researchers tend to be cautious. They do not feel comfortable out on the limb. The most dramatic wins of the anti-smoking campaign came about as the result of grass roots agitation. All over the country ordinary citizens, not public health professionals, have fought and won the battles to ban cigarettes from domestic airline flights and from offices and public buildings. Grass roots efforts like this are not only valuable in themselves, but they are a spur to the professionals involved in the fight.

We cannot expect the public health establishment to turn into fire-breathing radicals. While I might enjoy such a spectacle, it is not reasonable to count on this happening, and we do not have the time to wait for it to happen. I think grass roots efforts by necessity will have to be at the forefront of public health movements inciting physicians, researchers, and public policy experts to take more risks.

The way this kind of public-private interaction works can be seen by looking at Mothers Against Drunk Driving (MADD) inspired public health campaign to reduce drunk driving. The actions taken by police departments and courts all over the country to ferret out and to imprison drunk drivers did not come from Masters in Public Health. This effort was triggered by a group of angry, hurt, and disgusted mothers whose children had been killed by drunk drivers. These grief-stricken women rose up and shouted "No more, no more, no more!" Their moral outrage galvanized the nation, including the public health establishment, members of whom then jumped in to join the fray. The public health community then set to work creating many interesting anti-drunk driving interventions. My favorite is the collaboration between public health experts at Harvard's School of Public Health and Hollywood writers and producers. This partnership, orchestrated by my colleague at the school of Public Health, Jay A. Winsten, has led in recent years to the holiday-time blanketing of the airwaves with messages about designated (non-drinking) drivers. These were not just public service announcements. Winsten convinced the creators of many of television's most popular weekly series to dramatize incidents in which characters chose designated non-drinking drivers before heading off to holiday parties. How I long to undertake similar collaborations with television writers and producers around the issue of violence! Can you imagine the impact of showing adolescent viewers young characters like themselves who struggle to resolve their conflicts without resorting to violence?

We who are committed to using public health strategies to reduce violence cannot do the job alone. We need the anger, the energy, and the moral power of ordinary people demanding that we engage in this most important fight. There is no force on earth more powerful, more persuasive than that of plain people who have had enough. I think ordinary Americans have had enough violence, enough killing, enough crippling injury, enough dead children endlessly mourned. It is time now for all those weary of the violence to rise up and take a stand. We need to begin turning back the ugly tide of violence.

ONE DAY IN THE LIVES
OF AMERICAN CHILDREN

2,740 teenagers get pregnant
1,105 have abortions
  369 miscarry
1,293 give birth

  676 babies are born to women who have inadequate prenatal
      care
  700 are born at low birth weight (less than 5 pounds, 8 ounces)
  125 are born at very low birth weight (less than 3 pounds, 8
      ounces)
   69 die before one month of life
  107 die before their first birthday
2,407 are born out of wedlock

   27 children die because of poverty
    9 children die from guns
    6 teenagers die from suicide
7,742 become sexually active
  623 get syphilis or gonorrhea
1,375 drop out of school

1,849 children are abused
3,288 run away from home
1,629 are in adult jail
2,989 see their parents divorced*

* Statistics from "A Vision for America's Future," compiled and published by the
Children's Defense Fund, 1989.

10

HELPING FAMILIES PREVENT VIOLENCE

INTRODUCTION

VIOLENCE IS A PROBLEM THAT BEGINS AT HOME. THAT'S THE conclusion that nearly all the specialists who address the issue of violence in our society come to sooner or later. Sociologists, criminologists, epidemiologists, probation officers, welfare workers, bureaucrats in the juvenile justice system, research psychologists, clinical psychologists, media critics, police officers, "gangologists," psychopharmacologists, judges, physicians, community activists, youth workers—all agree that families play a vital (but not an exclusive) role in teaching children to use force to resolve their conflicts.

My own view could not be simpler. I believe if all the children born in America learned at home how to manage anger and aggression non-violently, our homicide and assault rates would decline by 50 percent—maybe even 75 percent. Mothers and fathers rarely put guns in the hands of their children and tell them, "go kill or be killed." *The destructive lessons parents teach when they are physically and psychologically abusive to their children and when they allow their children to be physically and psychologically abusive to others, in conjunction with our society's glorification of violence, the ready availability of guns, and the drug culture are an explosive combination that set our children up to be the perpetrators and the victims of violence.*

Individual parents cannot remove guns and drugs from our environment, nor can they halt the viciousness broadcast incessantly on the mass media, but teaching children how to function in a social setting without bashing those who stand in their way can make a big difference. As a physician, I consider children who have learned at home how to satisfy their own needs without resorting to force to be inoculated against violence. When they become adolescents, young people like this are more able than others to walk away from trouble. Trouble may still find these peace-loving young people—a stray bullet can find anyone, especially those living in impoverished neighborhoods—but children who know how to resolve conflict, rather than escalate it, stand a lot better chance of surviving to adulthood.

RAISING WELL-ADJUSTED KIDS

I CONSIDER PARENTING THE TOUGHEST JOB THAT I DO— the one that makes the most diverse and challenging demands on me. The list of children's needs can feel endless at times. Children need healthy food and clean clothing. They need housing that is dry, warm, sanitary, and safe. They need regular medical care. They need developmentally appropriate toys that help them perfect their gross and fine motor capabilities. They need care-givers who talk to them and read to them, helping to promote their inborn ability for spoken and written language. They need non-violent adults whose behavior they can imitate and model. Unless children possesses all of these basic necessities they are developmentally at risk—their physical, intellectual, social, or emotional growth may be stunted because of factors having nothing to do with their innate capacity to flourish and to learn.

A child is not a machine. Adequate maintenance and fuel are not enough to guarantee maximum functioning. For a child to thrive his or her physical needs must be met in the context of a loving relationship with at least one parent or care-giver. "Someone who is crazy about the kid," is how one wise professor described the kind of care needed by a developing child. Bonding. Attachment. These are the terms specialists use to describe what happens between the adult who is "crazy about the kid" and the kid herself during infancy and childhood.

Babies need someone whose presence is predictable, someone who gazes into their eyes when they are being changed, or fed and delivers the unspoken message, "You are good. You are wonderful. I am glad that you are here on earth." All through childhood and well into adolescence, children depend on one or more special people to cement their positive feelings about themselves and others. A child's capacity to feel love, to give love and to mature into a responsible, participating adult requires the presence of loving adults who stay put year after year. Tragic consequences may await children who lack such people in their lives.

Even love is not enough. In order for children to thrive emotionally they need limit-setting and non-violent discipline nearly as much as they need love. The lack of these two is disorienting and frightening to children and to adolescents alike. Young children need to know (you can see them begging to be told) that the adults in their life are in control, not of the smaller issues such as what color t-shirt to wear, but of the larger issues related to health and safety. Adolescents, too, hunger, though perhaps less obviously, for parental limits. Most want their parents to save them from their own most extreme impulses. They are disappointed and hurt when parents do not care enough to pay attention to what they are doing and to intervene when they disapprove.

Many parents assume if they do "what comes naturally" they will raise their children right. Unfortunately, our species is not genetically pre-programmed with child-rearing skills. When we hold our babies during their first weeks of life we do not "naturally" discriminate between a hungry cry and a tired cry. When we face a tantrumming toddler, we do not "naturally" know how to help this child resolve his rage without capitulating to his demands. Later, when we confront a rebellious adolescent, we do not "naturally" know how to give our child enough freedom to separate from us, but not so much that he or she is adrift and alone, susceptible to unsavory peers. Not knowing what to do, we often adopt the parenting strategies of our parents. Unfortunately, not all parents are worthy of emulation.

In societies in which roles are clear cut, values are undisputed, and morality is as unblinking as an eye for an eye, rearing children may be easier. In our complex society, rearing children tests the wisdom of each and every one of us. All parents need help some of the time. Confronted by siblings who fight, a child slacking off at school, and other common, but confounding problems, I have often sought advice from my mother, child-care providers, nurse-practitioners, pediatricians, teachers, and other experts. All these figures are important resources whom I would find it difficult to do without.

In the area of family dynamics, there are no experts for whom I have more respect than the team of psychologists and family therapists, headed by Gerald Patterson, Ph.D. at the Oregon Social Learning Center (OSLC). In the past twenty years, Patterson and his colleagues at OSLC have penetrated some of the mysteries of family life. Their work is based on social learning theory, which states that children learn how to behave by imitating role models. What children learn this way is then "reinforced" by other people. Behavior that is positively reinforced will be repeated often and added to a child's normal repertoire. Behavior that is not reinforced will disappear.

By minutely studying the interactions of parents and children in troubled and untroubled families, the Patterson team concluded that the parents of untroubled kids have certain skills that enabled them to "control" their children's behavior most of the time without excessive screaming or hitting. They knew intuitively how to positively reinforce desirable behavior. *The parents of troubled kids were not necessarily bad, or neurotic, but they lacked these crucial parenting skills. They did not know how to get their children to comply with their requests. They did not know how to reinforce good behavior; without intending to, they reinforced undesirable traits.*

Compliance, the time a child does what he or she is asked to do, turns out to be a crucial indicator of how a young person is faring and how well he or she is likely to fare in the future. Following the rules is an essential part of social functioning. Children who are noncompliant trigger the ire of their parents, they alienate their peers by their inability to play by the rules, they anger their teachers by their oppositional and disruptive behavior, and they short-circuit their own capacity to master other more sophisticated social and cognitive skills. Patterson and his colleagues observed 100 families with normal 10 and 11-year-old sons—these were children who got along well with their parents, were able to make and keep friends and were doing average or better work at school—to find out how much compliance parents ought to expect. Among the sample families, the sons obeyed their mothers 57 percent of the time and obeyed their fathers 47 percent of the time. (Only 3 of the boys obeyed their mothers every time.) Patterson defined 50 percent as a normal amount of compliance. He suggests that parents whose children comply much less than that ought to reconsider the techniques they are using to encourage good behavior and discourage unpleasant behavior.

Sometimes parents seeking compliance unwittingly encourage the opposite. (This is one I do more often than I am proud to admit.) "Would you like to set the table?" we ask our kids. "Isn't it time to do your homework?" we ask. We turn what ought to be simple declarative statements, such as "Please set the table," or "It is time to do your homework" into questions that allow our kids to answer, "no." Patterson and his colleagues suggest that parents use positive statements with simple verbs like "go" and "start" instead of phrases that begin with negative words like "stop" and "don't." Instead of, "don't hit your sister," tell your son to "Go to your room and start your homework." Instead of, "Turn down that damn music," tell your daughter to "Go brush your teeth, and get ready for bed." The positive statements are less challenging to the child. They give the child a way to stop or alter his course without losing face. Children, misbehaving or not, have a lot of pride. Finding a way to demand their compliance that leaves their pride intact makes it easier for them to comply.

Few children do what they are told the minute they are told to do it. Responding to their children's resistance, parents have two choices. They can threaten punishment if the job is not done, or they can offer a reward. The specialists at the Oregon Social Learning Center strongly believe that offering small rewards contingent to the completion of the task is a far more effective strategy than threatening punishment. They believe that making demands contingent is one of the hallmarks of effective parenting. "Set the table now and there will be ice cream for dessert," you might say to a young child. "Do your homework now and then you can watch television for a half an hour before bedtime," would be a reasonable way to deal with a 9 or 10-year-old. "After you have cleaned up the kitchen, you can borrow the car," is a sure-fire method of getting action from a teenager.

Contingent requests always have two parts to them—the request and the reward, the *if* and the *then*. The reward need not be large, expensive, or difficult to grant, but it must be something desired by the child. *If* you make your bed, *then* you can go out and play. This method of getting children to obey removes parents from the weak and unpleasant position of constantly threatening their children with dire and usually unenforceable consequences. Children know that parents who threaten a great deal rarely follow through, and that's not surprising. Most punishments are just as unpleasant for the parent as for the child. An adult who punishes an adolescent by grounding him has to stay home to enforce the punishment or else the punishment is meaningless. Punishments often turn out to be too much trouble and parents who issue them in the heat of their anger— "You are grounded for a month"—usually stop enforcing them when the flush of their anger has passed. By using contingencies, parents have a first line of defense—a way to induce compliance without threats. On the rare occasions when punishments are used, Patterson and his colleagues urge that they be enforceable and that they are enforced. Mild punishments, they say, are just as effective, maybe more so, than draconian ones. They recommend short work "details"—scrubbing the bathtub, mowing the lawn—as appropriate punishments for adolescents who break the rules. What counts isn't the severity of a punishment. What counts is parental follow-through. From a Social Learning perspective, parents who don't follow through are training their children to disregard them.

Making privileges contingent on good behavior is an especially important tactic with teenagers. While a 10-year-old may be intimidated by a bellowed, "Clean up your room this minute, young lady," with adolescents shouting is not very effective. You cannot force your will on teenagers. When yelled at and "abused" teenagers feel justified in defying you, lying to you, and doing precisely what they want. Unless teenagers are involved in your strategies to parent them, they will most likely "yes" you to death and do what they want as soon as they leave the house. Contingencies give the adolescent some of the power and the parent some of the power. The parent sets the ground rules—always—but the child has power over where and when he complies. If he complies right away, he can have the car right away. If he doesn't comply until tomorrow, well, that's his choice; but no car until tomorrow.

After more than twenty years of doing research and treating families as a therapist, Patterson says with great certainty that children who are socially competent come from homes where the rules are enforced contingently and the parents provide a rich supply of love. Other researchers using the Patterson technique of directly observing family interactions have come to the same conclusion. The combination of warmth and firmness is what works when raising children—adolescents included. Parents who bring up their children in this way are saving themselves and their children from trouble and even tragedy.

Like most experts, Patterson is not in favor of using coercion to enforce family rules. While taking a less rigid stand than some academics who believe that every swat on the bottom is an act of child abuse, the OSLC team does not favor spanking. I, too, take a dim view of spanking. On a few occasions when my children were small, I lost control and gave one or the other a swat to the rear. Doing so certainly did not make me feel good about myself as a parent. I knew spanking was not the best I had to offer. I understand that many parents believe very strongly in the efficacy of spanking. Others, being human, occasionally succumb to the anger every child is a master at eliciting.

My own view is that, although not the best means of discipline, small children are not likely to be damaged by an occasional slap on a spot where nature and fashion conspire to provide several layers of padding. A quick spank to the bottom, however, is very different from planned or protracted spankings and beatings. These forms of punishment are unwise and unacceptable; they may, if severe enough, be illegal. Beatings can cause grave harm. They are also likely to be entirely ineffective, bringing about temporary apparent compliance and long-term defiance. Other forms of physical punishment such as shaking, or throttling with an object, can cause serious physical harm and should never be done. Spanking, moreover, is never appropriate for adolescents in whom it is likely to ignite feelings of fury and humiliation and lead to acts of rebellion.

One of the problems with spanking is that it may fail to communicate to the child what is really expected of him or her. Children do not think like adults and they often do not understand what parents want them to do. Claude Brown expressed this juvenile bewilderment with the wishes of the adult world in his memoir, *Manchild in the*

Promised Land. "When I was a little boy," he wrote, "Mama and Papa would beat me and tell me, 'You'd better be good,' but I didn't know what being good was. To me, it meant that they just wanted me to sit down and hold my hands or something crazy like that. Stay in front of the house, don't go anyplace, don't get into trouble. I didn't know what it meant and I don't know if they knew what it meant, because they couldn't ever tell me what they really wanted."

Spanking becomes a serious problem when it is the only item in a parent's bag of tricks. If the only way you know to compel your child to do what you want is to spank him or threaten to spank him, then you must either spank him many times a day, or you must passively accept most of his misbehavior. This is an extremely ineffective way to parent. The child routinely misbehaves, but is punished only intermittently. From a social learning perspective, when parents tolerate a great deal of whining, yelling, hitting, tantrumming, and so forth, exploding violently only occasionally, they are teaching their child that *most transgressions go unpunished.* They are teaching other destructive lessons as well: That violence is the only way to get what you want when others resist. That violence is an adult's first and only response to anger. That violence, not words, is the language of family interaction. Moreover, when the spanking is capriciously delivered, unconnected to a specific transgression, the child may be taught "learned helplessness." This form of destructive passivity is exhibited by laboratory animals and, it is believed, by human beings when the penalties they receive are unconnected to their own behavior. Animals and humans in such stressful circumstances give up and cease trying to interact with or alter their environment.

Other forms of coercion can be nearly as destructive as too much spanking. Gerald Patterson urges parents to speak as politely to their children as they speak to strangers and co-workers. I myself find that I am more effective as a parent when I am speaking in a calm voice. When I start to shout, I have a tendency to regress to my child's level. For adolescents, parental ranting and raving sets up a hostile environment in which neither side can hear what the other is saying. Not yelling does not mean capitulating. "No" can be said in a normal tone of voice quite as well as it can be shrieked. If a parent is so angry that she cannot speak in a normal voice, she should give herself a few moments to compose herself before addressing her child.

Using contingencies, in fact, often takes away the necessity for parents' yelling because it gives parents a sense of their own power. Yelling and screaming often come out of the parents' feelings of helplessness. The parent who coolly says "When the kitchen is cleaned up, then you can borrow the car," does not feel compelled to yell. The one who yells is the one who watches his teenager take off in the family car, totally disregarding the messy kitchen.

Another of Patterson's most vigorously held beliefs concerns monitoring teenagers. He believes, and so do I, whole-heartedly, that parents ought to know where their children and teenagers are, all the time. Who they are with? Where they are going? What they are doing there? When they will be home? The more unsupervised "street time" a child is allowed, the more likely he or she is to get into trouble. Because even the best teenager will occasionally lie to their parents about where he is going and with whom he will be (I have never heard of a teen who does not lie now and then), it is wise to make a phone call occasionally to check up on them.

RAISING ANTI-SOCIAL KIDS

"When the fussy infant, instead of being rocked and soothed, is shaken and told that he is bad. . . .

When the 1-year-old, triumphantly standing up in her crib, is not applauded, but ignored.

When her frustrated screams at not being able to let herself down again are not met with assistance.

When the 2-year-old, trying to get a drink from the faucet, is not shown how to make the water flow into the cup, but is cursed and slapped . . .

When the 5-year-old, venturing out the front door, finds not a brother who might read to him but huddled bodies of junkies sleeping in the doorway . . .

When the 8-year-old, bringing home a truancy complaint discovers that no one cares.

These are the experiences of early family life that create adolescents . . . who are quick to yield to impulse, to seek immediate gratification of desires, to find minor obstacles at school, work, or training insurmountable, to see little reason to finish school or postpone early childbearing, to show no regard for others' feelings, and to become easy recruits to the ranks of crime."

Lisbeth Schorr, from *Within Our Reach*

Aggressive, anti-social adolescents are not born. They are slowly made over many years. Researchers in this country, in Britain, and in Scandinavia have repeatedly tracked the development of the kind of teenager who cannot get along at home or in school, who assaults those who get in his way, and who winds up getting in trouble with the police. In every instance, they discovered that trouble starts for these aggressive kids long before adolescence.

Psychologist Dan Olweus reports that as early as the age of three, the symptoms of excessive aggression show up in children. Olweus, Leonard Eron, and Gerald Patterson have all conducted longitudinal studies that look at aggression in large numbers of children over the course of decades. These studies have shown that the youngsters who are named by their parents, peers, and teachers as having trouble with self-control and aggression when they are 8 and 10 are the same young people who fight and get in trouble with the law when they are 17 and 18. These difficulties do not stop when young males move out of adolescence. One recently published study of 1,000 young males in Sweden found that fully half of all the subjects who had numerous police contacts as adolescents continued in a life of crime as adults. Once the seeds of excessive aggression are planted in a young person's personality, this trait takes root and is difficult to remove.

How do children as young as 8 or 10 learn to be violently aggressive? Some learn by brutal example. There is a clear, undisputed, (although empirically difficult to prove) correlation between child abuse and aggression. Children who are abused and children who see their mothers and siblings abused are hurt terribly by the experience. Therapists say that as they grow, some of the most seriously abused children are driven to repeating what happened to them, inflicting pain on others as helpless as they were. Adults and children like this feel no empathy for those they hurt. For them, the cycle of nurturance that predisposes those who were tenderly cared for as children to tenderly care for others is replaced by a cycle of abuse. Boys who see their fathers abuse their mothers may learn that it is the prerogative of men to "rule the roost" by using physical force. Other victims of abuse are damaged by their experiences in less global ways. They are likely to be frightened by anger. They are likely to assume that the world is made up of victims and victimizers. They may believe that intimacy inevitably leads to victimization. Doubting their own worth, fearing their own capacity to abuse, they may avoid intimate relationships and avoid becoming parents.

Not all the children who are abused grow up to become violent or enact their rage on society. The majority do not, but a significant portion, we do not know an exact percentage, of those who were abused become abusers. What is easier to establish quantitatively is the high instance of severe abuse among the most violent members of our society. In a study of juvenile murderers on death row, Dorothy Otnow Lewis found that all 14 of her subjects had been abused and in some cases tortured by parents and stepparents. This death row study confirmed earlier findings by Lewis that nearly 80 percent of a cohort of extremely aggressive juveniles had as children been the victims or the witnesses of unusually brutal family assaults. Interestingly, only 20 percent of a group of less violent children interviewed in the same study had been exposed to this kind of vicious attack.

Abuse is the most ugly and dramatic way that families "teach" children to be abusive to others. Many young people who cannot manage their anger and aggression do not have abuse, per se, in their backgrounds. Instead, they do have parents who regularly deliver harsh discipline. Over 25 studies have associated parental punitiveness with excessive displays of aggression in children.

Often the parents of aggressive children feel so overwhelmed by their own problems—money problems, work problems, marital problems, problems with drugs and alcohol—that they do not pay a great deal of attention to their children. They do not notice good behavior and reward it with what in better functioning families are the often entirely unconscious smiles, pats, and praise that help to reinforce positive behavior. This apparent indifference is punctuated by episodes of verbal and physical lashing out.

There is a similarity between the parenting practices of abusive parents and those of the parents of anti-social children, whether these parents are abusive or not. In both instances, parents fail to notice and praise what their children do right. In both cases communication between parent and child is impoverished. Violence may be the only way in which parents address their children. A study conducted by family therapists at the Oregon Social Learning Center found that abusive parents routinely ignored attempts of their children to talk to them. It is as if these parents, perhaps because of their own poor parenting, had not learned how to build positive bridges to their children. Instead, the parents were enclosed with their children in a psychological universe that was destructive to both.

In troubled families like this coercion is the driving force. Fathers beat mothers and children. Parents shout at each other and at their children. Children are beaten by adults. Children hit each other. Children control parents with tantrums, screaming, nagging, whining. Gerald Patterson and his colleagues describe these interactions between parents and children as "coercive family processes." In such a system children are "taught" by their environment to use coercion. Each lesson can be minute. Parents ignore a request for help made quietly. They ignore a drawing proudly displayed. They give in to a child's demand for candy when he whines and begins to tantrum. Interactions like these, thousands of them in a young lifetime, are what teach aggressive children to be aggressive and set them apart from the mass of youngsters who learn quite different lessons in their family and social interactions.

Once a child has established a pattern of using verbal and physical force to get what he wants, breaking that pattern is extremely tough. Research confirms what every good pre-school teacher knows: That the negative attention aggressive children receive gratifies them and reinforces their behavior. When Mom shouts at Johnny to stop bothering his brother, Johnny may be pleased that Mom is paying attention. Similarly, when Johnny grabs Paul's truck and the teacher intervenes and spends five minutes talking to Johnny, Johnny feels even more powerful than he did before.

Once coercive processes begin to dominate what takes place among family members, the pattern is difficult to change. We all cling to the way we do things long after our behavior has proven ineffective. The parents of troubled youngsters are no different. The problem, they say, is *not enough* spanking, *not enough* harsh discipline, *not enough* shouting. Rarely does it occur to an adult in a troubled family, an adult who was probably poorly parented himself, that what is needed is *less* hitting, *less* shouting, and more firm and reasonable limiting-setting and compliance training. In a coercive family context the outcome is predictable, so predictable that Patterson and his colleagues have created a chart that shows the tragic developmental ladder of a child who has been taught by his environment to use aggression to control the adults and the other children in his life:

This chart illuminates how the aversive behavior learned at home cripples the child's chances outside the home. Patterson says that children who learn aggression at home suffer from a kind of "learning disability." Their nasty behavior and their refusal to comply with the rules prevents them from learning to function in the world. Because they do not behave in acceptable ways, they are rejected by their teachers and by their peers. The more they are rejected by others, the more vicious their behavior becomes. They are caught in a cycle that they did not originate, they do not understand, that is carrying them further and further from a reasonable, responsible, and decent life.

Training like this doesn't happen overnight or in a week or two. It

FIGURE 1

A Developmental Progression on Antisocial Behavior

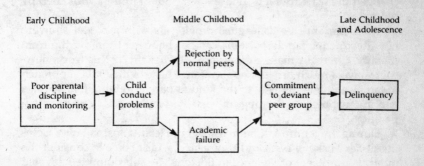

"A Developmental Perspective on Antisocial Behavior" G. R. Patterson, B. D. DeBarysche, E. Ramsey

takes months and even years of destructive family interactions to cement the beliefs, behaviors, and attitudes that will ultimately create a young adult who does not get along with others and cannot make his way in the world without smashing people and things.

Patterson and his colleagues in Oregon have proven that this destructive course can be interrupted when intervention is provided early enough. The behavior of aggressive, anti-social children can be improved, not by experts and outsiders, but by their own parents. The OSLC family therapists believe that parents, not paid specialists whose involvement with families is time-limited, have the power to change the lives of their difficult offspring. When outsiders do the job, when troubled children are sent to residential treatment centers, for example, research shows that the changes wrought are temporary, lasting only so long as the child remains away from home. When he is re-introduced into his coercive home environment, he will revert to his old way of behaving, unless his parents change as he changes.

The OSLC therapeutic intervention is a form of parent retraining. With children who are young and whose difficulties are mild, therapy can last for as brief a stint as 6 or 8 weeks. With more severely disturbed children, the therapeutic intervention can run for several years. The point of all OSLC therapy is to teach parents how to identify positive behavior and reinforce it, while weaning their children from their "aversive" behaviors through the use of contingent rewards. The results of these therapies are impressive with children and young teens. (Older teens who are more influenced by their peers than their parents do not fare as well.) Controlled studies have been conducted comparing the OSLC family therapy with traditional psychotherapy. When conducted by a highly skilled therapist (the skill of the therapist turns out to be crucial), the OSLC treatment changed the way troubled children behaved. Traditional talk therapy did not.

Patterson and his colleagues provide us with a model showing how destructive family patterns can be changed. Therapy, the right therapy, can really make a difference. The benefits of this work, however, have a much broader application. I believe the OSLC approach to families points the way to the kind of parent training that we as a nation must begin providing universally, to all parents and potential parents.

During my tenure as Commissioner of Health, Boston Police Commissioner Mickey Roach and I convened a Task Force to consider the mounting problem of violence in Boston. The subcommittee devoted to families came to the conclusion that much of the youth violence enacted on our city's streets originated in our homes. The subcommittee recommended that a standardized course teaching parenting skills be created along the lines of the Red Cross CPR courses. This standardized course with standardized teaching materials could be

presented before hundreds, thousands, of community groups—
PTAs, church groups, housing projects, parents groups, YMCAs,
YWCAs.

I would go even further. I believe that parent training ought to be
a mandatory course in every high school in our nation. This form of
teaching is not outside our educational tradition. We used to teach
home economics. Every girl in the nation learned to sew and cook.
Today we need to teach every girl and boy how to parent, how to love
and care for children, how to discipline them, how to provide for their
developmental needs. I cannot think of any addition to our school
curriculum that would be more useful. Most of us become parents.
Few of us are prepared for the job. I loved the moment in the the the
movie *Parenthood*, when one of the characters noted that you need a
license to fish, a license to hunt, a license to drive a car, but any two
fools can get together and have a baby. We can no longer afford to
have "fools" in charge of our most precious resource, our young.

SECOND CHANCE KIDS

Shakur Ali is a 42-year-old black man who knows what poor black
kids, kids without fathers, are up against. He knows, because he was
one of them. He knows about violence, too. And gangs and drugs.
His life has been touched by all these calamities.

Shakur Ali, who is the co-owner of a Roxbury security business, lives
in a big old house in Roxbury with six of his own kids and five former
gang members he has informally adopted. Another twenty young
people in Roxbury consider him to be their surrogate father.

Shakur Ali began rescuing kids after the violence that is endemic in
Roxbury almost carried away one of his own sons. In 1989, a gang of
local teenagers reigned over Ali's Fort Hill neighborhood—mugging,
robbing, assaulting, terrorizing residents. In November, one of these
youngsters plunged a knife into the abdomen of Ali's 18-year-old son
Alexander, nearly killing him. Alexander Ali was stabbed because his
assailant resented being looked at. There was no other motive.

Shakur Ali was enraged. He went looking for the kids who had done
this to his child. The gang heard he was on the prowl and evaded
him. Eventually a meeting was arranged. Ali says, "I went in very
angry, with fire in my eyes. I came out meek with tears in my eyes."

What moved Ali to tears were the life stories of the violent young
troublemakers. None had a father living at home. Some had mothers
who were hooked on alcohol or drugs. Most had brought themselves
up. All were fooling with drugs, using and selling. They all had criminal records—car theft, assault and battery, illegal gun possession.

Something in the youngsters stories, so similar to his own, moved Ali
and made him take a big chance. He offered the gang members the

chance to move into the two upper floors of his house. He would provide them with food, love, discipline, and direction. In exchange, they would have to go straight. Totally. No drugs. No criminal activity. No hanging out. Instead, they would have to return to school, get a job, make something of themselves.

The gang of young males said yes.

Since then big changes have taken place. The crime rate in Fort Hill has leveled off. Local merchants say the streets are less violent. Customers are not fearful to venture out. Probation officers of the five "adoptees" say the kids appear to be changing. No new charges have been pressed against them. They are going to school, studying for their high school equivalency diplomas. They work. They attend house meetings, and they abide by Ali's strict rules—most of the time, but then, what teenager abides by the rules all of the time?

The work has just begun. But Ali is full of hope. "I'm not gullible enough to think we're not going to lose some of these kids," he says. But, "I know one of these boys will be a state representative . . . One will be a congressman . . . One might be a senator . . . a governor . . . a doctor . . . a lawyer." Other young males, ones who don't live in, have also turned to Ali for help and guidance.

Money is tight. Shakur Ali has run through his savings, but he doesn't mind. Helping these kids find themselves, he has found his own true calling. Their need for some one after whom to pattern themselves perfectly matches his need to teach and to nurture. He has found himself, in the deepest sense. And he has found something else, too, some elusive secret of manhood—a manhood having to do with inner strength, a manhood shaped by commitment, compassion and belief, a kind of manhood in tragically short supply throughout our society, a model of manhood desperately needed by our young black men.*

When I think about Shakur Ali and his new "family," I cannot help recalling the phrase used by psychoanalyst James Herzog to describe the loneliness of boys without fathers. "Father hunger" is the evocative phrase Herzog coined to describe the emotional state of the boys he treated whose families had been ruptured by divorce. Father hunger. It is a phrase that resonates throughout poor black communities, throughout every American community, black and white. In our nation at least half of all children spend part of their childhood in single parent families, most often families headed by women.

Of course, girls and boys alike hunger to be close to fathers they do not know and are hurt when fathers are absent, but the socialization of boys appears to be jeopardized, as that of girls is not, when

---

* Based on the reporting of Pamela Reynolds in *The Boston Globe*, Tuesday, April 3, 1990.

fathers are missing. Psychoanalytic theory states and common sense confirms that fathers help boys manage their aggression. Experiencing and accepting the non-violent authority of a male parent or other male figure who is a part of a boy's everyday life requires that boy to keep his own unruly impulses under control. Fathers do not have to hit or bully sons to keep them in line; simply by being close to their male offspring they have a pacifying effect on their behavior. Modeling surely plays a part in this. Watching their non-violent fathers master anger and aggression, boys learn how to cope with their own feelings. Boys who can count on their non-violent dads to be there know that they will not be allowed to act out endlessly. No doubt the world feels like a much safer place to them than to boys who lack close relationships with men. The presence of a father or father figure gives boys the feeling of being protected and "contained," which all children need.

Fathers play another unexpected role in the lives of their children. New research on empathy has pointed out that children who spend a great deal of time with their fathers are more likely than other children to grow up to be highly empathetic adults. This is important because empathy is such a socially desirable trait: People who feel for others tend to be good parents, good citizens. The researchers who conducted the study that revealed the connection between fatherhood and empathy say they are at a loss to explain the connection between father availability and empathy. Perhaps this finding is related to another interesting discovery about empathy: that children who develop empathy are ones who have been warmly nurtured within a family context in which limits are firmly enforced.

Of course, you don't have to have a father living at home to have a father. In the years following divorce, boys who continue to see their fathers often and maintain close relationships with them tend to do very well psychologically. These boys tend to function well in the world and have high self-esteem. Boys who see their fathers infrequently are far more likely to be depressed and suffer from low self-esteem.

Even when fathers are unknown to their children, the presence of other caring, non-violent mentors like Shakur Ali can make a huge difference. Human beings seem to have an amazing resilience. Emmy Werner's longitudinal study of "high risk" infants on Kauai island in Hawaii, begun in 1955 and continuing today, confirms what Shakur Ali's story implies—that the lives of troubled teenagers can be turned around with the help of "surrogate parents." Werner and her colleagues discovered that a large number of males in her study did poorly in school and had trouble with the law as adolescents, but in later years were able to reform. Those males who changed usually had the support of an adult mentor—a stepfather, a Big Brother, a teacher, anyone willing to make the commitment. These mentors were instrumental in helping their young friends take advantage of what Werner calls "second chance opportunities," which often meant joining the military and getting an education. By the time they reached their thirties, the majority of these once troubled teenagers were working and married. Werner says they were raising their children "appropriately" and had made decent lives for themselves.

We have every reason to believe that the lessons Emmy Werner learned on the remote island of Kauai hold true in Roxbury, the south side of Chicago and in Watts. Hope is not an illusion. Most experts believe that most "high risk" children are redeemable, especially when help is offered when they are still young. The problem is not proving that intervention works, it is providing intervention to all the hundreds of thousands of children, millions of children, who need help. The federal government estimates that half a million teenagers in our country are runaways and what are called "throwaways," kids who have been kicked out of their homes. Another half million are thought to be in foster care, juvenile detention facilities, or mental health facilities. Many of the incarcerated teens are being held on "status offenses," crimes like running away, which would not be crimes if they were adults. Many of these kids, like the delinquents in Werner's study, could be saved if just one adult took an interest in them, made a commitment to them. One Shakur Ali is not enough. We need one thousand, ten thousand Shakur Alis, and where private heroes are not available, we need institutional solutions.

11

HELPING SCHOOLS
PREVENT VIOLENCE

PUBLIC HEALTH HAS A LONG HISTORY OF COLLABORATION
with public schools to safeguard the lives of children. At school,
many young people are gathered together at one location; public
health takes advantage of this "captive" audience to promote a health
agenda. To protect children from measles, mumps, polio, and dipthe-
ria, public health officials use the legal clout and administrative resources of schools to require that parents have their children
inoculated. Public health clinicians screen children in school-based
clinics for vision and hearing difficulties, for tuberculosis, for scolio-
sis, and for other remediable conditions. In the classroom, public
health-sponsored health education is a staple. Children are taught
about fitness, human reproduction, nutrition, substance abuse, and
so forth. Education programs operate on the assumption that individuals who understand the health risks confronting them are more
likely to make healthy decisions.

When I began to think about creating a behavior modification
program that would teach adolescents how to avoid fighting, I did not
doubt that this program belonged in the public schools. I believed
then and I continue to believe that high schools have a responsibility
to help students understand, avoid, and survive the lethal menaces of
childhood and adolescence—not only infectious diseases, but drugs,
AIDS, alcohol abuse, teenage pregnancy, suicide, and violence, as
well. The violence prevention curriculum I created was designed to fit
within a tenth grade health course. I assumed that truthful information about the risks of fighting could and would change students'
attitudes about fighting and, over time, their behavior. I was not
aiming at miracles. I did not think that a single intervention would
save the world. I saw the curriculum as a beginning, a first step, that

would eventually be joined with other interventions inside and outside the schools. I kept the successful campaign to reduce smoking as my model: In 25 years, using an imaginative array of public health strategies, we had reduced the number of smokers in the United States by 30 percent. Health education in the schools had been an important component in the anti-smoking effort. I believed health education in the schools would play a similar role in the effort to reduce adolescent violence. Once the campaign to reduce violence was fully engaged, I expected it to be joined by many allies, including grass roots activists. In the meantime, we had to start somewhere. For me, that "somewhere" was the classroom.

Back in those early days of my violence prevention work, there was a piece of the school picture that I had missed. At first I did not realize that learning itself is a vital form of violence prevention. The cognitive skills children slowly develop during years of studying English, social studies, math, and science help them to reason their way through stressful and dangerous situations. Young people whose language skills and analytic abilities have been well developed in the classroom are likely to think before striking and use words instead of force to persuade. As they grow, their developing brain power can help them transcend their teenage inability to imagine another's point of view. Their capacity to think can help them see beyond the prevailing assumption that *one has no choice but to fight.* In poor neighborhoods, all adolescents are at risk for violence, but children who have been taught to think decisions through clearly are less at risk than others. In poor urban neighborhoods, circumstances that prevent children from learning how to reason promote violence. Circumstances that promote learning promote the survival of our children.

KIDS WHO DO NOT LEARN

African-American boys are by far the most isolated group in most of the nation's urban schools, even within systems that are predominantly African-American. Few school systems have detailed the carnage as has Milwaukee. Of the city's 5,716 African-American males in high school, only 135 earned a B average or higher last year.

Overall, African-American children had a grade point average of D-plus. While African-American children account for 55 percent of the system's population, they were handed 94 percent of suspensions from 1978–1985. Milwaukee's failures are particularly painful, after nearly three decades of attempted desegregation.

The Boston Sunday Globe, Oct. 7, 1990

These disheartening paragraphs about the school performance of young black males were written by *Globe* columnist Derrick Jackson. They present information about academic failure that is as true in

Boston, Atlanta, and Chicago, as it is in Milwaukee. Milwaukee has decided to do something about what Jackson calls these "horrid statistics." The Milwaukee school board has agreed to open two experimental schools in the fall of 1991, a primary school and a middle school, geared to the specific needs of African-American males. The school's curricula will be designed to provide pupils with positive information about their African heritage. Students will wear uniforms. The school day will include an after-school enrichment program. There will be mandatory Saturday classes. Each of the male students enrolled in the two schools will spend time every day with adult mentors, all male.

I find the Milwaukee experiment of great interest, not only for its academic implications but also for its implications concerning violence prevention. Children who succeed at school are at less risk for violence than their non-successful peers. The young males who fail and drop out of school are the ones who are dying on our streets. This correlation between violence and school failure is true for all groups of young people in our society, but it is most true for young black males who perform more poorly in school than any other segment of our population and are more likely to die the victims of homicide.

In our nation's schools, as on our streets, young black men are truly an endangered species. Nationally, they do worse on all standardized tests, including the tests needed to enter college, than members of any other group in our nation. They are expelled and suspended more frequently. They drop out of high school more frequently. They drop out of college more frequently, and their grades in high school and college are worse than any other segment of the school population.

Tragically, there are more young black males in prison than in college. Approximately one in four African-American males between the ages of 20 and 29 is incarcerated, on probations, or on parole. One in five is enrolled in a two- or four-year college program. In 1988, nearly 700,000 African American women were enrolled in colleges and universities; fewer than 450,000 young black males were in college. These figures should not be interpreted as meaning that young black females are doing as well as they should be.

While the number of African-American females attending colleges and universities is growing, the number of African-American males at colleges and universities is not. David L. Evans, a senior admissions officer at Harvard College, an African-American, describes an information session that he hosted in St. Louis. Such meetings familiarize high school students with Harvard and help the university recruit qualified minority students. Of the 55 African-American students who attended the meeting, only one was male. Evans is terribly disturbed by what he calls the "vanishing black male." In some recent years *twice* as many black females as males have entered Harvard. Evans explains the black male trend away from school and into prison saying, "There is an antagonism in this society toward the black male that is not present toward the black female. It is racism, plus . . . antagonism."

This "antagonism" not only excludes young black males from higher education, it also misshapes their early educational experience as they are labeled academically and behaviorally deficient and driven out of college track courses. Of the students labeled behavior disabled, 73 percent are young black males. Suspension rates for young black males far exceed those for any other group. So do drop-out rates. In Boston, school officials say 46 percent of students who enter the ninth grade do not graduate. In Los Angeles and Chicago 45 percent do not graduate. In New York City the "official" drop-out figure is 34 percent. For young men of color in these cities the percent of non-graduates is much higher. In Detroit's poorest neighborhoods, for example, school officials say that as many as 80 percent drop-out.

Many teachers and administrators blame black kids personally for their failure to learn, saying peers, drugs, and gangs, have created an urban black youth culture that is completely incompatible with intellectual pursuits. No doubt, black youth culture plays a part in keeping black kids, especially males, outside the educational mainstream. Still, blaming this problem on black kids themselves seems absurd. Most teachers will tell you that every child begins first grade excited and hungry to learn. This is as true for black children as for white, as true for boys as for girls. All children want to learn, but for poor black children, especially black males, all too often circumstances in their lives dampen and then kill their excitement.

A significant body of research indicates that prejudice about their abilities plays a significant role in snuffing out the intellectual ardor of African-American school kids. Social scientists and educators have proven time and again that children tend to perform academically as they are expected to perform. By and large, children who are expected by their parents and their teachers to work hard and achieve, do just that. When teachers, administrators, and parents do not expect much, children do not rouse themselves. Children who are labelled as "C" students, tend to do "C" work. Children who are labelled "dumb," tend to become dumb to meet the expectations of those in authority. This process works for all children, regardless of race or socio-economic status. For black children low expectations are especially destructive. One lingering legacy of slavery and racial injustice is the idea, often unstated but present nevertheless, that black people are intellectually inferior. Many white people consciously or unconsciously believe this. Many black people consciously or unconsciously believe it, too. This idea is a powerful barrier to school achievement.

Negative and even hostile notions about the academic proficiency of young blacks are put into practice by teachers who are not aware of their own prejudices. In one study carried out in Illinois, 66 student teachers were told to teach a math concept to four pupils—two white and two black. All of the pupils were of equal, average intelligence. The student teachers were told that in each set of four, one white and one black student was intellectually gifted, the others were labelled as average. The student teachers were monitored through a one-way mirror to see how they reinforced their students' efforts. The "superior" white pupils received two positive reinforcements for every negative one. The "average" white students received one positive reinforcement for every negative reinforcement. The average black student received one positive reinforcement for every 1.5 negative reinforcement, while the "superior" black students received one positive response for every 3.5 negative ones. Jeffrey Howard, Ph.D., a Harvard-trained social psychologist who works with school systems all over the country in an effort to improve black school achievement believes that the Illinois study raises very important issues. The heavy dose of negative "reinforcements" heaped upon the "superior" black students delivers the message, Howard says, that being black and being intelligent are not reconcilable. Superior intelligence was nurtured in the "superior" white pupils; they received praise twice as often as criticism. Superior intelligence was crushed in the "superior" black pupils, who were criticized three and a half times more often than they were praised. The teachers delivering these disheartening messages to young blacks were not from an older, "burned-out" generation. They were young people, presumably eager and idealistic, but blind to their own cultural biases.

The negative expectations and negative reinforcement of teachers clearly plays a part in destroying the enthusiasm of young blacks for school. "Spirit murder," Jeff Howard calls this process. Many observers have noted that by the third or fourth grade African-American children, particularly boys, begin to shut down academically. At this point significant differences between the school performance of young whites and young blacks start to emerge. These differences continue and broaden over the years. They appear to be unrelated to the natural talent of African-American students. The results of a study by the educational consultant Kawanza Kunjufu illustrated this point. Kunjufu looked at the school records of 20 randomly selected young black males who had been in the same school for five years. Each child's score on the Iowa Reading Test at the beginning of the third grade was compared to his score at the end of the seventh grade. Students who scored very high in the third grade collapsed academically by the time they were tested again. Four young males who were reading in the 98th, 97th, 92nd, and 91st percentiles at the time of the first test, sank to the 35th, 54th, 24th, and 68th percentiles respectively when tested four years later. Kunjufu says his study shows that the males of color who fail in school are not necessarily the least intellectually gifted. They may be the most gifted.

No one knows all the reasons that cause black students, especially boys, to tune out as their years in school progress. We can surmise that as children move toward adolescence, the attitudes of their teachers toward them probably grows more negative. Students who are nine and ten years old are a lot less cuddly and charming than six-year-olds. In the inner city, children this age may start to exhibit the cool, street-wise attitude they feel they need to survive. These changes in behavior and attitude may further estrange students from their teachers. No doubt there are other reasons as well. Developmentally, children in the third and fourth grades are increasingly able to make judgements about themselves in relation to the world. James Comer, M.D., a professor of child psychiatry at Yale University says that at this age children begin to understand where they stand in the American hierarchy. When kids realize that they are not part of the economic and social mainstream, Comer believes, they stop trying to bond with school and with teachers. They lose faith in the school's power to educate them, in their own power to become educated, and in the notion that any of it matters. A tragic cynicism seems to fall over them. They opt out of school and the values embraced by teachers. Instead, they cultivate an air of aloof "cool;" they talk, walk, and dress "cool." What counts, they say, is "getting mine now."

By the time kids like this reach high school, many cannot read or do math at anything approaching grade level. Some get assigned to unchallenging Special Education classes. Others warm chairs in academic classes in which all who show up receive a passing grade, especially those with athletic ability. Many students drop out. For those who continue, school may be unpleasant and dangerous, a place where the code of the street is allowed to rule indoors. Violent attacks on students and teachers are common in many urban schools. Kids join gangs and arm themselves for "protection." Drug dealing may surround the school or even enter it. In a setting like this, students, teachers, and administrators feel betrayed and endangered. Students say teachers and administrators do not care about them. Teachers and administrators say students do not care about learning. Teachers and administrators, unable to feel pride or satisfaction in their work, may wind up hating themselves and hating the children they are supposed to be teaching. At its worst the relationship between students and adults in the schools is as laden with resentment and rage as the relationship between young black males and some police officers.

For some teachers, the students become the enemy. One teacher from the Bronx who taught in both elementary and high schools spoke about his feelings in these two environments:

"When I walked into an elementary class, my heart went out to the kids. I'd do anything to make their lives better. When I walked into a high school class, with a lot of tough, angry black kids, my heart nearly stopped. If I closed my eyes I could imagine myself getting into an argument with one of these guys and getting punched out. After I had words with a kid and I'd see him in the hall or in the parking lot, I'd think, shit, here comes the switchblade."

For students, the interaction is just as fraught with emotion. Many feel disliked, misunderstood, and used by teachers and administrators. A young man who went to college and became a youth worker in Newark described his high school experience this way:

"Inside I was really hurting, although I didn't want to admit it. . . . I was hurting myself in the streets. I was hurting all over. I just didn't want to be part of that (school) anymore. I wanted to escape. I wanted to change my life. The first semester in high school I scored high in my classes, but I couldn't see myself continuing up to the twelfth grade. I was saying, I'll be nineteen when I get out of here, twenty. So I wanted a way out—and the school and me, we worked out a way."*

The young man got drunk, entered the school and committed serious acts of vandalism. He was expelled. His feelings about what he did are revealing:

"I was striking back at the educational system and it felt good. I could be just as tough and rough with them as they was with me."

HELPING KIDS SUCCEED IN SCHOOL

You don't need a lot of rules to run a school, but the ones you have need to be clear and they need to be enforced. At our school every kid knows what the rules are: You have to be in class on time. No hats are allowed inside the building. No Walkman inside the building. No gold jewelry visible inside the building. And no students roaming the corridors. If you are caught outside of class without a pass you are written up immediately and given a warning.

> Albert Holland, Principal
> Jeremiah E. Burke High School
> Boston

There are schools in every city of our nation where children feel safe and where they learn a great deal. There are teachers, thousands of them, who know how to teach, who love to teach, who do teach every day. There are poor youngsters of color, tens of thousands of them, who do well in school. The formula for success is no mystery.

* Both of these quotes were taken from Bernard Lefkowitz, *Tough Change*, N.Y., Macmillan, 1987, pp. 105 and 150.

Research shows that schools with strong principals; schools that are not too large; schools where discipline is fair, but firm; schools where teachers are imbued with high expectations for every child; schools where parents are drawn into the educational orbit, are schools where learning takes place.

The first requirement is that students, teachers, and administrators feel safe. It does not take a Joe Clark patrolling the hallways of Eastside High in Paterson, New Jersey with a bullhorn and a baseball bat, expelling hundreds of "leeches and parasites," to create a safe environment, but it does take commitment. Safety has to be the first priority. If students are carrying guns to school, metal detectors are required. At the Jeremiah E. Burke School there is no metal detector. The presence of Mr. Holland, the principal, many teachers, and a staff of security guards in the hallways is sufficient to maintain order. Security personnel have friendly relations with the students. This also helps adults know what is going on inside the school at all times.

Making schools secure is easier than raising the academic performance of students. While one good principal can control the diverse forces that shape the ability and willingness of students to commit themselves to their schoolwork. Learning, moreover, is a cumulative process. Even in a firm-but-fair school environment, teenagers who have not mastered the basics have a difficult time performing on or near grade level.

Gifted teachers, when supported by their principals and a challenging curriculum, are able to burst through some of these impediments. The best known of this impressive breed is Jaime Escalante, of Garfield High School in Los Angeles, once a haven for gang members and school failures. Escalante, whose story was told in the film *Stand and Deliver*, teaches advanced placement math, including calculus, to poor black and Hispanic kids whom many, including officials in the office of the Los Angeles school superintendent, thought were too "dumb" to learn these subjects. Each Escalante class begins with warm-up music and hand clapping as students ceremonially drop their homework into a basket. Advanced placement students are given special t-shirts and satin jackets proclaiming their membership in the academic elite. When Escalante joined the faculty in 1976, Garfield was close to losing its academic accreditation. Thanks to his commitment to excellence and his belief in the capability of his students, the school now boasts more than a dozen advanced placement teachers. Hundreds of kids take and pass advanced placement tests each year, earning college credit. Of the student body, 70 percent go on to college.

Escalante nudges, tugs, and cajoles parents, who often feel intimidated by teachers and schools, into committing themselves to their children's educational goals. Escalante reaches out to parents. When pupils cut class, Escalante calls their parents at home. He also visits students' homes, inducing parents to sign contracts pledging that they will use their authority to see that their children do extra hours of homework. In effect what Escalante does is teach parents how to be involved with their children's educations.

A certain kind of parental involvement appears to be the most important factor determining academic success of poor children and probably all children. Researcher Reginald Clark conducted an in-depth study of ten poor black families, five with high achieving high school children, five with low achieving offspring, to find out how the home lives of academically successful African-Americans differed from the home lives of young African-Americans who were failing. As a result of this work, Professor Clark believes race, socio-economic status, and parental marital status are irrelevant to a child's academic achievement. What counts, he says, is a certain style of high profile parenting. Clark discovered that the parents of the academically successful young people in his study, all of whom were poor and lived in poor neighborhoods, shared certain traits: They all believed that education could make the lives of their children better, and they shared this belief with their children. They helped prepare their young children for school by talking to them, reading to them, playing word and math games with them. They trained their small children to do homework by setting aside a time and place for them to work everyday, so that by the time their children were in high school, disciplining themselves to do their work came naturally. They supervised their children's leisure time, limiting their access to risky peers and activities, and they encouraged their children's efforts with love and support. Though poor, these parents and their offspring were not defeated by poverty. What protected them was their shared belief in their own ability to make life better.

Only a relative few children have parents whose belief in education is so powerful that it can overcome poor schools, indifferent teachers, and peers who are hostile to education. Such parents are a national treasure, and they are important role models to all of us who want our children to do well, but parents alone cannot remake our schools. Institutional change is also needed.

Someone who fervently desires to change the way our public schools operate is Jeff Howard, the social psychologist whose Efficacy Institute based in a suburb of Boston works with dozens of school systems to improve academic achievement. Dr. Howard's critique of public education, which transcends race, originated when he discovered how poorly black children perform academically as compared to whites. His fundamental insight concerns the unwritten assumptions made by all schools in this country about the capabilities of the mass of children. In Japan and Israel, he points out, countries with universal literacy and very highly educated work forces, every child, not just a small percentage of "gifted" ones, studies foreign languages, science, literature, and math, including calculus. Howard says children in these countries are not smarter than American children. What is different is the fundamental principles on which the public school systems in Japan and Israel are constructed: Those systems operate on the assumption that every child can learn sophisticated material. Our schools, on the other hand, operate on the assumption that only a minority of students is bright enough to learn complex material. This confidence-assailing assumption is "operationalized" in our schools; in time, expectations create reality.

Dr. Howard says American education is predicated on the belief that all children fall into one of three immutable categories:

—VS (very smart)

—SS (sort of smart—the category into which most teachers fell as children)

—KD (kinda dumb).

Just as every first grader knows whether he is in the best or the worst reading group, so, says Jeff Howard, do all children know precisely where they have been pigeon-holed in this ranking-for-life-by-intelligence. Moreover, these categories are a one-way ticket: children can slip a notch or even two, as do many young blacks after the third or fourth grade, but they cannot rise. When children fail, educators fall back on their pre-conceived ideas about them. Failure means that a child was born "kinda dumb." By relying on this model, educators are relieved of responsibility for the failure of their students. Within this model, intelligence is seen as a commodity that is dispensed once, at birth. Some folks, usually the "haves" of our society, "got it," the rest "don't got it."

In the days when the United States economy was dominated by heavy industry, business needed the public schools to produce a few "very smart" leaders, a percentage of "sorta smart" white collar workers and a majority of "kinda dumb" blue collar workers. In today's global economy these categories make no sense. Today the nation requires skilled workers, workers who understand science, who can do mathematics. Instead of helping us produce the educated workforce we need to compete internationally, these outmoded classifications justify the academic failure of many of our citizens—blacks and Hispanics, working class whites, and females in math and science.

Howard and his colleagues at Efficacy say "Hogwash!" to this traditional way of looking at children's capacity to learn. They say that anyone who is smart enough to learn a spoken language by the age of three or four is smart enough to learn anything. Including calculus. They point to the success of teachers like Jaime Escalante to prove their point. Intelligence, the Efficacy people say, is not something you are born with, like blue eyes. Intelligence in their view is a kind of muscle that is *developed* with use. *You are not born smart, you get smart.* Confidence in yourself, plus serious effort, they say, makes people smart. Jeff Howard and his colleagues came to this conclusion after careful study of the "very smart" children at the academic pinnacle. Decades of research into human motivation shows that children who perform well at school come from environments (like the families of the successful African-American students described by Reginald Clark) that have filled them with the confidence needed to commit themselves to hard work. Because these children think they can do the job, they work hard and prove to themselves that they can do the job. The more they succeed, the more inspired they are to work hard and succeed more. The opposite kind of "feedback loop" is at work when students fail. If they think they cannot do the job, if the environment delivers messages telling them that they haven't got "what it takes," they will not work hard; why should they? As they did not work hard, they will fail and that failure appears to be proof that they are dumb. The more they and their teachers believe they are dumb, the less incentive they have to work hard. The less they work, particularly in cumulative subjects like math and foreign languages, the "dumber" they will become. The children who think they are smart go to school and get smarter. The children who think they are dumb go to school and get dumber. The success of one group and the failure of the other has nothing to do with any half-baked ideas about the relative intelligence of one race, or one sex, or one class as compared to the other.

The consultants at the Efficacy Institute work with teachers and school administrators, helping them peel away layers of destructive thinking about intelligence and achievement. During an intensive week-long seminar, teachers learn how erroneous assumptions about academic capability has damaged their own self-concept. After all, every teacher was once a child in school who learned that he or she belonged in a niche, often well below the top. Realizing how they themselves have been hurt by these assumptions, teachers begin to empathize with their less successful students. Efficacy shares with teachers all the social science research highlighting the way the unconscious biases of teachers shape their interactions with minority students. When teachers realize the kinds of destructive forces that have been holding their students back, they can begin to change what takes place in their classrooms. Once they begin to believe in every child's ability to learn, they can convey with conviction that they *expect* success, not failure, from each and every student.

Efficacy also works with children. A third grade curriculum and a high school curriculum present grade school students and high schoolers with developmentally-appropriate versions of the Efficacy program. These semester-long courses are taught after school; follow-up is built into the program. The two courses delineate how internal and external forces conspire to prevent young people from learning and achieving. The goal is to re-motivate students who have been demoralized by failure. Children who do not believe in their own capacity to work productively and shape a bright future for themselves are said to be in "The Box"—controlled by a set of negative assumptions about who they are and what they may aspire to. Youngsters are led to understand how they help to keep each other in "The Box" by destructive, anti-intellectual peer practices called "bringing each other low." Children and adolescents can be vicious with one another, especially when circumstances conspire against their feeling good about themselves as individuals. Black students, Howard believes, are masters at keeping each other in "The Box." They chide, taunt, and threaten to ostracize peers who study and try to get ahead, accusing them of trying to "act white." To help pupils understand how destructive "bringing low" behavior is, Efficacy students are told to think about crabs in a bucket. Every time one crab tries to crawl out of the bucket, it is attacked by the others who "brings him low." If the crabs left each other alone, each would be able to escape. Instead, none escape and all eventually die in the bucket.

Jeff Howard and his colleagues at the Efficacy Institute are not pie-in-the-sky theorists planning to fix our schools at some unspecified future date. They are interested in improving the grades and the test scores of American school children *this year*. Almost without exception, the school systems with which they have worked have registered improvements in student performance. Other educators and consultants around the country are doing similar work with positive results. These fledgling efforts are of enormous political and economic significance. Within the public schools, two of our nations most pressing needs converge: the need of American business for an educated workforce and the need of all children, especially young black males, for a route out of academic failure, self destruction, and violence. If our government were truly committed to educating all of our young, the global competitiveness of our economy would be insured and young black males would be able to find their way out of "The Box" in which so many are dying.

PREVENTING VIOLENCE

SCHOOLS CAN PREVENT VIOLENCE BY INSURING THAT ALL children are well served academically and by teaching children to manage conflict and anger. When children learn how to assert their own needs and opinions without trampling on the rights of other people, when they learn to express their angry feelings without losing control or hurting other people, they have mastered skills that enhance their lives and the life of the community. There is no better place than school, where diverse groups of children congregate, to learn these important lessons.

Children can be very mean to one another. They insult, belittle, and berate each other. They have no inkling that their words can hurt. They do not understand that other people have feelings, too. They do not understand that apologizing or excusing themselves does not make them a chump. Nor do they know that not every argument must have a loser—that there are win/win ways to resolve disagreements. How can our children know all this when so many adults behave so badly? Anyone who saw Red Sox pitcher Roger Clemens mouth obscenities at the home plate umpire during the concluding game of the American League pennant race in 1990 will understand how entrenched our culture is in the idea that verbal—and even physical—violence is an appropriate response to conflict. For children in homes already troubled with violence and discord such ugly incidents are doubly destructive, for they confirm what these children already know—that life is a struggle in which the strong assert their will over the weak.

Programs in many schools all over the country have been designed to help school children with what one school teacher calls "the fourth R—Relationships." The goal of these "conflict resolution" programs is to teach children how to get along with one another peacefully. All of these programs share certain ideas:

—That conflict is a normal part of human interaction.

—That when people take the time to explore their prejudices, they can learn how to get along with (and enjoy) people whose backgrounds are different.

—That most disputes do not have to have a winner or loser. Win/win is the ideal way to resolve most disputes.

—That children and adults who learn how to assert themselves non-violently can avoid becoming bullies or victims.

—That the self-esteem of children will be enhanced if they learn to build non-violent, non-hostile relationships with their peers.

Public School 321 is an integrated grade school in the Park Slope section of Brooklyn, New York. The school's elaborate "Peacemakers" program is sponsored jointly by the New York City Board of Education and the independent Educators for Social Responsibility.

One-quarter of the 1,000 students at P.S. 321 are African-American. One-quarter are Hispanic. One-half are white. Some children are rich, some are middle-class, some are poor and some are very, very poor. Different groups of kids play together, and they are required to get along.

"Peacemaker" teachers are trained in "conflict resolution" techniques, observed and critiqued in the classroom, and then receive follow-up training. Children as young as five and six are taught how to stand up for themselves without triggering an aggressive response from their peers. Children learn to assert what they need, using the pronoun I: "I wish you would stop using my toys," a first grader might say, instead of, "Gimme back my truck, you creep." Children learn "strong, instead of mean" ways to respond: "Don't bother me," instead of, "Get your ugly face out of here." The lessons of assertion and civility are taught formally and then incorporated into the daily life of the classroom. Interestingly, the research shows that children who learn to assert themselves without verbally or physically attacking others are not only less likely to become bullies, they are also less likely to become the victims of bullies.

The kinds of interpersonal skills children develop when schools make a commitment to "the fourth R" can be impressive. During a demonstration of the Peacemaker program at P.S. 321, my co-author saw the following interchange take place, in an integrated fifth grade classroom. The children had been given an assignment to analyze a conflict from their own lives or from television, telling whether it had been resolved aggressively; as a result of avoidance (meaning one party retreated); or assertively. Most of the children described conflicts with their siblings. Then an African-American girl spoke. She described an incident that had occurred in her home over the weekend involving her cousin, her aunt, and the aunt's estranged husband. A dispute broke out. The police were called. The entire experience was terribly upsetting to the fifth grader. For a moment after she spoke there was silence in the classroom.

"Someone say something positive," the teacher coached.

"I'm so sorry that happened," said a young Hispanic girl.

The black girl began to cry. She rose from her seat.

The teacher nodded, "It's alright," she said, "you can leave."

The child fled to the bathroom.

The Hispanic girl rose to her feet, "I'll go with her. I want to give her a hug."

The teacher nodded and the lesson resumed. (The incident would be discussed again by the teacher and the children at a "sharing circle.") Years of training had taught these students how to be kind to one another. What occurred was not group therapy. No one was prodded to air overly intimate emotions, but the teacher and the students were not frightened when emotion was expressed.

Mediation is the second component of the "Peacemakers" program. At P.S. 321, fourth and fifth grade children are elected by their classmates and trained to negotiate settlements when disputes break out among their peers. A faculty adviser helps the young mediators to improve their listening skills and teaches them how to help disputants resolve their differences. Working in pairs and wearing special t-shirts, young mediators are assigned to patrol the playground and the lunchroom. When they see children arguing or fighting, they approach and ask if their help is needed. The disputants can either agree or disagree to mediation. The program provides all the children in the school with a model of a successful non-violent strategy for resolving disputes. The mediators themselves are changed by the job: they see themselves as peace-promoting leaders.

Peer mediation on the high school level is known to reduce fighting and reduce suspensions and expulsions. Generally when a fight breaks out in a high school with a well organized mediation program, the disputants are given a choice between mediation and, say, a one-week in-school suspension. Most students choose mediation. The mediators, who are trained and supervised by faculty advisor's, work in teams. The mediation itself takes place quickly (to prevent rumors from complicating the process) and in private. Both sides agree to confidentiality. High school mediators, with their advisor present, also mediate disputes between teachers and students. The mediation process has several steps: each side is allowed to air its grievance, uninterrupted; mediators help each side clarify its grievance—often the issue at the heart of the dispute is not immediately apparent; the mediators keep both sides talking to one another until together they agree on the nature of the problem; the mediators help the two sides work out a balanced settlement that each side accepts as fair; the mediators write up the settlement and have it signed by both sides. Students who have had a fight settled by mediation may be asked to become mediators.

Mediators can sometimes intervene before the fact, preventing violence from occurring. Fights almost always have an escalation period; sometimes this period lasts for several days. Events during this time have an almost choreographed quality. Insults are exchanged. Students take sides. Rumors fly. Excitement grows. Teachers and school administrators often know what is going on, but feel powerless to halt the process leading up to a fight. If student mediators can talk with the rivals when the fight is brewing and convince them to submit their dispute to mediation, a peaceful solution can sometimes be worked out. Mediations like this can be life-saving.

"Conflict resolution," and mediation go hand and hand with my violence prevention curriculum. Violence prevention, however, is more crisis-driven. If all children mastered the lessons taught at P.S. 321 and we stopped glamorizing violence in the media, teaching violence prevention might not be necessary. Until that happy day, I think it is extremely important to help teenagers understand the risk of violence to their survival, to learn about their own anger, and to learn some practical skills for deflecting angry confrontations and fights.

In my experience, students *want* to know about violence prevention. Many of them have never had the chance to talk to anyone about fighting, violence, or death. When the subject is violence sleepy and indifferent young people snap to attention. This is not just my perception. In an unpublished paper about improving the lives of at-risk black males, Ron Ferguson, the Associate Professor of Public Policy at Harvard's Kennedy School of Government, reports on the conversation he had with the leaders of a mentoring program for black males in Pittsburgh. The adult mentors told Ferguson that they were surprised by the kind of program their young friends wanted:

> "What they wanted from us was help with intellectual and emotional development. They wanted to deal with issues of manhood—what being a man is all about—with issues like sexuality and drugs. They wanted to deal with violence in the schools and protecting themselves. . . .
>
> "A number of them had a desire to learn how to control their emotions. For example, when they don't agree with a teacher or don't appreciate the way a teacher or an authority figure 'comes off' to them, belittling them or making them feel like they're stupid. They wanted to know how to react to that. Typically, if it's a teacher their usual reaction was to get smart, get into an argument, and to get kicked out of class. If it's a fellow student who they have a problem with, they get into an argument and it breaks out into a fight. In other words, in reaction to feeling put down they would lose control of their emotions and get into trouble."[*]

The point of the violence prevention course is to provide these young people with alternatives to fighting. The first three lessons of the ten-session curriculum provide adolescents with information about violence and homicide. Urban teenagers are not surprised to learn that most homicides occur among people of the same race, people who know each other. This fact corresponds to their experience. They are surprised to find out that gangs and drugs do not cause 80 or 90 percent of all homicides. This misperception is as self-serving for them as it is for the rest of society. Like adults, young people would rather think that UZI-toting, crack-selling gang mem-

---

[*] R. Ferguson, "The Case for Community-Based Programs that Inform and Mentor Black Male Youth," An Urban Institute Research Paper, Distributed by the Urban Institute, Washington, D.C.

bers are responsible for the violence. No one wants to face how ordinary most assaults and most homicides are. No one wants to admit that the mass of these crimes involves plain people; acquaintances, family members, who drink, who disagree, who have a gun.

Some of the most interesting classes occur in the next set of lessons. These deal with the nature of anger. The goal is to help students understand that anger is a normal emotion that they will not outgrow, an emotion that each of us must learn to handle without hurting ourselves or others. We start by having the students list all the things that make them angry. Many have never had a chance to reflect in this way before. A fast-writing teacher can travel around the room filling up blackboard after blackboard with things that students say make them angry. Among the approximately 100 entries compiled by one class of inner city youths were extremely serious items such as drugs, gangs, and teenage pregnancy, and items that were silly and "adolescent:"

> *Someone dies. . . V.D. . . . ignorant people . . . drug addicts . . . police . . . teachers who accuse you of cheating . . . teachers who have favorites . . . girls who have short hair . . . girls who won't buy you anything . . . girls who try to get you to support a baby that's not yours . . . threat of nuclear war . . . no money . . . parents who try to tell you what to do . . . gangs . . . men who talk to young girls . . . people who don't wash . . . dandruff . . . boys who are homosexuals . . . boys who "stick and kick"—(get a girl pregnant and then leave her) . . . people who think school is a beauty parlor . . . smoking on the bus . . . boys with pierced ears.*

The next lesson is designed to help teenagers think about the way they deal with their own anger. Students list all the ways they respond when angry and then rate them as healthy or unhealthy. Students tend to be quite imaginative in their healthy strategies. Some of the healthy ways students report responding to anger include:

Read a book . . . walk . . . Leave—walk away

(kids saw this as potentially healthy and potentially unhealthy)

. . . listen to music . . . have sex

(Young people tend to see sex as a "healthy" way to deal with anger. Adults do not. The discussion that follows can be interesting.)

. . . lock yourself in your room . . . hang out . . . argue

(arguing they see as healthy or unhealthy depending on the circumstances)

. . . sleep . . . watch T.V. . . . slam doors . . . talk on phone . . . bite nails . . . grit teeth . . . yell/scream . . . sing. . . eat. . . play ball . . . do homework . . . take a bath . . . count to ten . . . lift weights . . . talk it out . . . cry . . . meditate . . . throw things that can't be broken . . .

Their unhealthy list included:

Take it out on someone else . . . drink alcohol . . . take drugs . . . fight/kill . . . attempt suicide . . . mark on walls . . . rob people . . . .

Fighting, of course, is always on the list. In the next lesson we do a cost/benefit analysis of fighting. We have students create two lists describing what is good and what is bad about fighting. This leads students to the realization that they have more to lose than to gain from fighting. This conclusion is drawn from the student's list; it is not a teacher-imposed insight. Inevitably, the list describing what is bad about fighting is longer and more impressive than the list telling what is good about fighting. There really is much more to lose than to gain from fighting. Here is the list created by one class:

WHAT'S GOOD AND WHAT'S BAD ABOUT FIGHTING

Good	Bad
winning	kill someone
prove your point	get killed
get a reputation	might lose
get attention	get embarrassed
enjoyment	get suspended from school
relieves tension	get expelled
evens the score	lose a job
satisfaction	get a bad reputation and no one
earn money (become a pro)	wants to hang out with you
	because you're always fighting
	have an enemy coming after you
	revenge cycle begins
	get clothes dirty or torn
	get scarred for life
	may have to pay for broken things
	lose respect of friends
	parents responsible for medical bills
	get punished
	hurt innocent bystanders
	hurt person (then be sorry)

Looking at this list—their own list—students begin to think about fighting. Many of the males have never before considered *not* fighting. They begin to question their own values. They also question mine. They want to know where I stand. "Does this mean," they ask me, "that you would never fight?" I tell them that I am not a pacifist, that I do think there are issues that are worth fighting for and perhaps even dying for. I would fight to protect my husband and children if I believed that fighting was the only way to save them from imminent danger, I tell them, but I would not fight because someone called me, or my husband or my children a name. Many of the students attribute my attitude about fighting to my sex. "What about your husband?" they want to know. One student asked me what I would expect Charles to do if he were walking down the street with our daughter and a man *on the other side of the street* started calling her names." For me, of course, the answer is easy. I would expect Charles to ignore the insults, explain to Mimi that they were not going to listen to such foolishness and then walk in the other direction as quickly as possible. The mere asking of this question is an important reflection of the level at which many adolescents think about these issues. The combination of their age-appropriate narcissism and the special emphasis that poor males put on respect, hobbles their ability to make distinctions between real threats and trivial ones. The head of the mentoring program in Pittsburgh who was interviewed by Professor Ron Ferguson had an interesting comment that illuminates the issue of respect: *One of the things that we observed*," he told Professor Ferguson, "*was that the young men had a difficult time respecting one another: . . . They wanted to receive respect, but they didn't have proper training to respect one another. We had to work on this with them.*" Many young black men seem to feel that showing respect for someone else is a form of toadying. The combination of their super-sensitivity to slights and their lack of sensitivity to the feelings of others sets the stage for fights and violence.

Another question that students often ask is "What if someone calls your mother a bad name? Don't you *have* to fight then?" There is a certain sweetness and loyalty to their mothers inherent in this question that I find touching, but of course completely wrong-headed. "Look," I always answer, "so you get into a fight because someone calls your mother a bad name. You get your clothes torn, or you get thrown out of school for fighting, or maybe you get killed. Is that respectful of your mother? Don't you think your mother would rather that you come home alive, in one piece, that you stay in school and graduate? Isn't that the real way to show her respect?" "Yes," they say, "But . . . but . . . but. . . . This way of thinking makes inner city young people uneasy. I have never had a student convert to non-violence right before my eyes, but I know they do think about what

I am saying. In fact, you can see them thinking really hard, during the classroom discussion, and that is the whole point of the curriculum—to engage them, to make them think about their behavior, to make them understand the control they have over their behavior and to begin to question the inevitability of fighting.

A third question I am often asked by high school students is what I would do if someone just came up to me and hit me for no reason. Again, this question is interesting as it highlights the psychological concerns of young people, especially young males, and their sense of being perpetually vulnerable—not only to the potential assaults of known foes, but to the potential assaults of strangers. I usually answer this question by saying that I do not know what I would do if randomly assaulted, but I would hope, given how common gun-carrying has become, that I would be self-possessed enough to retreat. When facing any combatant in a fight, especially a stranger, one has no way of knowing if he or she is armed. The point to be remembered, I say, is that there is almost always more to be lost than gained from fighting, and the list of what you can lose is topped by your most precious possession—your life. Then I explain that fights almost always have a history. Rarely does a stranger smack a stranger. I tell them that I feel certain that no one in the classroom has ever been the victim of a completely random assault. The students usually assent to this point. We can then talk about the kinds of fights they have had, the facts of which generally corroborate the statistics relating that most fights occur between people who know each other, who argue.

This discussion is a good lead-in to the concluding set of lessons in which mock fights—"role plays"—are created, staged, videotaped, analyzed, discussed, and then re-worked with different endings. Students break down into small groups to create their skits and rehearse. Each group of "actors" is asked to decide:

—Who is going to fight?

—What will they fight about?

—Where will the fight take place?

—Who will be the friends, girlfriends/boyfriends and onlookers?

The sketches must describe real-life circumstances. Students are not allowed to create role plays about strangers and criminal violence. Nor do we allow profanity. Skits continue right up to the moment in which the first imaginary punch is thrown. At that moment the teacher shouts, "Cut" and the "role play" is over.

The goal of the "role plays" is to show kids—in reality to have kids show themselves:

—that most fights are imbedded in a series of relationships

—that most fights have a history

—that the best and safest time to intervene to stop a fight is early in its genesis when the antagonists' animosity is just building

—that there are techniques for preventing fights, once you recognize the patterns.

Each group of students presents their four or five minute playlets before the entire class. Videotaping, if the school owns the equipment, greatly improves the ability to analyze the "role plays." At the next class, if the role plays have been videotaped, the tape is played back and discussed. (If not the role plays can be discussed.) First, however, the teacher must let the students get their fill of watching themselves "on television." Once students have settled down, the teacher replays the tape and asks the class to decide where each fight could have been prevented.

Students pick out the spot where a friend instigates the dispute by shouting, "Are you going to let that jerk stomp on your shoes?" where he could just as easily have said one of these to his friend:

—"Hey man, a little dirt on your sneaker is not worth fighting about,"

—"Hey man, take it easy, it was an accident,"

—"Hey, man, let's give this hothead some room to chill out."

Students learn the most when they come up with their own strategies for stopping fights, but often it takes a lot of adult prompting for a teenager to see that he or she does not have to rise to every insult. One of the most talented people teaching the violence prevention curriculum, Ann Bishop, from Cathedral High School, always tells her students that the best way to respond to insults is with a non-defensive question:

—"Why would you want to say that?"

—"Why would you want to tell me I am ugly (or dumb, or fat) and hurt my feelings?"

This response stops the insulter short. Suddenly he (or she) is on the defensive.

By talking about these issues in the classroom, students have a chance to think up non-violent strategies for getting out of hot spots, before they are in a crisis. Another one of my violence prevention colleagues, Peter Stringham, M.D., a family practitioner who works in a health center in a poor, white neighborhood with a great deal of violence talks to all his adolescent patients about fighting and tries to get his young patients to memorize a few stock answers that can help them avoid fights.

—"This isn't worth fighting about."

—"If you've got a problem with me, I'll talk, but I don't want to fight."

—"I have nothing against you and I don't want to fight."

Humor seems to be the best strategy for diffusing potentially violent situations. Some kids are absolute masters at using humor to lower the temperature of a tense interaction. They do it intuitively. During one role play about a fight between two young males who were rivals for the same girl's attention, I saw a young male, "who'd just been called a 'dumb, ugly blank-head,' " by his rival turn sweetly to his foe and say, "I know you couldn't be talking to me." Everyone broke up—the other "actor," the whole class, me. For the quick-witted, this tactic works wonderfully to halt heated exchanges. Laughter removes the desire to hit. Unfortunately, not all of us have the talent to think of the perfect rejoinder when we are in a high-pressure situation.

Many students have a difficult time when we get to the end of the curriculum. They want a perfect strategy for avoiding fights that won't cause them any embarrassment or loss of social standing. Unfortunately, there are no such strategies. Not for kids living in a society that largely condones violence. Children who choose not to fight are bucking the trend, or rather, they are beginning a new trend. It's not easy. Ann Bishop tells the story of one of her students who really connected with the curriculum. Sometime after he took the course, he got into a conflict with another kid in which he was expected to do battle. The student used the techniques he had learned to prevent the fight. He probably prevented an injury, or maybe even a death. When the incident was over, however, the young man's friends did not praise his efforts. They thought he was a coward and told him so. Even his parents did not approve of his peace-making. Afterward, the young man became depressed. He felt terrible. Part of him believed what the others were saying—that not fighting was unmanly. Ann had to work with him for many months before he could begin to feel good about what he had done.

Educating students about violence is not an easy process. Not in this society, but if we do not tell kids that it is alright not to fight, no one else will. I think often about a young man I taught in one of my early violence prevention courses. The student talked about a friend of his who had been stabbed in a fight. The ambulance took about twenty minutes to arrive. The friend bled to death while waiting for medical help. The student was terribly hurt and angry about this death, which he felt was preventable. During the discussion that followed I understood not just with my head, but with my whole body, what I mean when I tell students that the violence prevention curriculum challenges them to claim their anger as normal and to use it to better themselves and their families.

In class that day we listed the young man's options:

1. He could beat up the ambulance driver.
2. He could slash ambulance tires and break ambulance windows.
3. He could take out his anger on a cat or dog.
4. He could beat up a little brother or sister or someone else.
5. He could write a letter to the city. (This is the typical adult, middle-class response, which has little meaning to poor kids. Letter writing, however, can work and adults should offer to help teenagers do it.)
6. The young man could get so angry that he decided to finish high school, become an ambulance driver and hope to chart the response times of ambulances in every neighborhood in the city. If the response times in poor neighborhoods were longer than in rich ones, he could blow the whistle.

This last option is a strategy of the oppressed which works. All of our great black leaders, from Harriet Tubman to Martin Luther King to Nelson Mandela, have channelled their anger at injustice into a force to reshape the world. This is what the violence prevention curriculum is all about. It is not about passivity. It is about using anger not to hurt oneself or one's peers, but to change the world.

12

HELPING COMMUNITIES PREVENT VIOLENCE

"Within each and every one of us there is a fear. Maybe a fear of flying, a fear of an animal or even the fear of death.

"My worst fear is dying in the street. Every morning I wake up and I kiss my daughter and I thank God we have made it through the night. I live in Spanish Harlem, and I am surrounded by crack heads and drug dealers. This is not the type of environment I want to raise my child up in. But I'm stuck here until I get to a higher level.

"Every night I can hear loud explosions. The children run through the street screaming and cursing as though fighting were going on. And you know, a lot of times, they're just doing that for fun because they want to be heard. They enjoy disturbing people at 4 o'clock in the morning by throwing bottles at cars just to hear the alarms go off.

"Sometimes I sit in the dark and I think about when is it all going to end. Or is this the end? I just keep feeling pain in my heart when I look at all the children in the street suffering. It just keeps getting worse and worse. Tears run down my face when I embrace my daughter and I pray she doesn't become another victim of life.

"Everyone is born an innocent baby that is full of joy. All they want is to be loved and comforted and they want to have playtime and food. I began to wonder what goes through the minds of these teenagers that still receive love and comfort and playtime from their parents. Why do they resort to violence as a baby resorts to crying when hungry? What are they hungry for?. . .

Tanya Parker
Member of
"The Writing Crew"*

---

* "The Writing Crew" is a group of young writers in New York City. The urban ethnologist Terry Williams organized the "crew" and is a friend and mentor to its members.

A young writer named Tanya Parker wrote this essay. She is 20 years old and resides with her infant daughter in public housing on East 100th Street, in East Harlem. In Tanya Parker's neighborhood, there is no place to hide. At night, an army of young men carrying guns controls the streets. Young "soldiers" use rooftops, empty parking lots, and the scruffy open spaces between housing project buildings as firing ranges and as battlefields. They shoot powerful semi-automatic weapons at the night sky and at one another. For these youngsters, guns talk; guns mediate disputes; guns equalize the large and the small, the weak and strong, the rich and the poor. The peace-loving stay at home to avoid the carnage, but they cannot prevent stray bullets from crashing through triple locked doors or careening through the lattice work of the metal window gates installed to bar intruders. They cannot prevent the sounds of gunfire, the wails of police sirens and ambulances from violating the night. They cannot be certain that they or the people they love are safe.

Tanya Parker does not carry a gun, or believe that fighting is the best way to resolve conflicts. She does not use drugs or drink to excess. She does not sell drugs. Many of the most common risk factors for violence do not apply to her. Still, violence overwhelms Tanya's daily existence. The fear of dying in the street is always with her. She is not free, as we expect Americans to be free, to live her own life, to pursue her own happiness, to make her own decisions based on her own wishes.

Risk factors beyond her control make Tanya vulnerable to violence. These risk factors are poverty and geography. She was born poor in an extremely poor neighborhood. In her neighborhood and in many urban neighborhoods, violence has made life a waking nightmare.

Turning the tide of violence for Tanya and for all the frightened and beleaguered residents of very poor neighborhoods will not be easy. The economic, political, social, and familial problems that breed violence in these communities are formidable. No single form of intervention, no single institution can bring about the kind of change needed to restore a sense of safety and order to everyday life. What is required are comprehensive, multi-institutional, community-wide solutions that address the violent behavior of the young, while redressing the social conditions in which violence flourishes. Before we can mobilize the instruments of change within our society, we must understand that violence is not inevitable. Poor people do not choose to live in a battle zone, their lives constricted by tragedy and hopelessness. And poor teenagers are no different from other adolescents. Most teenage males are at risk for violence; most are narcissists defending their overweening pride; most are concrete thinkers who may have trouble differentiating silliness from a principle worth dying for.

What separates armed teenagers in inner city neighborhoods from their more affluent peers are the choices that are available to them. Most teenagers understand and respond to real opportunity when it is offered. But when there is no real opportunity available, adolescents by default choose what make them feel better, what the media portrays as glamorous and exciting, what counteracts the grinding boredom of poverty. Our poorest adolescents have armed themselves and become guerrilla fighters in a war against each other that has no name, no political ideology, and no end in sight. In their despair, to use Tanya Parker's eloquent words, *"they resort to violence as a baby resorts to crying when hungry."* The hunger of these children is not insatiable; we can feed them. We can nourish them by providing them with better choices.

HELPING TO MAKE COMMUNITIES SAFE

THE HIGH SCHOOL VIOLENCE PREVENTION CURRICULUM I created was designed to teach young people, especially inner city males, two important lessons: 1) They are at risk of becoming the perpetrators and the victims of violence. 2) Violence is not inevitable—they have choices. Reaching adolescent males with this life-saving message is not the sole responsibility of public schools, however. A large proportion of the adolescents who are *most* at risk are no longer in school. Many have dropped out. Others are incarcerated in juvenile detention facilities or in adult prisons. Young people operating outside the academic mainstream tend to be those who have the most difficulty containing their physical aggression. Even more than their peers, these youngsters need to learn about managing anger and resolving conflict peacefully. As public health officials interested in reducing violence we must find ways to make contact with these high-risk adolescents.

For this reason and because I understood that raising the public consciousness about violence would require numerous exposures at many developmental stages, I wanted my violence prevention curriculum to be disseminated as broadly as possible. In 1985 even before the curriculum was formally published, I began to look for ways to make it available to public and private community agencies, as well as to high schools. By this time I had an institutional base at Boston City Hospital and a close collaborator, pediatrician Howard Spivak. Our organization, the Health Promotion Project, funded by grants, had the broad goal of promoting health among impoverished adolescents. Dr. Spivak and I agreed that no health goal for poor teens was more critical than reducing homicide and assault. When we started working together in the early 1980s, I believe we were working on the only public health project in the entire country that aimed at reducing violence among inner city adolescents.

With the support of the Boston Foundation, Howard and I set about creating a community-based violence prevention pilot project using an adapted version of my high school curriculum as a starting point. Our goals were to change the attitudes of adolescents toward violence and to change their violent behavior. We tried to organize the project in such a way that it would produce quantifiable results. A measured outcome, we believed, would inspire other communities to undertake their own violence prevention initiatives.

Our intervention was aimed at two neighborhoods: Roxbury, which was poor and black and had the city's highest homicide rate, and South Boston, which was poor and white and had the city's fastest growing homicide rate. Two community organizers, Paul Bracy and Mark Bukuras, were hired to identify and make contact with appropriate community agencies, inspiring youth workers to take part in the violence prevention pilot project. Paul, who is black and had roots in Boston's black community, took the lead in Roxbury; Mark, who is white, and had graduated from high school with students from South Boston organized that community. Among the agencies that took part in the project were boys and girls clubs, YMCAs, church groups, health centers, and tenants organizations. Only agencies from Roxbury and South Boston were allowed to participate. Other Boston neighborhoods were excluded because they were to be the "control." We wanted to prove that incidents of violence in the target communities could be reduced by saturating them with the prevention message. For a variety of reasons, we were unable to scientifically prove this point. "Saturating" two communities is difficult when your budget has room for only two community organizers. Moreover, the boundaries between "target" and "control" communities proved to be porous, undermining the accuracy of our results.

The evaluation of the community-based program was designed by George Kelling Ph.D. and Alice Hauman Ph.D., MPH and carried out by Dr. Hausman. This book-length project was funded by the Kaiser Foundation. Dr. Hausman is still working on the final manuscript, but she has released some preliminary findings. Her most interesting discovery is this: The community-based project had its largest impact not on the young people who were clients of the agencies involved but on those who provided young people with services.

The study revealed that providers possessed attitudes about anger and violence that were quite similar to those of their young clients. Prior to attending a two-day violence prevention training session, many believed that violence was an appropriate and often an inevitable response to human conflict. The training succeeded in changing the youth workers' beliefs and attitudes toward violence. We can expect that the training may also have changed the way youth workers handle their own anger when they interact with the adolescents in their charge. This would be especially important because of the role these adults play as models and mentors to at-risk adolescents.

Dr. Hausman says that the evaluation proves that the public health approach to violence prevention is doable. Agency personnel can be converted to violence prevention. Once they are converted, they can be instructed how to teach young people about violence prevention. What proved to be false was our assumption that front-line youth workers intuitively believed the importance of changing adolescents' attitudes toward violence. Just as doctors and police officers have trouble accepting the idea that violence can be prevented—so do youth workers, many of whom come from similar backgrounds to their clients and tend to regard violence as an inevitable, though tragic, outcome of conflict. Until service "providers" are converted to the public health point of view, they are not very effective violence prevention teachers. The smoking analogy pertains: Doctors who smoke cannot be expected to convince their patients to quit. Only when a physician undergoes a personal conversion and quits smoking, does he or she become an effective agent of change for others. The same kind of mechanism is at work with alcoholics. People who have come to grips with their own addiction to alcohol are best able to help others. That's the Alcoholics Anonymous model. Violence and the ideology of violence are so pervasive in our society that without formal training many people cannot imagine other ways to respond to conflict.

Dr. Hausman's findings about "providers" have many interesting implications. We probably need to carefully consider how to change the attitudes and ideas about violence possessed by many of the adults who shape the thinking of teenagers—teachers, health care professionals, police officers, and parents—especially parents. I am sure we will discover that even adults who, on one level, recognize violence to be a problem for teenagers, may be as confused and as fatalistic about the inevitability of violence as teenagers themselves on a less conscious level. Given the teaching most of us had as children and the constant presentation of violence by the media as a glamorous and desirable way to respond, I believe that most of us, on some level, accept the idea that the right response to being shoved is to shove back. This idea is so deeply ingrained in our culture, that its expression is reflexive. Until tested most of us may never realize that we operate on violence-embracing assumptions. Until challenged, we do not question our belief that the world is made up of victims and victimizers.

The Roxbury/South Boston project was an example of what public health planners call "secondary intervention." Secondary preventions are aimed at an entire population that is at risk. Because they were poor and lived in neighborhoods in which violence was common, all the adolescents in our target communities were at risk for violence. The Violence Prevention Project also contained tertiary interventions.

Tertiary violence prevention interventions are those aimed at young people who have already been labeled as the perpetrators or victims of violence. Detention facilities housing youths accused or convicted of serious offenses were among the sites we chose to locate our tertiary interventions. Counselors and youth workers at these facilities (which in Massachusetts are small and generally well run) were trained to teach the violence prevention curriculum to their young charges. Similar trainings were conducted at court-ordered programs for young offenders and at the Barron Center, the facility where students from the Boston Public Schools are sent for a mandatory observation and assessment when they are found carrying weapons into their schools.

We also attempted to create a sophisticated tertiary intervention at Boston City Hospital, but our reach exceeded our grasp. Our goal was to make contact with adolescents who entered the hospital through the emergency room following an assault. We knew that these young victims were at the highest risk for future violence both as repeat victims and as potential perpetrators. Once we had identified these high-risk patients, we intended to provide them with appropriate referral services—either counseling or membership in a violence prevention self-help group. I am convinced that this sort of emergency room intervention will eventually prove to be extremely effective. With our limited resources, we were unable to execute our plan back then, although a small-scale intervention of this kind is being tried now.

A program like this requires the commitment of emergency room doctors and nurses, for it is they who must ask the probing questions, who must record the answers on patients' charts, who must "red-flag" the charts of violence-prone patients and who must refer. In general, frantically busy doctors and nurses will not voluntarily increase their work load without a great deal of in-house education and training, and perhaps, as with the issues of attempted suicide and suspected child abuse, without the help of legal instruments requiring cooperation. In years to come I hope that health care providers will consider adolescent violence as much as a "syndrome" demanding their attention as is attempted suicide or child abuse today. We want every health care worker to feel compelled to be on the lookout for at-risk adolescents. When young people do appear to be at risk, emergency room personnel ought to know precisely to whom to refer patients for counseling and follow-up. Right now, even if we could convince every physician and nurse to identify their violence-prone adolescent patients, we do not have adequate services to offer. There is not yet a therapeutic protocol outlining how a young male who has been getting into fights since he was 11, who routinely carries a gun, and who enters the emergency room with a gunshot wound should be treated. I believe in the coming years emergency medicine will evolve in this direction.

A media campaign, including two public service commercials, accompanied our violence prevention efforts. Free-of-charge, Hill, Holliday, Connors, and Cosmopulos, one of Boston's leading advertising agencies, created two public service announcements aimed at teaching at-risk young people about the tragic consequences of fighting. I found working with the creative team at Hill, Holliday instructive and interesting. The writers and art directors told us that they had never been asked to market a product directly to poor adolescents before. (It occurs to me, however, that the industry that has convinced poor youngsters that what brand of sneakers a youth purchases is a decision of crucial concern, may know more than it thinks it knows about marketing to the poor.) This incipient understanding, however, was not apparent in the first campaign proposed by the creative team at Hill, Holiday. Members suggested that we build a campaign around the slogan, "Blow the Whistle on Crime." To us this suggestion revealed how little most Americans understand the causes of violence, not to mention the motivations and feelings of adolescents. We rejected this "Just Say No" approach, and spent some more time educating the creative team about violence. Their next effort was far more successful.

The "spots" ultimately created by Hill, Holliday were quite agonizing to watch. Each highlighted the role that friends and bystanders play as catalysts to violence. One shows a young male as he realizes his best friend has just been shot in a fight he encouraged. Leaning over the body of his friend, the young man wails, "I didn't know he had a gun." The other "spot" shows a young female equally distraught, following a fatal incident in which her boyfriend has been shot to death. "Why did I tell you he was coming on to me?" she moans. Both these commercials dramatize the central role that peers play in encouraging violence, while illustrating the grievous emotional consequences of violent acts. Because they are dramatic, highlight peer relationships, and do not preach, the spots grab the attention of young people. Accompanying the media campaign were posters and t-shirts carrying the slogan: "Friends for life don't let friends fight." I think the entire campaign was quite effective. Sadly, the commercials did not run for long. Union rules make even public service commercials quite expensive to air, and there was another problem. Because of the planned evaluation of our violence preven-

tion efforts in Roxbury and South Boston, we were supposed to iso-
late our message. You cannot restrict a television campaign to two
neighborhoods, however. Creating these spots, though, was an education. We learned how to tell the violence prevention story in thirty
second bites. Next time I would like to promote the violence prevention message nationally, creating a set of public service spots for
prime time network television, where the impact is greatest.

While the Roxbury/South Boston pilot project was still underway,
I was named Commissioner of Public Health for the state of Massachusetts. I asked Dr. Spivak to serve as Deputy Commissioner of
Health and he agreed. We both continued to take a significant interest
in the Violence Prevention Project, although our own efforts were
henceforth enacted on a different stage. Under Dr. Spivak's supervision, the Massachusetts Public Health Department established a state
office of violence prevention—the only one in the nation. Now having
left state service, Howard and I continue to be allies, friends, (and to
the degree that we are needed) advisers, to our colleagues at the
Health Promotion Project. The work of our old and new friends at the
Health Promotion Project continues unabated, now supported by the
city of Boston. One new initiative involves eliminating the middle
man and working directly with adolescents, providing them with
violence prevention information and training. Efforts to have an impact on health care professionals also continue. Project coordinator
Joanne Taupier is working on an adolescent violence prevention protocol for health center physicians and nurses. She has discovered that
it is not easy to convince primary care physicians that violence is a
health problem with which they ought to be concerned. (One of the
few physicians I know who has whole-heartedly embraced this position is Peter Stringham M.D., MPH. Dr. Stringham works in a health
center in a white, working-class neighborhood in Boston. Dr. Stringham routinely includes questions about violence when he talks to
parents and children. He asks new mothers how much fighting children are exposed to in their households. He asks parents of toddlers
how they discipline unruly 2-year-olds and he counsels them to use
"time out" (removing the child from the scene for a brief span) instead of hitting. He asks young teens about fighting and teaches them
techniques for avoiding fights. He counsels older teenagers against
using coercion to compel girls to have sex. Using an approach I find
charmingly sly, he tells his young male patients it is widely known
that guys who force girls to have sex are bad lovers. Dr. Stringham's
violence prevention efforts take advantage of the high regard patients
generally feel for their physicians, especially physicians they know
for many years, to induce parents and children to begin to question
their assumptions about physical aggression and to interact non-
violently with one another.)

In the years since Dr. Spivak and I established the Violence Prevention Project, a national movement to prevent adolescent violence has been born. Physicians, epidemiologists, nurses, community workers, teachers, criminologists, probation officers, police officers, social scientists from all over the nation have clambered aboard. Hundreds of school systems and community agencies in every state have become interested in the public health approach to preventing adolescent violence. Many of them are using the violence prevention curriculum. Thousands of teachers and community agency "providers" have been trained to use the curriculum to teach adolescents about violence prevention. In cities as diverse as Little Rock, Arkansas and Seattle, Washington the violence prevention curriculum is being used as part of comprehensive, community-wide efforts to provide teenagers with alternatives to violence. In many instances communities have shown a great deal of imagination in the ways in which they have adapted the curriculum to their own needs. A number have scaled the material down to meet the needs of primary and middle school children. Some communities have devised their own interventions. Other curricula have been produced. These take various approaches. Some are mentoring programs, some are conflict mediation programs, some emphasize job skills and teenage parenting skills. The Education Development Corporation (EDC), the non-profit organization that published the curriculum, has compiled a list of 85 church-based and community-based organizations all over the nation that are already working to reduce adolescent violence.* All over the country, the idea that communities can take steps to curb adolescent violence is beginning to take root.

The accomplishments of a community determined to combat adolescent violence can be inspiring. In Little Rock, Arkansas, a city of 160,000, a school bus stabbing by a girl in which a ninth-grade boy was nearly killed roused Suzanne Hicks, the mother of another ninth-grade student, to action. Mrs. Hicks organized a broad-based, interracial committee, the Coalition for Violence Prevention, to combat the growing problem of adolescent violence.

I am proud to say that my curriculum has played a role in the Coalition's impressive and successful campaign. Mrs. Hicks saw me on the *Today* show, talking about the school-based curriculum and my violence prevention work in Boston. She got in touch with my colleagues at the Health Promotion Project. Eventually a two-day training was organized to teach youth leaders in Little Rock about violence prevention and about teaching violence prevention. The training was attended by a notable array of professionals—youth workers and their supervisors from numerous agencies including two umbrella agencies

---

* See Appendix for the names and addresses of these and other organizations working to prevent adolescent violence.

that coordinate services to young people; police officers; school officials. The training and the effort didn't end when the out-of-state "experts" went home. Instead, those who had been trained, trained others in their agencies and departments. The violence prevention message radiated outward, deep into the agencies and departments whose workers have an enormous impact on the lives of young people.

The Little Rock school system made an extraordinary commitment to violence prevention. Every school in the system has been encouraged to take part. At the elementary level there are anti-fighting campaigns with school-wide rewards for not fighting. One school that introduced a peer counseling and mediation program went for an entire school year without a single fight and the principal threw a pizza party for the entire student body at the end of the year.

In every Little Rock junior and senior high school, the violence prevention curriculum is taught. The goal is to teach all the junior and senior high school students in the system during the same ten week period, although this effort in the high schools has not been totally implemented. Poster contests and other rewards are part of the system-wide campaign. Suzanne Hicks reports that the program has been particularly successful in the junior high schools where the same teachers teach the curriculum all day long for ten weeks. Teachers like this really get to know the curriculum and can share its contents very effectively with students. This is my experience, too; to be effective the curriculum must be taught by people who have explored their own feelings and attitudes towards violence and who are committed to violence prevention. The adoption of the violence prevention curriculum in Little Rock junior highs is credited with helping to reduce the number of fights and the number of suspensions within the system.

What is taught in school is reinforced outside in all the agencies providing social services and recreation to school age children in Little Rock. The health department, too, has taken part in the violence prevention effort, producing two violence prevention pamphlets, one educating kids about the risks of violence in general and one discussing the impact of television violence. The local television station and the city's two newspapers have been induced to report on the violence prevention campaign, although Suzanne Hicks expresses disappointment that she has been unable to convince these media outlets to provide weekly updates to parents on the violence prevention curriculum that would explain and illuminate what is being taught in school.

As impressive as all this is the Coalition still wants to do more. Members would like to see the curriculum incorporated more successfully into the high school. They are eager to involve the local university medical center, where many young stabbing and shooting victims are treated, in their violence prevention efforts, but thus far have not succeeded.

In Massachusetts, the Educational Development Corporation (EDC) is continuing its commitment to violence prevention. A three-year grant from the Centers for Disease Control has provided funding for the development of a formal middle school violence prevention curriculum aimed at young teens, 11 through 14 year olds. The need for a curriculum aimed specifically at young adolescents has long been felt. Research psychologist Ron Slaby PH.D. is the principal investigator for the middle school curriculum. His goal is to incorporate the most important social science research findings about aggression into the making of this new curriculum. He seeks to create an instrument that will re-educate aggressors, victims, and by-standers, teaching them new, more socially acceptable and personally satisfying ways to relate to one another.

Social science is only one of the specialties to which we in public health are reaching out. There are experts in the juvenile justice system and experts in the mental health system who also have a great deal to teach us about helping adolescents manage their anger and physical aggression. We need to work with specialists from these fields to create treatment protocols for adolescents who have difficulty containing their physical aggression. The public health perspective provides professionals in many fields with a way to understand adolescent violence and condemn physical aggression without condemning or blaming kids. In cities all over the country, when I speak about preventing adolescent violence, I sense a great wellspring of interest. People want to talk about kids killing kids. They want to understand why so many of our children are dying and they want to find a way out of this abyss. As saddened as I am by the mounting death toll on our streets, I am also heartened, as I feel that the will and the energy finally exists to face this terrible problem.

COMMUNITY POLICING

REDUCING ADOLESCENT VIOLENCE IN POOR NEIGHBOR-hoods requires the effort of all the institutions that shape people's lives—especially the police. The police are inextricably involved in the violence that bedevils poor communities. Many poor people blame the police for instigating violence and for failing to curtail violence in their communities. They think that if the police really cared they would restore order and end the mayhem on city streets. African-Americans in particular resent the way their sons and other males are demeaned by the police. They interpret the search-on-sight policies of many urban police forces as proof that the police despise and assail black manhood. For their part, many white police officers look at non-white communities and all they see is trouble and disarray. They do not recognize the strength, the health, the diversity, and the resilience in minority families, in minority churches, and in other minority institutions. Many police officers have trouble even seeing that poor people of color are victimized by violence and by crime more than any other of our citizens. Instead, the police focus on the hostile attitude with which their presence is often greeted and they feel betrayed by the very citizens they say they are risking their lives to protect.

Neither side in this round robin of dislike and misunderstanding has much sympathy for the other, and neither side approaches the other in a manner likely to reduce violence. Instead, there is a stalemate. Those in desperate need of police services and those who are paid to provide desperately needed police services often do not understand, like, or communicate with one another. In general, this is the case even when the police officers in question are members of minority groups.

So long as police officers spend their shifts in patrol cars, I think this stalemate will continue. Inside a car police officers are basically anonymous unaccountable, and far removed from the life of the street. Much of the ill will between police and local people stems from the absence of contact between them. When police officers walk a beat the relationship is changed for the better. Anyone can approach a cop on the beat. People get to know one another. Officers become part of the community they serve. The sense of menace disappears from the relationship.

A new brand of policing that advocates the return of foot patrol interests me very much—not only as a tactic for improving police-community relations, but also as a method of combatting crime. Community policing, as it is called, is the public health of police work. Like public health, community policing emphasizes prevention. Numerous police departments are already experimenting with this far-reaching new method of police work. The most prominent convert is New York City's Police Commissioner Lee Brown, who served as the chief of police in Houston from 1982 to early 1990.

Community policing is based on a handful of hard-hitting realizations about the failure of modern police techniques to curb crime, violence, or social decay. Each of these insights is supported by computer-generated data. Among them:

—As many as half of all police calls come from as few as 3 percent of locations, or "hotspots."

—A vast increase in the number of arrests has over-crowded courts and prisons, but done nothing to reduce crime.

—Deploying officers in patrol cars to respond to radio calls is a poor way to fight crime and an ineffective way to make the streets safe.

—The 911 system is an albatross. Responding quickly to crimes that have already occurred does nothing to make the streets safe.

—The current police emphasis on responding to major crime such as murder, rape, and robbery, while ignoring minor crime such as vandalism, purse snatchings, and public drinking hastens the decline of deteriorating neighborhoods, while failing to lead to an increase in public safety.

Supporters of community policing say the first crucial step toward improving big city policing is restoring foot patrols. The second even more radical step on the community policing agenda is to reorganize the way police work is done. Instead of reacting to every criminal act as if it were a unique occurrence, supporters say officers need to approach the problem more wholistically. What are the larger problems connecting apparently unrelated events? Instead of intermittently arresting the low-level drug dealers who congregate on a darkened basketball court in the park, community policing boosters suggest police should approach this "hotspot" analytically. If night after night dealers gather on a darkened playground, instead of arresting them only to see them released a few hours later, why not change the circumstances that create the problem? One community policing solution might be to flood the park with high density light, creating a desirable environment for basketball, softball, and rugby, but an undesirable one for dealing drugs.

The community policing approach does not measure success by the number of arrests made. In fact, a successful solution can mean a reduction in the number of arrests. When the now brightly lit park is used for recreation instead of drug dealing, the number of violent incidents and arrests there will decline. In their book, *Beyond 911*, Mark Moore, Malcolm Sparrow, and David Kennedy report that this is just what happened in the Link Valley section of Houston in 1988 when a coalition of community activists and a local police sergeant joined forces to drive the cocaine dealers out of the neighborhood. Link Valley is near the freeway. Most of the users who purchased drugs there were white suburbanites who took a quick detour off the highway on their way home from work. Believing that this kind of user would do anything to avoid exposure, the coalition heavily publicized the fact that they would be setting up roadblocks and arresting drug buyers in Link Valley, and that's just what they did. After several months of planning, police sealed off most access routes into the neighborhood. Residents received stickers so they could enter and

depart unbothered. Everyone else who entered the neighborhood
was questioned politely by police. Few drug purchasers showed up to
buy drugs that day, or ever again. There were few arrests.

The coalition, of course, considered this a success, not a failure.
The anti-buyer initiative, however, was only one piece of an overall
strategy. Other steps included tracking down the landlords of the
abandoned buildings where drug dealers did their business and le-
gally compelling them to raze or secure their structures. The police
and community also organized a highly successful garbage cleanup.
In one day, ten semitrailer-sized dumpsters full of filth were hauled
out of the neighborhood. This is hardly the way the police fight drugs
on *Miami Vice*, but it worked! Before, police had made hundreds of
arrests in Link Valley. Still, the community was dying a drug-induced
death. After the campaign, the community was revived. Residents
felt safe again. Calls for police service in this neighborhood decreased
by 44 percent. Nor did the dealers simply move next door. Calls for
service in surrounding communities also declined significantly.

What worked in Link Valley would not necessarily work in East
Harlem. Each police problem requires different solutions. One of the
strengths of the community policing model is that it sets free the
intelligence of the police. Officers no longer simply react to events.
They look for root causes. Within a specific community the mission of
the police becomes one of stopping crime by preventing crime. When
police and community people work together to solve problems, the
result can heal old wounds. Officers who work side by side with local
residents get to know young black males as someone's son, someone's nephew. The ill will between anonymous cop and anonymous
kid can be defused. Young males, too, can get a chance to know
police officers as people who are present in the community to help. In
this new police context, I hope some of the terrible bitterness that has
poisoned relations between police and inner city communities can
begin to recede.

CONTROLLING GUNS

THERE IS ONE AREA ABOUT WHICH MANY BLACK AMERICANS
and most police officers agree completely. Guns and gun control. The
need to limit the sale and distribution of non-sporting firearms. No
two groups are more passionate on this subject than African-
Americans and the members of the nation's urban police forces. This
shared passion stems from both groups' awareness that they have
lost so much, and that they have so much to lose. Police officers
quake before the high-powered semi-automatic handguns that have

replaced "Saturday night specials" as the weapon of choice in many inner city neighborhoods. Many police officers, formerly supporters of the pro-gun National Rifle Association, have become strong advocates of gun control. The National Association of Chiefs of Police has become a powerful voice in the gun control lobby. African-Americans, too, are completely disgusted and enraged at the number of high powered weapons that have entered their communities and are killing their children. I travel a great deal all over the country, speaking about violence prevention at meetings and conferences. At every meeting I hear the same message from blacks: We have to get rid of guns. We have to control the sale and distribution of guns. We have to ban non-sporting guns.

My own view on gun control is simple. I hate guns and I cannot imagine why anyone would want to own one. If I had my way, guns for sport would be registered and all other guns would be banned. I do not have high hopes, however, for the adoption of my agenda. Until the day when America undergoes a major change in its attitudes toward gun possession, I think those of us who favor gun control need to be extremely realistic about our opponents. The National Rifle Association (NRA) is a very powerful and very rich organization. We need to selectively choose our fights with the NRA. There are two battles I think we can win. I think we can gain passage in Congress of the Brady Amendment, which calls for a seven-day waiting period during which a background check can be conducted, prior to the purchasing of a handgun. This measure was named for Press Secretary Jim Brady, who was shot in the head during an assassination attempt on President Reagan, and his wife, anti-gun activist Sara Brady. While opponents of the Brady amendment contend that one week is not enough time to conduct a meaningful background check, knowledgeable people tell me that in the coming years information will be processed so quickly that two days, let alone seven, will be adequate to learn a great deal about a gun buyer. The other national initiative I think we should and must support vigorously is a national ban on the sale of all assault rifles, whether they are manufactured in this country or overseas. I think this measure has the emotional clout to overcome all disagreement.

On the non-legislative front, I am very intrigued by and I heartily support the gun-control efforts of two veteran gun opponents, Garen Wintemute, M.D., MPH from the University of California at Davis who is known for his work documenting the number of children killed and injured in gun accidents and Stephen Teret, J.D., MPH, who is the director of the Injury Prevention Center at Johns Hopkins University. These two have decided to launch a campaign not against the NRA and gun "users," but against domestic gun manufacturers, many of which are located in the Connecticut Valley. Stephen Teret says that to date gun opponents have let themselves be "suckered" into a debate with users, while the producers of guns have been left to continue manufacturing and selling guns unquestioned. It is time, he says, that gun manufacturers who are growing rich making weapons with which our children are killing one another be held accountable.

Wintemute and Teret are approaching this problem from a number of different directions. To publicize their side of the story they have planned a protest march through the Connecticut Valley, at which they intend to launch a campaign in favor of safety regulations for the gun industry. At the present time, due to the power of the pro-gun lobby, the Consumer Produce Safety Commission is expressly forbidden from regulating the manufacture of guns in any way. Gun producers cannot be compelled to install safety devices or child-proofing devices on their products. Interestingly, from 1888 to 1937 some Smith & Wesson guns were manufactured in such a way that they were "child-proof"—a child could not operate them. Why was this safety practice abandoned? Wintemute and Teret want to use the power of public opinion to compel gun manufacturers to once again produce accident-proof products.

I have high hopes that this new gun control strategy can yield fruitful results. While it takes 51 percent of Congress to win a legislative gun control battle, it only takes a small decline in profitability to make a company extremely nervous. No company, not even a profitable one, likes bad publicity. Moreover, this approach speaks to a concern of the public—safety. It is in the areas of product safety; toy safety; auto safety, including seat belts; bicycle helmets; smoke alarms, and so forth that the public health movement has had some of its most impressive victories in recent years. We have every reason to believe that the public's concern for safety will extend to the manufacture of firearms.

CREATING A COMPREHENSIVE FAMILY POLICY

WE LIVE IN A NATION THAT PRACTICES ORWELLIAN "DOUblethink" so far as families are concerned. Our government, our schools, our health care system, many of our employers operate on the assumption that our children live in two-parent families, with fathers who go to work and support them adequately and mothers who stay home and raise families. Children like this may need relatively few outside supports. They and their families may not need childcare, preschool, nutritional counseling, afterschool care, medicaid or respite care. But most children do not live in these types of households. Most children live in families with working mothers.

Money is tight. Schedules are complicated. Parents do not always get along. Sometimes they divorce and remarry. Half of all children will live in a single-parent household for part of their childhoods. Nearly 60 percent of African-American youngsters are born into single parent households. These female-headed households, of course, are very often poor. Working women still only earn two-thirds of what is earned by working men. One in two black children are poor. One in three Hispanic children are poor. The fastest growing group of poor children is white.

Reciting these mind-numbing facts always make me angry. I have a difficult time understanding the blindness of a country that cannot see that the funds we spend putting hundreds of thousands of our young males in prison could be so much better spent supporting families in need. We spend our money on piecemeal programs that make no sense, that increase dependency and despair, that leave children grossly unprotected. By failing to underwrite the costs of decent childcare we drive poor, working women out of the labor force and onto welfare roles where they are deprived of the opportunity to be self-sufficient and their children are deprived of the opportunity to see them live independent lives. By failing to insist that our schools truly teach, we create children who are illiterate and unable to compete in an international economy that daily grows more competitive.

What is needed is a comprehensive family policy of the sort that every other developed nation possesses, one that guarantees certain minimal standards of care for every child.

—We need universal health care for families

—We need subsidized high quality childcare

—We need nutritional services for poor children

—We need universal preschool programs for children who are educationally at risk

—We need universal, after-school programs for the children of working parents

—We need schools that are open and serving children educationally, recreationally and socially from morning until night, twelve months a year

Our children are our most important national resource. If we do not provide for their basic needs when they are small, they will repay us for our laxity by spending the rest of their days as predators dependents upon us all. This is not speculation. We know this to be true. A significant portion of our children are withering on the vine before they have even bloomed a little. An article in the *New York Times* speaks about children dropping out, not of high school, not of middle school, but of primary school—kindergarten. These are babies. We cannot abandon them to bring themselves up in a harsh and cruel environment.

The one cheering fact in this sea of sadness is that we know we can make a difference. When social programs are designed with the real needs of real people in mind we *know* we can make life better for poor parents and for their at-risk children. In her book, *Within Our Reach*, Lisbeth Schorr describes dozens of social programs that accomplish what they set out to accomplish. Programs that succeed, she comments, have certain traits in common. "They are intensive, comprehensive, flexible, and staffed by professionals with the time and skills to establish solid relationships with their clients." We need these successful programs not only as models to be replicated elsewhere, but as beacons shining the light of truth on the lie that says nothing works, trying to improve the lives of the poor is hopeless.

The grandmother of all successful social programs is Head Start which for twenty-five years has been preparing at-risk youngsters for school. One long-term study found that Head Start "graduates" dropped out of school one-third less often than the young people in a control group. Young people in the control, meantime, were placed in Special Education six time more often than members of the Head Start cohort. Another Head Start study found that at the age of 19, twice as many Head Start "graduates" were employed, in college or receiving more training than those in the control group.

One of the most interesting of the successful programs Lisbeth Schorr describes provides young at-risk mothers in Elmira, New York with at-home visits by well-trained nurses during pregnancy and afterward. When compared to a control group, the visited mothers had healthier, heavier babies; they had fewer cases of child abuse or neglect; they returned to school more rapidly after delivery; they were employed more often; they had fewer repeat pregnancies; they cared for their babies more "appropriately," and they punished their babies less frequently.

It works. Caring and providing services works. When the services respectfully and truly address the real needs of families in trouble, we can help family members rewrite their fates. We already know how to do it.

THE MASTER KEY

"What we wanted to do was try to give kids a fresh start—that is, to grow up learning about themselves, their bodies, how they grow, how they mature, what makes sense in developing and negotiating friendships. At first, the program was generally focused around the

202 ■ Deadly Consequences

issues embodied in most traditional prevention programs. There were
four concepts, but we have added a fifth. We call the first four concepts keys: decision-making; problem-solving, planning, and goal
setting. In the process of talking with the kids and finding out a lot
about what they felt regarding growing up in the environment that
they're in, we added another key: feelings. We call it the Master
Key."

Amos Smith
Program Director
Hartford, Ct.*

As individuals we do not have the power to protect all the children. We do not have the power to ban the sale of handguns, end the
sale of illicit drugs, or require that violence be portrayed realistically
in the mass media. Collectively, we must struggle toward these ends.
As individuals we only have a little power, but the power that we
have is profound nevertheless: It is the power to care.

Teenagers, especially ones who are young and poor, are hungry
for emotional contact and nurturing. Young black males especially
need the sincere attention of other black males—males who are responsible, males who embody a set of values that are deeper and
truer than the values of the street. They need to know that they have
not been abandoned to their adolescent posturing—that our caring
can contain their anger and their aggression. They need to know that
we are there to explain a world that is frightening and overwhelming.

As a physician and public health educator dedicated to combatting
adolescent violence, I turn to science to help me understand why our
children are dying in the streets. But for the leadership that will save
our children, I do not turn to my fellow physicians. I turn instead to
ordinary people, parents and others who care. I am convinced that
coiled in the passion for children of parents, grandparents and aunts
and uncles is a storehouse of energy that when released will be powerful enough to remake the world.

We in public health can advise and augment the popular movement to prevent violence, but few professionals have the rage or the
vision born in grief that Clementine Barfield possesses. In 1986 two of
Mrs. Barfield's sons were shot in the same incident. One of them
survived. Her sixteen year old son, Derick, was killed. Mrs. Barfield's
sorrow drove her to join forces with the five other mothers of slain
children to found SOSAD—Save Our Sons and Daughters.

Today SOSAD provides crisis intervention and bereavement support to the families and friends of slain children; it provides services

---

* Ronald Ferguson, "Case for Community Based Programs that Inform and Mentor
Black Male Youth," Urban Institute Research Paper, Distributed by the Urban Institute,
Washington, D.C.

to at-risk young males and works with incarcerated youth prior to release; it organizes public education and cultural campaigns; it lobbies in favor of gun control and crime victims compensation; and it stands as a daily aching reminder of all the young life that has been needless, tragically, lost to violence in Detroit and in all the cities of our nation. The dedication of Clementine Barfield and the other parents in SOSAD to curtailing youth violence is as relentless and endless as their heartache. I expect this organization and others like it to be catalysts in the crusade to curtail adolescent violence, just as MADD was a catalyst in the struggle to reduce the incidence of drunk driving.

"The children who are dying are real kids," says Clementine Barfield. "They are real kids, from real families. Some were doing foolish things. And some were just caught in the wrong place at the wrong time. But all kids have a right to make mistakes. All kids have the right to live. Somebody has to wake up and see that our children are dying. My child is dead. Your child could be next."

All of us who care about our children, who care about all of the children, need to heed these frightening words. Our children are dying. Only we can save them.

NOTES

Chapter 1

p. 3. Statistical material on homicide drawn from: "Public Health Problem of Violence Receives Epidemiologic Attention," *Journal of the American Medical Association*, Vol. 254, No. 7, Aug. 16, 1985; "International and Interstate Comparisons of Homicide Among Young Males," by L. A. Fingerhut and J. C. Kleinman, *Journal of the American Medical Association*, Vol. 263, No. 24, June 27, 1990; and "Homicide Among Young Black Males," *Morbidity and Mortality Weekly*, Vol. 34, No. 41, Oct. 18, 1985.

p. 4. The *Violence Prevention Curriculum for Adolescents* was published by the Educational Development Corporation of Newton, Ma., in 1987.

pp. 4–5. For a general discussion of the criminal justice approach to violence, see: J. Q. Wilson and R. Herrnstein, *Crime and Human Nature*, Simon & Schuster, 1985.

pp. 5–7. For a readable discussion of the mental health approach to anger and the research data about anger, see: C. Tavris, *Anger The Misunderstood Emotion*, Simon & Schuster, 1982.

pp. 6–7. Information about Lewis Ramey's theory of "free-floating anger," was presented in a symposium, "Homicide Among Black Males," sponsored by The Alcohol, Drug Abuse and Mental Health Administration on May 13th–14th, 1980. To my knowledge, this was the first national conference on violence organized to explore the victimization of black males. Proceeds were published in *Public Health Reports*, Nov.–Dec. 1980, Vol. 95, No. 6., pp. 549–561.

pp. 7–9. For information concerning the biology of violence, see the forthcoming review paper by A. F. Mirsky and A. Siegel, "The Neurobiology of Violence and Aggression." This paper was commissioned by the National Rsearch Council for its April 1990 symposium, "Understanding and Control of Violent Behavior." Publication is expected in late 1991 or 1992. For a copy of the paper, contact: A. Mirsky, Laboratory of Psychology and Psychopathology, National Institute of Mental Health, Building 10, Room 4C-110, Bethesda, Md. 20892. Additional information on the biology of violence may be found in: D. Goleman, "When Rage Explodes, Brain Damage May Be the Cause," *The New York Times*, Aug. 7, 1990.

p. 8. For more about the work of Drs. Vernon H. Mark and Frank R. Ervin, see: V. H. Mark and F. R. Ervin, *Violence in the Brain*, New York, Medical Dept., HarperCollins, 1970.

p. 9. "Cocaine stimulates epileptic electrical outbursts . . .": "Grand Rounds: A Case of Intractable Rage," *Behavioral Medicine*, July 1981, p. 32.

p. 9. For a discussion of the relationship between violence and head injury, see: D. O. Lewis, M. Feldman, and A. Barrengos, "Violent Juvenile Delinquents: Psychiatric, Neurological, Psychological and Abuse Factors," *Journal of the American Academy of Child Psychiatry*, Vol. 18, 1979, pp. 307–319; D. O. Lewis and S. Shanok, "Medical Histories of Delinquent and Non-Delinquent Children: An Epidemiological Study, *American Journal of Psychiatry*, Vol. 134, No. 9, 1977, pp. 1020–1025; and C. Bell and R. P. Kelly, "Head Injury with Subsequent Intermittent Nonschizophrenic, Psychotic Symptoms and Violence," *Journal of the National Medical Association*, Vol. 79, No. 11, 1987.

pp. 9–10. For a discussion of the relationship between gender and violence, see the forthcoming review article by C. Kruttschnitt, "Gender and Interpersonal Violence." This paper was commissioned by the National Research Council for its April 1990 symposium, "Understanding and Control of Violent Behavior." Publication is expected in late 1991 or 1992. For a copy of the paper, contact C. Kruttschnitt, The Department of Sociology, University of Minnesota. For additional information in the general press, see: M. Konner, "The Aggressors," *The New York Times Magazine*, Aug. 14, 1988; and L. Shapiro, "Guns and Dolls: Scientists Explore the Differences between Girls and Boys," *Newsweek* cover story, May 28, 1990.

Chapter 2

p. 11. J. C. McKinley Jr, "Teen-Ager Slain Trying to Shield Brother From Bullies," *The New York Times*, Dec. 2, 1989.

p. 12. Data on annual number of homicides: FBI: Uniform Crime Reports.

pp. 12–13. Newspaper stories describing the deaths of young males: Carl West: "A Week's Killings: A Profile of Violent Death," *The New York Times*, April 8, 1988; Richard Bailey: "A Life Taken, a Hope Lost," *The Boston Globe*, Aug. 20, 1988; Raymond Tersignis: "Teen Sentenced to 4 Year Term in Friend's Death," *The Fort Lauderdale Sun Sentinel*, Aug. 23, 1989; Donald White: "A Neighborhood Mourns a Young Dreamer," *The New York Times*, Nov. 9, 1989; and Thomas Viens: "South Boston Youth is Charged in Shooting," *The Boston Globe*, July 13, 1990.

p. 13. Sources for 1989 and 1990 homicide data: The FBI: Uniform Crime Reports; "1990: the Bloodiest Year Yet?" *Newsweek*, July 16, 1990; "The Perpetual Crime Wave Crests, and a City Shudders," *The New York Times*, Aug. 1, 1990; "Record U.S. Murder Rate Seen," *The Boston Globe*, Aug. 1, 1990; "Many Cities Setting Records for Homicide in Year," *The New York Times*, Dec. 9. 1990; and "Record Year for Killing Jolts Officials in New York," *The New York Times*, Dec. 31, 1990.

pp. 13–16. Comparison of international, interstate and interracial homicide rates for young males, including data on handguns: L. A. Fingerhut and J. C. Kleinman, "International and Interstate Comparison of Homicide Among Young Males," *Journal of the American Medical Association*, Vol. 263, No. 24, June 27, 1990.

pp. 15–16. International comparison of overall homicide data: M. L. Rosenberg and J. A. Mercy, "Homicide: Epidemiologic Analysis at the National Level,"

Bulletin of the New York Academy of Medicine, Vol. 62, No. 5, pp. 376–399, June, 1986.

p. 16. Thirty year increase in homicide rate: "Homicide, Suicide, and other Violence Gain Increasing Medical Attention," *Journal of the American Medical Association*, Vol. 254, No. 6, Aug. 9, 1985.

pp. 16–17. "Who are the over 20,000 Americans who die each year in homicides?": Centers for Disease Control, *Morbidity and Mortality Weekly Report*, "Homicide Among Young Black Males," Vol. 34, No. 41, Oct. 18, 1985; Centers for Disease Control: *Homicide Surveillance*, Summary 1970–1978; Centers for Disease Control: *Homicide Surveillance*, "High Risk Racial and Ethnic Groups—Blacks and Hispanics," 1970 to 1983.

pp. 16–17. Analysis of victims and data on risk: M. L. Rosenberg, "Violence Is a Public Health Problem," book chapter from *"Unnatural Causes: The Three Leading Killer Diseases in America,"* editor R. C. Maulitz, New Brunswick: Rutgers University Press, 1989. (In its published form, the comparative data on black, white, male and female risk was derived from 1981 homicide statistics. In 1990, using updated statistics, Rosenberg reworked this data for oral presentation.)

p. 16. Cities with highest homicide rates for different groups: FBI: Uniformed Crime Reports.

p. 17. Poverty as a risk factor for homicide: W. J. Wilson, *The Truly Disadvantaged*, Chicago, University of Chicago Press, 1987; R. J. Sampson, "Urban Black Violence: The Effect of Male Joblessness and Family Disruption," *American Journal of Sociology*, Vol. 93, No. 2, pp. 348–382, Sept. 1987; and B. Centerwall, "Race, Socioeconomic Status and Domestic Homicide, Atlanta, 1971–72." *American Journal of Public Health*, Vol. 74, No. 8, pp. 813–815, 1984.

p. 18. "It's just guns now." Quote on handguns in Detroit: T. Rosenberg, "Eight Lives," *The New York Times Magazine*, June 12, 1988.

p. 18. Statistic on number of Americans killed in accidental shootings: The National Coalition to Ban Handguns, 100 Maryland Avenue NE, Washington, D.C. 20002.

p. 18. Vancouver–Seattle homicide comparison: J. H. Sloan, A. L. Kellerman, D. T. Rea, J. A. Ferris, T. Koepsell, F. P. Rivara, C. Rice, L. Gray, J. LoGerfo, "Handgun Regulations, Crime, Assault, and Homicide: A Tale of Two Cities," *New England Journal of Medicine*, Vol. 319, N. 19, p. 256, Nov. 18, 1988.

p. 18. "It is estimated that fifty million handguns are now in circulation . . .": No national data on the number of handguns circulating is kept. This estimate comes from the Coalition to Stop Gun Violence, 100 Maryland Avenue NE, Washington, D.C. 20002 and is based on polling samples.

p. 18. Half the households in U.S. armed: "Firearms and Violence in American Life," a staff report submitted to the National Commission on the Causes and Prevention of Violence, Franklin E. Zimring, Director of Research, July 1969.

p. 18. "Firearms used in 80 percent of homicides among young black males . . .": L. A. Fingerhut and J. C. Kleinman, "International and Interstate Comparison of Homicide Among Young Males," *Journal of the American Medical Association*, Vol. 263, No. 24, June 27, 1990.

pp. 18–19. Prevalence of powerful weapons: "Epidemic in Urban Hospitals: Wounds from Assault Rifles," *The New York Times*, Feb. 21, 1989; "A Tide of Drug Killing," *Newsweek*, Jan. 16, 1989; "Youths Dying Violently in War Zone on City Streets," *The Boston Sunday Globe*, Feb. 21, 1988; G. Hackett,

"Kids: Deadly Force," *Newsweek*, Jan. 11, 1988; M. Barnicle, "Even the Police Feel Outgunned," *The Boston Globe*, Feb. 4, 1988; K. Cullen, "Glut of Guns a Menacing Sign," *The Boston Globe*, April 29, 1990; and T. Loey and J. Thomas, "Weapons in the Hands of Children Spawn a Culture of Fear," *The Boston Globe*, May 2, 1990.

p. 19. Boston Commission Survey of weapons-carrying: The Boston Commission on Safe Public Schools, *Making Our Schools Safe for Learning*, Nov., 1983, pp. 12–16.

p. 19. National Student survey of weapons-carrying behavior: K. Zinsmeister, "Growing up Scared," *The Atlantic Monthly*, June, 1990.

p. 19. Increase in number of pre-teens accused of homicide: "When Children Kill Children," *The New York Times*, Aug. 27, 1990.

pp. 19–20. Data on guns and knives: The FBI: Uniform Crime Reports.

p. 20. Estimate of number of gun injuries yearly: The National Safety Council, 1050 17th Street NW, Suite 770, Washington, D.C. 20036.

pp. 20–21. Comparison of assaults to homicides: J. I. Barancik, "Northeast Ohio Trauma Study," *American Journal of Public Health*. Vol. 73, No. 7, pp. 746–51, July 1983.

p. 20. Cost of treating gunshot wounds: "Epidemic in Urban Hospitals: Wounds from Assault Rifles," *The New York Times*, Feb. 21, 1989.

p. 20. Cost of treating violent injuries: M. L. Rosenberg, "Cost of Injury in the United States: A Report to Congress 1989," Dorothy P. Rice, Allen J. Mackenzie, Associates, San Francisco, California: Institute for Health and Aging, University of California and the Injury Prevention Center, Johns Hopkins University, 1989.

pp. 21–22. Characteristics of homicide victims and perpetrators: Centers for Disease Control: *Homicide Surveillance*, Summary 1970–1978; Centers for Disease Control: *Homicide Surveillance*, "High Risk Racial and Ethnic Groups— Blacks and Hispanics, 1970 to 1983"; J. Rabkin, "Epidemiology of Adolescent Violence: Risk Factors, Career Patterns and Intervention Programs," Paper Delivered at the Conference on Adolescent Violence: Research & Public Policy, Arden House, Feb. 5–7, 1987, Columbia University, NYS Psychiatric Institute; M. L. Rosenberg, E. Stark, and M. Zahn, "Interpersonal Violence: Homicide and Spouse Abuse," book chapter from *Maxcy-Rosenau Public Health and Preventive Medicine*, 12th edition, John M. Last (ed.), Appleton-Century-Crofts, Norwalk, Conn. 1986; R. E. Dennis, "Homicide Among Black Males: Social Costs to Families and Communities," *Public Health Reports*, Vol. 94, No. 6, pp. 556–557, Nov.–Dec. 1980; R. A. Goodman, J. A. Mercy, F. Loya, M. L. Rosenberg, J. C. Smith, N. H. Allen, L. Vargas, R. Kolts, "Alcohol Use and Interpersonal Violence: Alcohol Detected in Homicide Victims," *American Journal of Public Health*, Vol. 76, No. 2, Feb. 1986; and G. A. Goodman, J. A. Mercy, M. L. Rosenberg, "Alcohol Use and Homicide Victimization: An Examination of Racial/Ethnic Differences," from *Research Monograph 18*, U.S. Department of Health and Human Services, DHHS Publication No. (ADM) 89–1435, pp. 191–202.

p. 22. "Both are likely to see themselves as persons under attack,": D. Offer, E. Ostrov and K. I. Howard, *The Adolescent*, New York, Basic Books, 1981.

pp. 22–23. How families teach children to behave aggressively: R. J. Gelles and M. N. Straus, *Intimate Violence*, New York, Simon & Schuster, 1988; and R. G. Slaby and W. C. Roedell, "The Development and Regulation of Aggression in Young Children," *Psychological Development in the Elementary Years*, J. Worell (ed.), Academic Press, Inc., 1982.

p. 24. University of Maryland study on the prevalence of violence in the live of poor, inner city kids: K. Zinsmeister, "Growing up Scared," *The Atlantic Monthly*, June, 1990.

pp. 24–25. Statistics on gangs and drugs: "Slaughter in the Streets," *Newsweek*, Dec. 5, 1988. Estimate of Gang Deaths: FBI: Uniform Crime Reports; "Number of Killings Soars in Big Cities Across U.S.," *The New York Times*, July 18, 1990; and "More Americans are Killing Each Other," *The New York Times*, Dec. 31, 1989.

p. 26. Story of Napier Traylor is paraphrased from an article by S. Jacobs in *The Boston Sunday Globe*, Feb. 21, 1988.

p. 27. "Violence is bigger than the police," Boston Police Commissioner Francis M. Roache, statement made during interview with author.

p. 27. "Homicide is a societal problem over which law enforcement has little control:" Quote from the FBI: *Crime in the United States: 1986*, Washington, DC, US Department of Justice, 1987.

p. 27. Quote from New York City Police Commissioner Lee Brown: "The Commissioner and Crime: Pressure Mounts for Results," *The New York Times*, Aug. 3, 1990.

pp. 27–28. The Surgeon General lists violence as a key health problem: "Healthy People—The Surgeon General's Report on Health Promotion and Disease Prevention," Background Papers: U.S. Dept. of Health, Education and Welfare, Publication No. 79-55071A, 1979.

Chapter 3

p. 29. V. Canby, "Now at a Theater Near You: A Skyrocketing Body Count," *The New York Times*, July 16, 1990.

p. 30. J. Maslin, *The New York Times*, July 20, 1990.

p. 31–32. Examples of Violence in the mass media: "Mess with me and I'll Kill you," headline for *People* cover story on Cher, Jan. 25, 1988; Revenger: "For Entrepreneur, Revenge is Sweet," *The New York Times*, Dec. 4, 1987; "Faces of Death": "Do Slasher Films Breed Real-life Violence?" *The Boston Globe*, Dec. 18, 1988; "The Confessions of Bernhard Goetz": "Goetz Confession Offered as Stocking Stuffer," *The New York Times*, Nov. 29, 1987; Geraldo Rivera: "Trash TV," *Newsweek* cover story, Nov. 14, 1988; and Robert Chambers: "Death in Central Park, Lives of 80's Youth," *The New York Times*, Sept. 22, 1989 and "Television and the Attack in Central Park," *The New York Times*, May 2, 1989.

pp. 32–33. Sex and violence on Television: "Trash TV," *Newsweek* cover story, Nov. 14, 1989; "Art or Obscenity," *Newsweek* cover story, July 2, 1990; N. Cobb, "Prime Time Sex: Why We're Seeing So Much on Network TV," *The Boston Globe Magazine*, April 4, 1989; "Dirty Words: America's Foul-Mouthed Pop Culture," *Time* cover story, May 7, 1990; and "TV Broadcast Grisly Scenes But Received No Complaints," *The New York Times*, Jan. 27, 1990.

p. 33. Glen Pierce: Conversation with the author.

p. 35. Teenage Mutant Ninja Turtles: J. F. McDermott, "Cowabunga," *The Boston Sunday Globe*, May 13, 1990.

p. 35. Toy-based "superhero" programs for kids: N. Carlsson—Page and D. E. Levin, *The War Play Dilemma*, Teachers College Press, Columbia University, New York, 1987; and P. Boyer, "Ethics of Toy-Based TV Shows Disputed," *The New York Times*, Feb. 3, 1986.

p. 36. The portrayal of enemies in "superhero" programs: P. Hesse and J. Mack, "The World Is a Dangerous Place: Images of the Enemy on Children's TV," book chapter from *Psychology of War and Peace: Images of the Enemy*, Robert Rieber, editor, Plenum Press, New York, 1991; P. Hesse and D. Poklemba, "The Stranger with Green Feet and Black Piggy Toes: Young Children's Conceptions of the Enemy," Center for Psychological studies in the Nuclear Age, Harvard Medical School; and J. J. O'Connor, Critics Notebook, "Insidious Elements in Television Cartoons," *The New York Times*, Feb. 2, 1990.

p. 38. Sources on Heavy Metal and Rap: J. Pareles, "How Rap Moves to Television's Beat," *The New York Times*, Jan. 14, 1990; J. Adler, "Rap Rage," and D. Gates, "Decoding Rap Music," both appearing in a *Newsweek* cover story on rap, Mar. 19, 1990; J. Pareles, "Have Rap Concerts Become Inextricably Linked to Violence?" *The New York Times*, Sept. 13, 1988; and S. Morse, "Writer Nelson George says Rap Gets a Bum Rap," *The Boston Globe*, May 24, 1990.

p. 40. For a discussion of the impact of television on behavior: R. G. Slaby and W. C. Roedell, "The Development and Regulation of Aggression in Young Children," *Psychological Development in the Elementary Years*, J. Worell, editor, Academic Press, Inc., 1982, p. 119.

p. 40. Data on hours per day that children watch TV: R. M. Liebert and J. N. Sprafkin, *The Early Window: Effects of Television on Children and Youth*, third edition, New York, Pergamon Press, 1988.

p. 40. TV as a baby-sitter: Slaby and Roedell, p. 122; and M. Winn, "The VCR: A New and Improved Babysitter," *The New York Times*, Aug. 27, 1989.

pp. 40–41. Television's impact on behavior: Liebert and Sprafkin; and Slaby and Roedell. J. Q. Wilson and R. Herrnstein, *Crime and Human Nature*, Simon & Schuster, 1985.

pp. 41–42. Examples of copycat murders: Details describing John Hinckley attack on President Ronald Reagan, Ronald Zamorra's attack on an elderly neighbor and the San Francisco gang rape of a young girl from Liebert and Sprafkin, pp. 135–161; details of the case against Rod Matthews from D. Golden's, "The Rod Matthews Case," *The Boston Globe Magazine*, May 22, 1988.

p. 42. "We are a suggestible species." See discussion of Social Learning Theory in Liebert and Sprafkin, pp. 65–73.

pp. 42–43. Mass murder: See J. Fox and J. Levin, *Mass Murder*, Plenum Press, 1985.

p. 43. "Parents and a Brother Slain by Self-Styled Rambo, 16," *The New York Times*, Mar. 23, 1989.

pp. 43–44. L. D. Eron, "Parent-Child Interaction, Television Violence, and Aggression of Children," *American Psychologist*, Vol. 37, No. 2, pp. 197–211; L. D. Eron, "Prescription for Reduction of Aggression," *American Psychologist*, Vol. 35, No. 3, March 1980, pp. 244–252; L. D. Eron, "Aggression Through the Ages," *School Safety*, Fall, 1987. Also see discussions of Eron's work in Liebert and Sprafkin and Slaby and Roedell.

pp. 44–45. See discussion of Social Learning Theory in Liebert and Sprafkin, pp. 65–73; and in D. Perry, "How Aggression is Learned," *School Safety*, Fall 1987.

pp. 45–46. Desensitizing and disinhibiting impact of television; Slaby and Roedell, pp. 121.

pp. 45–46. Discussion of George Gerbner's "mean world theory": G. Gerbner, "The Real Issue of TV Violence: It's Subversive," *Newsday*, Oct. 16, 1986; G. Gerbner, "Children's Television: A National Disgrace," *Pediatric Annals*,

Dec. 1985, pp. 822–827; G. Gerbner, L. Gross, N. Signorielli, M. Morgan, "Television's Mean World: Violence Profile No. 14–15," The Annenberg School of Communications, University of Pennsylvania; "Television Violence," *Newsweek*, Dec. 6, 1986; and H. Waters, "Life According to TV," *Newsweek*, Dec. 6, 1982.

pp. 46–47. Emmett Folgert's theory of television's role in the life of poor, fatherless boys: Articulated during interview with author.

Chapter 4

p. 49. ". . . A dangerous current runs back and forth as dark-skinned youths, suspects by virtue of race and age, are ordered to lie down, face on the pavement, while they are searched for weapons." Author observed this scene while riding with Boston police. For more information on this phenomenon, see: N. Meredith, "Attacking the Roots of Police Violence," *Psychology Today*, May, 1984, pp. 21–26.

p. 50. Developmental psychologists interpret the tasks of adolescence differently: Chad Gordon, in an essay on development, described the necessity of adolescent's exhibiting and developing, "autonomy, self-determination, accomplishment, control and self control." This assertion appeared in the book *Twelve to Sixteen*, J. Kagan and R. Coles (eds.), New York, Norton, 1972. J. Adelson, in another essay appearing in this volume, wrote of the adolescent's need to achieve, "abstractness, a sense of the past and an understanding of motivation." Jerome Kagan, in the same book, wrote of the adolescent's need to resolve his uncertainty over "sexual adequacy, interpersonal power, autonomy of belief and action and acceptability to peers."

p. 50. On the "normality" of adolescence: D. Offer, E. Ostrov and K. I. Howard, *The Adolescent*, New York, Basic Books, 1981.

p. 50. "Half of all children spend at least part of their childhood in a family headed by a single parent:" "A Vision for America's Future: An Agenda for the 1990's," Children's Defense Fund, Washington, D.C., 1989.

p. 51. Adolescence as culture-bound: Erik Erickson, *Childhood and Society*, New York, Norton, 1963.

p. 51. On Individuation and Separation: Erik Erikson, *Childhood and Society*; and "Youth: Fidelity and Diversity," from *Youth: Change and Challenge*, Erik Erikson (ed.), New York, Basic Books, 1963.

p. 53. Peers: P. Blos, *Twelve to Sixteen*, J. Kagan and R. Coles (eds.); and M. Csikszentmihaly and R. Larson, *Being Adolescent*. New York, Basic Books, 1984.

p. 53. C. Brown, *Manchild in the Promised Land*, New York, The MacMillan Company, 1965, p. 121.

p. 54. "The high incidence of teenage pregnancy, single-parent families, domestic violence, divorce . . . :" L. Dash, *When Children want Children: An Inside Look at the Crisis of Teenage Parenthood*, Penguin Books, 1989.

p. 56. Emerge: 18 Hurley Street, Cambridge, Ma. 02141.

p. 56. Erikson's discussion of "an open future" for youth: Erik Erikson, "Youth: Fidelity and Diversity," from *Youth: Change and Challenge*, Erik Erikson (ed.), New York, Basic Books, 1963.

p. 57. T. Cottle, from his essay appearing in *Twelve to Sixteen*, J. Kagan and R. Coles (eds.), p. 314.

p. 57. Competence: T. DeVaron from her essay appearing in *Twelve to Sixteen*, J. Kagan and R. Coles (eds.), p. 347; and M. Csikszentmihaly and R. Larson, *Being Adolescent*, New York, Basic Books, 1984.

p. 58. Adolescent need for adults: J. J. Conger from his essay appearing in *Twelve to Sixteen*, J. Kagan and R. Coles (eds.); and M. Csikszentmihaly and R. Larson.

p. 58. E. E. Werner and R. S. Smith, *Kauai's Children Come of Age*, Honolulu, University Press of Hawaii, 1977; *Vulnerable but Invincible: A Longitudinal Study of Resilient Children and Youth*, New York, McGraw-Hill, 1982; and A. Bass, "Kids Can Beat the Odds," *The Boston Globe*. This is a lengthy article about Werner's latest findings—that by age 30 many of her troubled subjects had been able to create decent lives for themselves with the help of mentors and other "second chance opportunities."

pp. 59–62. Forging a moral value system: J. Reimer, D. P. Paolitto, R. Hersh, *Promoting Moral Growth from Piaget to Kohlberg*, second edition, New York, Longman, 1983; W. Damon, *Social and Personality Development Infancy through Adolescence*, New York, Norton, 1983, p. 272–273; and B. Lefkowitz, *Tough Change*, pp. 211–212.

pp. 62–63. Risk-taking: Erik Erikson, "Youth: Fidelity and Diversity," from *Youth: Change and Challenge;* and J. T. Gibbs, "The New Morbidity: Homicide, Suicide, Accidents and Life-Threatening Behaviors," from the book, *Young Black and Male in America*, J. T. Gibbs (ed.), Dover, Ma., Auburn House, 1988.

Chapter 5

p. 64. A Kotlowitz, *The Wall Street Journal*, Oct. 27, 1987.

p. 64. The victims and witnesses of violence often become its perpetrators: J. Rabkin, "Epidemiology of Adolescent Violence: Risk Factors, Career Patterns and Intervention Programs," Paper Delivered at the Conference on Adolescent Violence: Research & Public Policy, Arden House, Feb. 5–7, 1987; R. J. Gelles and M. N. Straus, *Intimate Violence*, New York, Simon & Schuster, 1988, and R. G. Slaby and W. C. Roedell, "The Development and Regulation of Aggression in Young Children," *Psychological Development in the Elementary Years*, J. Worell, editor, Academic Press, Inc., 1982.

p. 65. Those most imperiled (by homicide) are poor, young males growing up in impoverished "inner city" neighborhoods: See R. J. Sampson, "Urban Black Violence: The Effect of Male Joblessness and Family Disruption," *American Journal of Sociology*, Vol. 93, No. 2, Sept. 1987, pp. 348–382.

p. 65. Black homicide rates: FBI: Uniform Crime Reports.

p. 65. Increase in black homicide rate, 1984–1988: "Short Lives, Bloody Deaths: Black Murder Rates Soar," *Newsweek*, Dec. 17, 1990.

pp. 65–66. Impact of gangs and drugs on homicide rates: FBI: Uniform Crime Reports.

p. 66. Data on Latino homicide rates: University of California at Los Angeles and the Centers for Disease Control: *The Epidemiology of Homicide in the City of Los Angeles, 1970–79*, Department of Health and Human Services, Public Health Service, Centers for Disease Control, August 1985.

pp. 66–67. "The Waltons:" Based on the reporting of A. Kotlowitz, *The Wall Street Journal*, Oct. 27, 1987.

pp. 58–68. The psychological impact of violence on children: R. Graham, "Amid Drugs and Death, Help for the Living," *The Boston Globe*, July 5, 1989; M. Wine, "Helping Victims of Violence Heal Their Psychic Wounds," *The New York Times*, June 13, 1988; and D. Kong, "Psychic Toll of Violence on Youth," *The Boston Globe*, Oct. 31, 1989.

pp. 68–69. Description of Roxbury's "Living After Murder" program; R. Graham, "Amid Drugs and Death, Help for the Living," *The Boston Globe*, July 5,

1989. Comments of psychologist Mohamed Seedat on the psychological impact upon children in the United States and in South Africa of living amidst violence made during interviews with the author.

p. 69. For information about Dr. Bell's work, see: C. C. Bell and G. Chance-Hill, "Treatment of Violent Families," *Journal of the National Medical Association*, Vol. 83, No. 3, Mar., 1983, pp. 203–208; C. C. Bell, E. J. Jenkins, "Preventing Black Homicide," in the book, *The State of Black America*, J. Dewart (ed.), New York, National Urban League, 1990; C. C. Bell, "Black on Black Homicide: The Implications for Black Community Mental Health," in the book, *Mental Health and Mental Illness Among Black Americans*, D. Smith-Ruiz (ed.), Westport, Ct., Greenwood Press, 1990; "Black on Black Murder Update," The Community Mental Health Council News Quarterly, Summer 1987, The Community Mental Health Council, 8704. S. Constance Avenue, Chicago, Il 60617; and D. Breo, "Chicago's Dr. Bell," *People*, Mar. 21, 1988.

pp. 69–73. "The Underclass:" Much of the data on the underclass appearing in this section was taken from the seminal work on this subject. W. J. Wilson's, *The Truly Disadvantaged; The Inner City, The Underclass and Public Policy*, Chicago, University of Chicago Press, 1987. Other sources on the emergence and the reality of life in the underclass include: W. J. Wilson, The Godkin Lecture, Delivered at the Kennedy School of Government, Harvard University, April 26, 1988; W. J. Wilson, "How the Urban Poor Got Poorer," *The New York Times*, Nov. 29, 1987; I. Wilkerson, "Growth of the Very Poor is Focus of New Studies," *The New York Times*, Dec. 20, 1987; R. Wilkins, "The Black Poor are Different," *The New York Times*, Aug. 22, 1989; and "A Vision for America's Future: An Agenda for the 1990's," Children's Defense Fund, Washington, D.C., 1989.

pp. 72–73. To understand the disastrous emotional and social impact of joblessness on the relations between black men and women, three early works of "urban ethnographers" are also extremely useful: C. B. Stack, *All Our Kin: Strategies for Survival in a Black Community*, New York, Harper & Row, 1974; Lee Rainwater, *Behind Ghetto Walls: Black Family Life in a Federal Slum*, Chicago, Aldine Atherton, Inc., 1970; and E. Liebow, *Tally's Corner*, Boston, Little Brown, 1967. Also useful is: J. Kozol, *Rachel and Her Children: Homeless Families in America*, New York, Crown, 1988.

pp. 72–73. R. J. Sampson, "Urban Black Violence: The Effect of Male Joblessness and Family Disruption," *American Journal of Sociology*, Vol. 93, No. 2, Sept. 1987, pp. 348–382.

p. 73. Glen Pierce, interview with author. For additional information on this subject, see, S. Daley, "For dropouts, Finding Jobs is a Tough Task," *The New York Times*, Aug. 1, 1988.

pp. 73–74. S. Rimer, "The Short Life of a Former Foster Child," *The New York Times*, Nov. 11, 1987. For information on community collapse, see: W. J. Wilson, *The Truly Disadvantaged;* R. J. Sampson, "Urban Black Violence;" "Violence, Youth and a Way Out," testimony of John A. Calhoun, Executive Director, National Crime Prevention Council, before the House Select Committee on Children, Youth and Families, Mar. 9, 1988; "A Vision for America's Future," Children's Defense Fund; L. Schorr, *Within Our Reach*, New York, Doubleday, 1988, Chapter 7; and J. Q. Wilson and G. Kelling, "Police and Neighborhood Safety: Broken Windows," *Atlantic Monthly*, Mar. 1982, pp. 29–38.

p. 77. Statistics on single parent families: "A Vision for America's Future," Children's Defense Fund.

pp. 77–78. What it means to have or to be a young, single Mom: L. S. Sadler and C. Catrone, "The Adolescent Parent: A Dual Developmental Crisis," *Journal of Adolescent Health Care*, 1983, Vol. 4, pp. 100–105. L. Dash, *When Children Want Children: An Inside Look at the Crisis of Teenage Parenthood*, Penguin Books, 1989. Also see J. Q. Wilson and R. Herrnstein, *Crime and Human Nature*, Simon & Schuster, 1985, on the effect of having "underdeveloped" parents who do not communicate well verbally.

pp. 78–79. Boys without fathers: J. Herzog, "On Father Hunger: The Father's Role in the Modulation of Aggressive Drive and Fantasy," from the book *Father & Child: A Developmental Perspective*, S. H. Cath, A. R. Gurwitt, and J. M. Ross, New York, Basil Blackwell, 1982; M. Connor, "Teenage Fatherhood: Issues Confronting Young Black Males," from the book *Young, Black and Male in America*, J. T. Gibbs (ed.), Dover, Ma., Auburn House, 1988; R. Jessor and S. L. Jessor, *Problem Behavior and Psychosocial Development: A Longitudinal Study of Youth:* New York, Academic Press, 1977; M. Shinn, "Father Absence and Children's Cognitive Development," *Psychological Bulletin*, 1978, Vol. 875, No. 2, pp. 295–324. Also see J. Q Wilson and R. Herrnstein's discussion of the research relating to the impact of growing up in a single-parent family.

Chapter 6

pp. 81–82. For a discussion of the wave of violence that swept across "Area B" in October 1989, see K. Cullen and T. Coakley, "A Month of Fear and Bullets," *The Boston Globe*, Nov. 5, 1989.

p. 83. "In New York City . . . four children . . . were shot to death by bullets fired outside their apartment walls.": S. Daley and M. Freitag, "Wrong Place at the Wrong Time: Stray Bullets Claim more Victims," *The New York Times*, Jan. 14, 1990.

p. 86. Source for statistics on police deployment: Boston City Councilor Charles Yancey.

p. 92. Bulhan, H. A., *Franz Fanon and The Psychology of Oppression*, Plenum, 1985.

pp. 93–94. More about Ferguson's study can be found in: R. Ferguson, "The Case for Community-Based Programs that Inform and Mentor Black Male Youth," Urban Institute Research Paper, Distributed by the Urban Institute, Washington, D.C.

Chapter 7

pp. 95–96. Information on Tony Johnson based on S. Jacobs and K. Cullen's, "Cool, Articulate, Savvy and Dead at 21," *The Boston Globe*, Mar. 26, 1990.

p. 96. "Gangs are not new:" See Erik Erikson, "Youth: Fidelity and Diversity," from *Youth: Change and Challenge*, Erik Erikson (ed.), New York, Basic Books, 1963; Walter B. Miller, "American Youth Gangs: A Reassessment," from the series, Crime and Justice, Vol. 1, *The Criminal in Society*, L. Radzinowicz and M. E. Wolfgang (eds.), New York, Basic Books, 1977, pp. 188–218; and J. M. Hagedorn and P. Macon, *People and Folks: Gangs, Crime and the Underclass in a Rustbelt City*, Chicago, Lake View Press, 1988.

p. 96. Gangs satisfy normal adolescent needs . . . but violent gangs are not normal: See discussion of peers in P. Blos's essay and in other essays in *Twelve to Sixteen*, J. Kagan and R. Coles (eds.), New York, Norton, 1972; Erik Erikson, "Youth: Fidelity and Diversity." For a discussion of the roles of economic, social and family dislocation in the formation of gangs, see M.

Morash's "Gangs and Violence," a review paper presented at a National Research Council Symposium on the Understanding and Control of Violent Behavior, April 5, 1989. For a copy of her paper, contact M. Morash at The School of Criminal Justice, Michigan State University, East Lansing, Mich.

pp. 97–98. "What differentiates pro-social groups from anti-social ones is violence:" M. Morash, "Gangs and Violence," a review paper commissioned by the National Research Council Symposium on the Understanding and Control of Violent Behavior for its April 1990 symposium on the Control and Understanding of Violence (For a copy of the paper, contact Dr. Morash at the School of Criminal Justice, Michigan State University, East Lansing, Michigan); C. S. Taylor, *Dangerous Society*, East Lansing, Michigan State University Press, 1990; and D. Gelman, "Going Wilding in the City: The Power of the Group Can Lead Teens to Mayhem," *Newsweek*, May 8, 1989.

p. 98. History of youth gangs in the U.S.: Walter B. Miller, "American Youth Gangs: A Reassessment," from the series, Crime and Justice, Vol. 1, *The Criminal in Society*, L. Radzinowicz and M. E. Wolfgang (eds.), New York, Basic Books, 1977, pp. 188–218; and J. M. Hagedorn and P. Macon, *People and Folks: Gangs, Crime and the Underclass in a Rustbelt City*, Chicago, Lake View Press, 1988.

pp. 98–99. "In recent decades, gangs have come to be associated with the entrenched poverty of inner city neighborhoods:" J. M. Hagedorn and P. Macon; J. W. Moore, "Isolation and Stigmatization in the Development of an Underclass: The Case of Chicano Gangs in East Los Angeles, *Social Problems*, 1985, Vol. 30, pp. 1–30; M. Morash, "Gangs and Violence;" C. S. Taylor, *Dangerous Society*, East Lansing, Michigan State Universtiy Press, 1990; I. Spergel, Principal Investigator, *Survey of Youth Gang Problems and Program in 45 Cities and 6 Sites*, The University of Chicago School of Social Service Administration in cooperation with the Office of Juvenile Justice and Delinquency Prevention, U.S. Department of Justice, May, 1990; R. Reinhold, "In the Middle of L.A.'s Gang Warfare," *The New York Times Magazine*, May 22, 1989; and S. Mydans, "Life in Girls Gangs: Colors and Bloody Noses," *The New York Times*, Jan. 29, 1990.

p. 99. Most gang members do not sell drugs: M. Morash, "Gangs and Violence;" and I. Spergel, Principal Investigator, *Survey of Youth Gang Problems and Program in 45 Cities and 6 Sites*, The University of Chicago School of Social Service Administration in cooperation with the Office of Juvenile Justice and Delinquency Prevention, U.S. Department of Justice, May, 1990.

pp. 99–101. Carl Taylor's description of three kinds of gangs—scavenger gangs, fighting or territorial gangs and corporate gangs: C. S. Taylor, *Dangerous Society*, East Lansing, Michigan State University Press, 1990.

p. 99. Taylor quote describing appearance of members at a Detroit rock concert: C. S. Taylor, *Dangerous Society*, pp. 27–28.

pp. 101–103. T. Williams, *The Cocaine Kids*, Reading, Masschusetts, Addison Wesley Publishing Company, 1989.

p. 103. In general, territorial gangs tend to remain territorial, not evolving into corporate gangs: C. S. Taylor, *Dangerous Society;* T. Williams, *The Cocaine Kids;* and M. Morash, "Gangs and Violence."

p. 103. "Some police officers and many reporters erroneously convey the idea that the members of territorial gangs are all on their way to becoming millionaires selling crack and other drugs:" M. Morash, "Gangs and Violence;" and H. L. Marsh, "Newspaper Crime Coverage in the U.S.: 1893–1988," *Criminal Justice Abstracts*, 1989, Vol. 21, pp. 506–514.

p. 103. Walter B. Miller, "American Youth Gangs: A Reassessment," from the series, Crime and Justice, Vol. 1, *The Criminal in Society*, L. Radzinowicz and M. E. Wolfgang (eds.), New York, Basic Books, 1977, pp. 188–218.

p. 103. "It does appear the rate of gang violence has increased:" M. Morash, "Gangs and Violence." I. Spergel, Principal Investigator, *Survey of Youth Gang Problems and Programs in 45 Cities and 6 Sites*.

pp. 104–105. Description of L. A. Gang Scene: J. W. Moore, R. Garcia, L. Cerda and F. Valencia, *Homeboys: Gangs, Drugs and Prison in the Barrios of Los Angeles*, 1978, Philadelphia, Temple University Press; J. W. Moore, "Isolation and Stigmatization in the Development of an Underclass; The Case of Chicano Gangs in East Los Angeles," *Social Problems*, 1985, Vol. 30, pp. 1–30; R. Reinhold, "In the Middle of L.A.'s Gang Warfare," *The New York Times Magazine*, May 22, 1989; and Transcript, *Gangs, Cops and Drugs*, an NBC News Special hosted by Tom Brokaw, August 15 and 16, 1989. For statistics on L.A. gang/drug scene, see: T. Morganthau, "The Drug Gangs," *Newsweek* cover story, Mar. 28, 1988: "Kids Who Sell Crack," *Time* cover story, May 8, 1988. Transcript, *Gangs, Cops and Drugs*, an NBC News Special, hosted by Tom Brokaw, August 15 and 16, 1989.

p. 105. Attitudes of Philadelphia gang members to violence: M. Morash, "Gangs and Violence;" and B. Krisberg, "Themes of Violence and Gang Youth," *Annales Internationales de Criminologie*, 1980, Vol. 18, pp. 9–18.

p. 106. Quote from Los Angeles school teacher, Pat Rice: *Gangs, Cops and Drugs*, an NBC News Special hosted by Tom Brokaw, August 15 and 16, 1989.

p. 106. Quote from Sneaky: R. Reinhold, "In the Middle of L.A.'s Gang Warfare," *The New York Times Magazine*, May 22, 1989.

p. 106. "They just want people to know their name:" P. Wen, "Boston Gangs: A Hard World," *The Boston Globe*, May 10, 1988.

p. 107. "Kids like to have their name in the paper:" P. Wen, "Boston Gangs: A Hard World." *The Boston Globe*, May 10, 1988.

p. 107. Young gang member describes himself as "public enemy number one:" "Life and Death with the Gangs," *Time*, Aug. 24, 1987.

p. 108. "Gang ideology defines a man as someone who is loyal to his friends and ruthless to his enemies:" M. Morash, "Gangs and Violence;" B. Krisberg, "Themes of Violence and Gang Youth," *Annales Internationales de Criminologie*, 1980, Vol. 18, pp. 9–18; P. Wen, "Boston Gangs: A Hard World," *The Boston Globe*, May 10, 1988; and L. Bing, "When You're a Crip (or a Blood)," *Harpers*, March 1989.

p. 109. Gangs relate to Kohlberg's stages of moral development: J. Reimer, D. P. Paolitto, R. Hersh, *Promoting Moral Growth from Piaget to Kohlberg*, second edition, New York, Longman, 1983.

p. 109. 14-year old gang member comments on drive-by shooting: "Child Warriors," *Time* cover story, July 11, 1990.

p. 109. The role of fighting in the lives of young gang members: M. Morash, "Gangs and Violence."

p. 109. Prison as a "ritual sacrifice," gang members seek out: J. M. Hagedorn and P. Macon, *People and Folks: Gangs, Crime and the Underclass in a Rustbelt City*, Chicago, Lake View Press, 1988.

pp. 109–110. The necessity of respect being shown: "In New York the member of one drug gang was shot to death after he refused to 'give five' to a rival:" J. C. McKinley, "Teenage Snub Ends in Killing of Youth," *The New York*

Times, Jan. 10, 1989; and "If you don't show 'em 'spect they get it by shooting or stabbing:" S. Jacobs and K. Cullen, "Gang Rivalry on the Rise in Boston," *The Boston Globe*, April 26, 1989.

p. 110. Glamorization of death: L. Bing, "When You're a Crip (or a Blood)," *Harpers*, March 1989.

p. 110. "Youth workers say when the patina of presumed immortality begins to wear off, young people can best be lured out of their gangs:" R. Reinhold, "In the Middle of L.A.'s Gang Warfare," *The New York Times Magazine*, May 22, 1989.

Chapter 8

p. 111. K. Sack, "The Short Life of 'Little Man': A Drug Dealer's Grim Legacy," *The New York Times*, Nov. 29, 1989.

pp. 112–113. Information about the life of Preston Simmons: K. Sack, "The Short Life of 'Little Man': A drug Dealer's Grim Legacy."

p. 113. "Neighborhood is a compelling element in the drug story:" R. J. Sampson, "Urban Black Violence: The Effect of Male Joblessness and Family Disruption," *American Journal of Sociology*, Vol. 93, No. 2, Sept. 1987, pp. 348–382.

p. 113. "As many die from heroin overdoses as cocaine:" Data from the Drug Abuse Warning Network, U.S. Department of Health and Human Services, Public Health Service. Alcohol, Drug Abuse, and Mental Health Administration. National Institute of Drug Abuse, Statistical Series, Semi-annual Reports, Trend Data, Series G, Nos. 22 & 23, 1988.

p. 114. Cocaine-based drugs were the drugs of choice of the 1980s: T. Williams, *The Cocaine Kids*, Reading, Massachusetts, Addision Wesley Publishing Company, 1989; M. Marriot, "After 3 Years, Crack Plague in N.Y. Only Gets Worse," *The New York Times*, Feb. 20, 1989; G. Kolata, "In Cities, Poor Families are Dying of Crack," *The New York Times*, Aug. 11, 1989; T. Morganthau, "The Crack Children," *Newsweek* cover story, Feb. 12, 1990; P. Bourgois, "Just Another Night on Crack Street," *The New York Times Magazine*, Nov. 12, 1989; and W. Finnegan, "A Street Kid in the Drug Trade," *The New Yorker*, Sept. 10 & 17, 1990.

p. 114. Heroin and other drugs make a comeback: "The Drug Gangs," *Newsweek* cover story, Mar. 28, 1988.

p. 114. Marketing history of crack cocaine: T. Williams, *The Cocaine Kids*.

p. 114. Why kids experiment with drugs: R. Jessor and S. L. Jessor, *Problem Behavior and Psychosocial Development: A Longitudinal Study of Youth*, New York: Academic Press, 1977.

p. 114. "Crack is a non-sexist addiction:" G. Kolata, "In Cities, Poor Families are Dying of Crack," *The New York Times*, Aug. 11, 1989; and S. Chira, "When Drugs and Despair View with 3R's," *The New York Times*, Nov. 15, 1989.

p. 115. Research of Dr. Jack Henningfield indicating that "one in six who try crack will become addicted:" G. Kolata, "Experts Finding a New Hope on Treating Crack Addicts," *The New York Times*, Aug. 24, 1989.

p. 115. "The taste for crack swept through urban neighborhoods in the 1980s:" M. Marriot, "After 3 Years, Crack Plague in N.Y. only Gets Worse," *The New York Times*, Feb. 20, 1989.

p. 115. "Crack put millions of children at risk for neglect and abuse:" G. Kolata, "In Cities, Poor Families are Dying of Crack," *The New York Times*, Aug. 11, 1989; J. Hart, "Child Abuse Found Tied to Drug Use," *The Boston Globe*, June 2, 1989; "Children of the Underclass," *Newsweek* cover story, Sept.

11, 1989; and S. Chira, "When Drugs and Despair View with 3R's," *The New York Times*, Nov. 15, 1989.

p. 115. "Kids use crack and kids sell crack:" "Kids Who Sell Crack," *Time* cover story, May 9, 1988; "Children of the Underclass," *Newsweek*. G. Kolata, "In Cities, Poor Families are Dying of Crack," *The New York Times*; T. Williams, *The Cocaine Kids*; and W. Finnegan, "A Street Kid in the Drug Trade," *The New Yorker*, Sept. 10 & 17, 1990.

p. 115. For an explanation of the "Rockefeller Laws," see: McKinney's 1973 Session Laws of New York, 196th session, vol. 1, ch. 276, vol. 2, ch. 1051.

p. 116. For descriptions of the jobs children do selling drugs, see: "Kids Who Sell Crack," *Time* cover story, May 9, 1988; "Children of the Underclass," *Newsweek*; G. Kolata, "In Cities, Poor Families are Dying of Crack," *The New York Times*; "The Drug Gangs," *Newsweek* cover story, Mar. 28, 1988; and K. Sack, "The Short Life of 'Little Man': A Drug Dealer's Grim Legacy," *The New York Times*, Nov. 11, 1989.

p. 116. D. Ribadneiro, "Eight Year old Busted," *The Boston Globe*, May 10, 1988.

p. 116. Kids impressed with drug dealers' wealth: A. F. Brunswick, "Young Black Males and Substance Use," from the book, *Young, Black and Male in America*, J. T. Gibbs (ed.), Dover, Massachusetts, Auburn House Publishing, 1988, p. 168; R. J. Reed, "Education and Achievement of Young Black Males," from same book, pp. 90–91; and W. Finnegan, "A Street Kid in the Drug Trade," *The New Yorker*, Sept. 10 & 17, 1990.

p. 116. "At the bottom of the drug trade, users and dealers are more or less interchangeable:" T. Mieczkowski, "Understanding Life in the Crack Culture," National Institute of Justice, Research in Action, Nov./Dec. 1989; and T. Williams, *The Cocaine Kids*.

p. 117. Quote from U.S. Attorney Roy Hayes on teenagers dominating crack market: "Kids Who Sell Crack," *Time* cover story, May 9, 1988.

p. 117. Drug distributors like to use adolescents because teens are willing to take chances: "Kids Who Sell Crack," *Time*.

p. 117. "In recent years many teenage drug dealers have begun to do business . . . outside their own states:" J. Kifner, "As Crack Moves Inland," *The New York Times*, Aug. 29, 1989.

p. 117. "On the West coast, many of the gang members colonizing new drug markets are associated with the Crips and Bloods:" W. Robinson, "Armed, Sophisticated and Violent, Two Drug Gangs Blanket Nation," *The New York Times*, Nov. 25, 1988.

p. 118. Statistics on percent of homicide victims found to have residues of drugs in their bodies: This data was gathered by the authors in telephone interviews with the medical examiners of Washington, D.C.; Wayne County, Michigan (Detroit); and New York City, New York.

p. 118. The correlation between cocaine and violence: L. Grinspoon and J. Bakalar, *Cocaine: A Drug and Its Social Evolution*, Basic Books, 1976; L. Grinspoon, Senior Psychiatrist, Mass. Mental Hospital and Associate Professor of Psychiatry, Harvard Medical School, interview with author, April 4, 1990; and R. Weiss, Clinical Director, Alcohol and Drug Abuse Program, McLean Hospital and Assistant Professor, Harvard Medical School, interview with author, April 6, 1990.

pp. 119–120. Drug violence is different from other violence discussed in this book: P. Bourgois, "Just Another Night on Crack Street," *The New York Times Magazine*, Nov. 12, 1989; L. Dash, "A Dealer's Creed: Be Willing to Die," *The Washington Post*, April 3, 1989; and L. Dash, interview with author, June 27, 1990.

p. 121. "Adolescent gunmen have itchier trigger fingers:" "Kids Who Sell Cocaine," *Time* cover story, May 8, 1988.

p. 121. The comments of "George," on how carrying a gun changes you: P. Wen, "Boston Gangs: A Hard World," *The Boston Globe*, May 10, 1988.

p. 122. Long Beach incident in which a black off-duty police officer from a nearby community was beaten and allegedly thrown through a plate glass window: Details of the allegations against Long Beach police officers were confirmed during a phone interview with author by a spokesperson in the office of the Long Beach police chief.

p. 122. "On both coasts, residents of the black community are beginning to speak out about the violent interaction between young males of color and . . . armed officers . . .": S. Monroe, "Complaints About a Crackdown," *Time*, July 16, 1990; P. Canellos, "From here to LA, Search Policies Stir Debate," *The Boston Globe*, Jan. 15, 1990; and P. Canellos, "Youth Decry Search Tactics," *The Boston Globe*, Jan. 14, 1990.

pp. 122–123. Philadelphia's "Operation Cold Turkey:" P. Canellos, "From here to LA, Search Policies Stir Debate."

p. 123. In Los Angeles civilian suits against police have skyrocketed: S. Monore, "Complaints About a Crackdown."

p. 123. Mexican-American gang members from Aliso-Pico district of L.A. describe their interactions with the LAPD: E. Shorris, "Sanctuary for L.A. Homeboys," *The Nation*, Dec. 18, 1989.

p. 124. P. Bourgois, "Just Another Night on Crack Street."

pp. 124–125. "There are invisible injuries sustained in 'the drug war' by poor families:" G. Kolata, "In Cities, Poor Families are Dying from Crack," *The New York Times*, Aug. 11, 1989.

p. 125. Drug money shifts power in poor families from parents to children: G. Kolata, "In Cities, Poor Families are Dying from Crack;" "Kids Who Sell Crack," *Time*; and D. Johnson, "Teenagers Who Refuse to Join Drug Dealers," *The New York Times*, Jan. 4, 1989.

p. 126. Skyrocketing incidence of abuse and neglect connected to crack: J. Hart, "Child Abuse Found tied to Drug Use," *The Boston Globe*, June 2, 1989; and L. Matchan, "Child Abuse Reports up 17% in 1990," *The Boston Globe*, Feb. 17, 1991.

p. 126. "One national study estimated that 375,000 babies a year are exposed to alcohol and illicit drugs while in utero:" "The Crack Children," *Newsweek*, Feb. 12, 1990.

pp. 126–127. Study comparing drug use of black and white pregnant women in Pinellas County, Florida: I. J. Chasnoff, H. J. Landress, M. E. Barrett, "The Prevalence of Illicit-Drug or Alcohol Use During Pregnancy and Discrepancies in Mandatory Reporting in Pinellas County, Florida," *New England Journal of Medicine*, Vol. 322, No. 17, April 26, 1990, p. 1202.

p. 127. Description of children born addicted to crack: "The Crack Children," *Newsweek;* S. Blakeslee, "Parents Fight for a Future for Infants Born to Drugs," *The New York Times*, May 19, 1990; S. Chira, "Crack Babies Turn 5, and Schools Brace," *The New York Times*, May 25, 1990; and J. Hoffman, "Pregnant, Addicted—and Guilty?," *The New York Times Magazine*, Aug. 19, 1990.

p. 127. Former Chief of New York City's 500-agent office of the DEA calls for more treatment services for addicts: P. Kerr, "Retiring Agents Sharply Attack Drug Policies," *The New York Times*, Mar. 1, 1990.

pp. 128–129. Treatment for crack addicts: G. Kolata, "Experts Finding New

Hope on treating Crack Addicts," *The New York Times,* Aug. 24, 1989; M. Marriot, "For Addicts, A Long Scary Wait for Treatment," *The New York Times,* Jan. 10, 1989; and A. Malcolm, "Affluent Addict's Road Back," *The New York Times,* Oct. 2, 1989.

p. 128. "Drug Money: Not What It's Cracked Up to Be:" T. Williams, *The Cocaine Kids;* and G. Kolta, "Despite Its Promises of Riches, The Crack Trade Seldom Pays," *The New York Times,* Nov. 26, 1989.

Chapter 9

p. 135. "Antibiotics, inoculations, and other advances in modern medicine had wiped out infectious diseases as the primary threat to health in this country.:" M. L. Rosenberg, E. Stark, and M. Zahn, "Interpersonal Violence: Homicide and Spouse Abuse," chapter from *Maxcy-Rosenau Public Health and Preventive Medicine,* 12th edition, John M. Last (ed.), Appleton-Century-Crofts, Norwalk, Conn. 1986; M. L. Rosenberg, R. Gelles, P. Holinger, M. A. Zahn, E. Stark, J. M. Conn, N. N. Fajman, T. A. Karlson, "Violence: Homicide, Assault, and Suicide," Division of Injury Epidemiology and Control, Center for Environmental Health and Injury Control, Centers for Disease Control, Atlanta, pp. 164–178.

pp. 135–136. ". . . Injury, not illness was the most significant threat to the health of young Americans in the latter half of the century.:" M. L. Rosenberg and J. A. Mercy, "Homicide: Epidemiological Analysis at the National Level," *Bulletin of the New York Academy of Medicine,* second series, Vol. 62, No. 5, June, 1986, pp. 376–399; R. Blum, "Contemporary Threats to Adolescent Health in the United States," *Journal of the American Medical Association,* Vol. 257, No. 24, June 26, 1987; and "Homicide, Suicide, Other Violence Gain Increasing Medical Attention," *Journal of the American Medical Association,* Vol. 254, No. 6, Aug. 9, 1985.

p. 136. "Suicide, accidents and homicides have much in common.:" J. T. Gibbs, "The New Morbidity: Homicide, Suicide, Accidents and Life-Threatening Behavior," from the book *Young, Black Male in America,* J. T. Gibbs (ed.), Dover, Ma., Auburn House, 1988, p. 270.

p. 136. "The Surgeon General . . . published his first national agenda for health promotion.:" "Healthy People—The Surgeon General's Report on Health Promotion and Disease Prevention," Background Papers: U.S. Dept. of Health, Education and Welfare, Publication No. 79-55071A, 1979.

p. 137. The CDC grouped assault and homicide along with other "intentional" injuries: M. L. Rosenberg, R. Gelles, P. Holinger, M. A. Zahn, E. Stark, J. M. Conn, N. N. Fajman, T. A. Karlson, "Violence: Homicide, Assault, and Suicide;" M. L. Rosenberg, E. Stark, and M. Zahn, "Interpersonal Violence: Homicide and Spouse Abuse."

p. 137. The first symposium exploring homicide among black males was called "Homicide Among Black Males," and was sponsored by The Alcohol, Drug Abuse and Mental Health Administration on May 13th–14th, 1980. Proceeds were published in *Public Health Reports,* Nov.–Dec. 1980, Vol. 95, No. 6, pp. 549–561.

p. 137. Every fight has a history: M. L. Rosenberg, E. Stark, and M. Zahn, "Interpersonal Violence: Homicide and Spouse Abuse."

p. 138. For information about the Surgeon General Conference on Violence as a Public Health Problem, see: *Report on The Surgeon General's Workshop on Violence,* Washington, D.C.: Health Resources and Services Administration

(HRSA), U.S. Public Health Service, U.S. Department of Health and Human Services (DHHS Publication No. HRS-D-MC 86-1), May 1986.

pp. 138–139. For a description of the four stages in which the public health mission is carried out, see: J. A. Mercy and P. W. O'Carroll, "New Directions in Violence Prediction: The Public Health Arena," from the book *Violence and Victims*, Vol. 3, No. 4, Springer Publishing, 1988.

p. 140. For a description of primary, secondary and tertiary preventions, see: M. Moore, B. Guyer and D. Prothrow-Stith, "Violence and Intentional Injuries: Criminal Justice and Public Health Perspectives on an Urgent National Problem." This paper was commissioned by the National Research Council for its April 1990 symposium. "Understanding and Control of Violent Behavior." Publication is expected in late 1991 or 1992. For a copy of the paper, contact: Mark Moore, Kennedy School of Government, Harvard University.

p. 143. For information about The Harvard Alcohol Project's Designated Driver Campaign, see the March 1990 *Status Report*, compiled by the Center for Health Communication, Harvard School of Public Health.

Chapter 10

p. 145. "Violence is a problem that begins at home.:" There are hundreds of sources to support this assertion. Among the most cogent are: G. R. Patterson, D. DeBaryshe, and E. Ramsey, "A Developmental Perspective on Antisocial Behavior," *American Psychologist*, Vol. 44, No. 2, Feb. 1989, pp. 329–335; J. Q. Wilson, "Raising Kids," *The Atlantic Monthly*, Oct. 1983, pp. 45–56. J. Q. Wilson and R. Herrnstein, *Crime and Human Nature*, Simon & Schuster, 1985; L. D. Eron, "Prescription for Reduction of Aggression," *American Psychologist*, Vol. 35, No. 3, Mar. 1980, pp. 244–252; R. J. Gelles and M. A. Straus, *Intimate Violence*, Simon & Schuster, 1988; and A. Vachss, "Today's Abused Child Could Be Tomorrow's Predator," *Parade*, June 3, 1990.

p. 146. "A child is not a machine.:" For an eloquent exploration of what children need from their parents and care-givers, see: L. Schorr, *Within Our Reach*, Doubleday, 1988.

p. 146. "Someone who is crazy about the kid." This statement, made by Professor Urie Bronfenbrenner, is quoted by L. Schorr in *Within Our Reach*, p. 146.

pp. 147–152. "Even love is not enough." Throughout this discussion of raising normal kids we have drawn heavily on the two-volume parenting guide written by G. R. Patterson and M. Forgatch: *Parents and Adolescents Living Together*. Part One, published in 1987, is called *The Basics*. Part Two, published in 1989, is called *Family Problem Solving*. To order these invaluable books, write to Castalia Publishing Company, P.O. Box 1587, Eugene, Oregon, 97440. Well-written and easy to read, these volumes provide parents with the distilled wisdom of Patterson and Forgatch and the hundreds of other researchers and clinicians at the Oregon Social Learning Center.

p. 147. For an exploration of Social Learning Theory, see: R. M. Liebert and J. N. Sprafkin, *The Early Window: Effects of Television on Children and Youth*, third edition, New York, Pergamon Press, 1988, pp. 65–73.

p. 150. C. Brown, *Manchild in the Promised Land*, Macmillan, 1969, p. 279.

p. 151. In addition to Patterson and Forgatch, see these other sources for discussions of spanking: R. J. Gelles and M. N. Straus, *Intimate Violence*, New York, Simon & Schuster, 1988; R. G. Slaby and W. C. Roedell, "The Development and Regulation of Aggression in Young Children," *Psychological Development in the Elementary Years*, J. Worell, (ed.), Academic Press, Inc., 1982;

and L. Kutner, "Dealing with the Impulse to Spank," *The New York Times*, June 21, 1990.

p. 151. For more information on "learned helplessness," see: L. Abramson, J. Garber and M. E. F. Seligman, "Learned Helplessness in Humans: An Attributional Analysis," in the book *Human Helplessness Theory and Applications*, J. Garber and M. E. F. Seligman (eds.), New York, Academic Press, 1980.

p. 152. Lisbeth Schorr, *Within Our Reach*, New York, Doubleday, 1988, p. 149.

p. 152. Aggressive children are made, not born: D. Olweus,"Stability of Aggressive Reaction Patterns in Males: A Review." *Psychological Bulletin*, Vol. 86, No. 4, 1979, pp. 852–875; G. R. Patterson, D. DeBaryshe, and E. Ramsey, "A Developmental Perspective on Antisocial Behavior," *American Psychologist*, Vol. 44, No. 2, Feb. 1989, pp. 329–335; J. Q. Wilson, "Raising Kids," *The Atlantic Monthly*, Oct. 1983, pp. 45–56; L. D. Eron, "Prescription for Reduction of Aggression," *American Psychologist*, Vol. 35, No. 3, Mar. 1980, pp. 244–252; L.D. Eron, "Parent-Child Interaction, Television Violence, and Aggression of Children," *American Psychologist*, Vol. 37, No. 2, pp. 197–211; and R. J. Gelles and M. A. Straus, *Intimate Violence*, Simon & Schuster, 1988.

p. 153. "One recently published study of 1,000 young males in Sweden . . .:" D. Goleman, "Taming Unruly Boys: Old Techniques and New Approaches," *The New York Times*, Feb. 1, 1990.

p. 153. "There is a clear, undisputed correlation between child abuse and aggression.:" R. J. Gelles and M. N. Straus, *Intimate Violence*, New York, Simon & Schuster, 1988; R. G. Slaby and W. C. Roedell, "The Development and Regulation of Aggression in Young Children," *Psychological Development in the Elementary Years*, J. Worell, (ed.), Academic Press, Inc., 1982; and J. Rabkin, "Epidemiology of Adolescent Violence: Risk Factors, Career Patterns and Intervention Programs," Paper Delivered at the Conference on Adolescent Violence: Research & Public Policy, Arden House, Feb. 5–7, 1987, Columbia University, NYS Psychiatric Institute.

p. 153. For data on the high rate of severe abuse among the most violent members of society, see: D. O. Lewis, M. Feldman, and A. Barrengos, "Violent Juvenile Delinquents: Psychiatric, Neurological, Psychological and Abuse Factors," *Journal of the American Academy of Child Psychiatry*, Vol. 18, 1979, pp. 307–319; D. O. Lewis and S. Shanok, "Medical Histories of Delinquent and Non-Delinquent Children: An Epidemiological Study, *American Journal of Psychiatry*, Vol. 134, No. 9, 1977, pp. 1020–1025; and A. Bass, "Head Injuries Found in Young Killers," *The Boston Globe*, June 20, 1988.

p. 154. "Over 25 studies have associated parental punitiveness with excessive displays of aggression in children.:" Slaby and Roedell, pp. 106–197.

p. 154. "There is a similarity between the parenting practices of abusive parents and those of the parents of anti-social children . . .:" K. A. Kavanagh, L. Youngblade, J. B. Reid, B. I. Fagot, "Interactions Between Children and Abusive Versus Control Parents, *Journal of Clincial Child Psychology*, Vol. 17, No. 2, 1988, pp. 137–142.

p. 154. For a clear and thorough explanation of "coercive family process," see: G. R. Patterson, D. DeBaryshe, and E. Ramsey, "A Developmental Perspective on Antisocial Behavior. *American Psychologist*, Vol. 44, No. 2, Feb. 1989, pp. 329–335; and K. A. Kavanagh, L. Youngblade, J. B. Reid, B. I. Fagot, "Interactions Between Children and Abusive Versus Control Parents."

p. 154. Negative attention can reinforce negative behavior: Slaby and Roedell, p. 128.

p. 155. Chart Illustrating the Development of Aggressive Behavior: G. R. Patterson, D. DeBaryshe, and E. Ramsey, "A Developmental Perspective on

Antisocial Behavior," *American Psychologist*, Vol. 44, No. 2, Feb. 1989, p. 331.

p. 156. "The behavior of aggressive, anti-social children can be improved . . . by their own parents.:" L. Bank, G. R. Patterson, and J. B. Reid, "Delinquency Prevention Through Training Parents in Family Management," *The Behavior Analyst*, Vol. 10, 1987, pp. 75–82; and A. E. Kazdin, "Treatment of Antisocial Behavior in Children: Current Status and Future Directions," *Psychological Bulletin*, Vol. 102, No. 2, 1987, pp. 187–203.

p. 157. ". . . Parent Training ought to be a mandatory course . . .:" R. J. Gelles and M. N. Straus, *Intimate Violence*, New York, Simon & Schuster, 1988, p. 199.

p. 158. "Father Hunger:" J. Herzog, "On Father Hunger: The Father's Role in the Modulation of Aggressive Drive and Fantasy," from the book *Father & Child: A Developmental Perspective*, S. H. Cath, A. R. Gurwitt, and J. M. Ross, New York, Basil Blackwell, 1982.

pp. 158–59. "The socialization of boys jeopardized when fathers are missing.:" J. Wallerstein and J. B. Kelly, "The Father–Child Relationship: Changes After Divorce," from *Father & Child: A Developmental Perspective*, pp. 454–455.

p. 159. Studies of empathy highlight importance of son-father relationship: D. Goleman, "Studies of Development of Empathy Challenge Some Old Assumptions," *The New York Times*, July 12, 1990.

pp. 159–160. "Second Chance Kids,:" E. E. Werner and R. S. Smith, *Kauai's Children Come of Age*, Honolulu, University Press of Hawaii, 1977; *Vulnerable but Invincible: A Longitudinal Study of Resilient Children and Youth*, New York, McGraw-Hill, 1982; and A. Bass, "Kids Can Beat the Odds," *The Boston Globe*. This is a lengthy article about Werner's latest findings—that by age 30 many of her troubled subjects had been able to create decent lives for themselves with the help of mentors and other "second chance opportunities."

p. 160. Half a million teens are runaways and "throwaways.:" J. C. Bardin, "Toll of Troubled Families: Flood of Homeless Youths," *The New York Times*, Feb. 5, 1990.

Chapter 11

p. 162. "Circumstances that promote learning, promote . . . survival,:" R. Ferguson, "The Case for Community Based Programs that Inform and Mentor Black Male Youth," an Urban Institute Research Paper, Distributed by the Urban Institute, Washington, D.C.; and R. J. Reed, "Education and Achievement of Young Black Males," from the book, *Young, Black Male in America*, J. T. Gibbs (ed.), Dover, Ma., Auburn House, 1988, pp. 37–96.

p. 162. Excerpt quoted is taken from a column by Derrick Jackson that appeared in the *Boston Globe*, Oct. 7, 1990.

p. 163. "Milwaukee school board has agreed to open two experimental schools . . .:" B. Kantrowitz, "Can the Boys Be Saved?," *Newsweek*, Oct. 15, 1990; and D. Johnson, "Milwaukee Creating 2 Schools Just for Black Boys," *The New York Times*, Sept. 30, 1990.

p. 163. "The ones who fail and dropout are the ones who are dying . . .:" R. J. Reed, "Education and Achievement of Young Black Males."

p. 163. Black males perform more poorly in school than any other group: R. J. Reed, "Education and Achievement of Young Black Males;" J. K. Bloom, "Fewer Black Men Attend College," *The Boston Globe*, Oct. 1, 1990; L. A. Daniels, "Tests Show Reading and Writing Lag Continues," *The New York Times*, Jan. 10, 1990; C. Black, "America's Lost Generation," *The Boston Globe*,

Mar, 1990; and G. I. Maeroff, "Withered Hopes, Stillborn Dreams: The Dismal Panorama of Urban Schools, *Phi Delta Kappan*, May 1988.

p. 163. School drop-out rates for black males: E. Bowen, "Getting Tough," *Time*, cover story, Feb. 2, 1988; and M. deCoury Hinds, "Cutting the Dropout Rate: High Goal But Low Hopes," *The New York Times*, Feb. 17, 1990.

p. 163. More young black males in prison than in college: C. Black, "America's Lost Generation," *The Boston Gloibe*, Mar. 4, 1990.

p. 163. Data on college attendance: M. Marriot, "Intense College Recruitment Drives Lift Black Enrollment to a Record," *The New York Times*, April 15, 1990.

pp. 163–164. David Evans talks about the "vanishing black male" on college campuses: J. K. Bloom, "Fewer Black Men Attend College," *The Boston Globe*, Oct. 1, 1990.

p. 164. "Of the students labeled behavior disordered, 73 percent are young black males." R. J. Reed, "Education and Achievement of Young Black Males."

p. 164. Suspension rates are highest for young black males: R. J. Reed, "Education and Achievement of Young Black Males."

p. 164. Drop-out data: E. Bowen, "Getting Tough," *Time* cover story, Feb. 2, 1988.

pp. 164–165. Expectations shape school performance: J. Howard and R. Hammond, "Rumors of Inferiority: Barriers to Black Success in America," *The New Republic*, Sept. 9, 1985.

p. 165. Description of study in which 66 student teachers were told to teach a math concept to pupils, black and white: R. Ferguson, "The Case for Community Based Programs that Inform and Mentor Black Male Youth," an Urban Institute Research Paper, Distributed by the Urban Institute, Washington, D.C., p. 14.

p. 165. Comments by Jeffrey Howard were made during the week-long Efficacy Institute seminar attended by Michaele Weissman. Also see the lengthy article on Dr. Howard and his work by C. Robb, "Teaching the basics of Motivation," *The Boston Globe*, Oct. 12, 1989.

pp. 165–166. More information about Kunjufu's study can be found in: K. Kunjufu, *Countering the Conspiracy to Destroy Black Boys*, Chicago, Afro-American Publishing Company, 1983.

p. 166. Comments of Dr. James Comer: W. Finnegan, "A Street Kid in the Drug Trade," *The New Yorker*, Sept. 17, 1990, pp. 64–66.

p. 166. "Violent attacks are common in many urban schools:" G. I. Maeroff, "Withered Hopes, Stillborn Dreams: The Dismal Panorama of Urban Schools," *Phi Delta Kappan*, May, 1988; S. Lyall, A Losing Fight on Violence in the Schools, *The New York Times*, Feb. 27, 1989; and S. Mydans, "On Guard Against Gangs at a Los Angeles School," *The New York Times*, Jan. 19, 1989.

p. 166. "Drug dealing may surround a school or even enter it:" R. Louv, "Hope in Hell's Classroom," *The New York Times Magazine*, Nov. 25, 1990.

p. 167. Mr. Holland's remarks were made to the author during a visit to the Jeremiah E. Burke School in October, 1989.

pp. 167–168. What research shows about successful schools. J. Q Wilson and R. Herrnstein, *Crime and Human Nature*. Simon & Schuster, 1985, pp. 281–282.

p. 168. For information about Joe Clark, principal of Eastside High School in Paterson, N.J., see: E. Bowen, "Getting Tough," *Time* cover story, Feb. 2, 1988.

p. 168. For information on metal detectors in schools, see: L. Jennings, "In an Era of Weapons, Districts Fighting Metal with Metal," *Education Week*, Mar. 16, 1988; and M. Marriot, "Detection Methods Raise Issue of Student Rights," *The New York Times*, Jan. 10, 1990.

pp. 168–169. Description of Jaime Escalante's teaching methods: E. Bowen, "Getting Tough," *Time* cover story, Feb. 2, 1988.

p. 169. For more about the work of Reginald Clark, see: R. Clark, *Family Life and School Achievement: Why Poor Black Children Succeed or Fail*, Chicago, The University of Chicago Press, 1983.

pp. 169–172. Information on the work of the *Efficacy Institute* was gathered by Michaele Weissman during the week-long Efficacy Institute seminar she attended in the fall of 1989. Those interested in obtaining more information can write: Efficacy Institute, 99 Hayden Avenue, Lexington, Ma. 02173. Also see the article on Dr. Howard and his work by C. Robb, "Teaching the basics of Motivation," *The Boston Globe*, Oct. 12, 1989.

pp. 170–171. For a deeper understanding of how erroneous assumptions about academic capability can damage a child's school performance, see: C. S. Dweck and B. G. Light, "Learned Helplessness and Intellectual Achievement," in the book *Human Helplessness Theory and Applications*, J. Garber and M. E. F. Seligman (eds.), New York, Academic Press, 1980.

p. 172. For more on "acting white," see: S. Fordham and J. U. Ogubu, "Black Students School Success: Coping with the Burden of 'Acting White,' " *The Urban Review*, Vol. 18, 1986, pp. 176–206.

p. 173. Children do not intuitively understand that there are win/win ways to resolve disputes: See the granddaddy of conflict resolution manuals: R. Fisher and W. Ury, *Getting to Yes: Negotiating Agreement Without Giving In*, Penguin Books, 1983.

p. 173. "Conflict Resolution programs share certain ideas:" N. Meredith, Conflict Resolution, *Parenting*, Aug. 1987; M. Roberts, "School Yard Menace," *Psychology Today*, Feb. 1988; A. Kohn, "P is for Pro-Social Teaching, *The Boston Globe Magazine*, Nov. 6, 1988; D. Olweus, "Schoolyard bullying—Grounds for Intervention," *School Safety*, Fall, 1987; and R. L. Selman and M. Glidden, "Negotiation Strategies for Youth, *School Safety*, Fall, 1987.

pp. 173–176. The "Peacemaker" and Conflict Resolution programs described in these pages were observed by Michaele Weissman during a visit in May 1989. For more information on these programs, contact Linda Lantieri, coordinator of Resolving Conflict Creatively, 163 Third Avenue, #239, New York, New York 10003. Phone: (212) 260-6290. You may also write to Educators for Social Responsibility, 23 Garden Street, Cambridge, Ma. 02138 or Educators for Social Responsibility, 490 Riverside Drive, Room 27, New York, NY. 10027.

p. 174. Children who assert themselves verbally are less likely to be victims or victimizers: R. G. Slaby and W. C. Roedell, "The Development and Regulation of Aggression in Young Children," *Psychological Development in the Elementary Years*, J. Worell, editor, Academic Press, Inc., 1982, p. 133.

pp. 177–183. Material presented in this section is based on: D. Prothrow-Stith, *Violence Prevention Curriculum for Adolescents*, published by Education Development Center, Inc., 55 Chapel Street, Newton, Ma. 02160.

p. 182. For more information on Peter Stringham's clinical violence prevention work, see: P. Stringham and M. Weitzman, "Violence Counseling in the Routine Health Care of Adolescents," *Journal of Adolescent Health Care*, Vol. 9, 1988, pp. 389–393.

Chapter 12

p. 185. "No single form of intervention . . . can bring about the kind of change needed to restore . . . safety and order:" L. Schorr, *Within Our Reach*, Doubleday, 1988.

p. 186. D. Prothrow-Stith, *Violence Prevention Curriculum for Adolescents*, published by Education Development Center, Inc., 55 Chapel Street, Newton, Ma. 02160.

p. 186. For information about the violence prevention work done by the Health Promotion Project, see: H. Spivak, D. Prothrow-Stith, A. Hausman, "Dying Is No Accident: Adolescents, Violence and Intentional Injury," *The Pediatric Clinics of North America*, Vol. 35, No. 6, Dec. 1988.

p. 191. For more information on Peter Stringham's clinical violence prevention work, see: P. Stringham and M. Weitzman, "Violence Counseling in the Routine Health Care of Adolescents," *Journal of Adolescent Health Care*, Vol. 9, 1988, pp. 389–393.

p. 192. Information about the coalition for Violence Prevention was gathered in a phone interview with Suzanne Hicks in Dec. 1990. For more information about the Coalition, contact New Futures for Little Rock, 209 West Capital, Little Rock, Arkansas, 72201. Phone: (501) 374-1011.

pp. 194–197. Community Policing: M. K. Sparrow, M. H. Moore, D. M. Kennedy, *Beyond 911; A New Era for Policing*, New York, Basic Books, 1990; B. Turque, "A New Line Against Crime," *Newsweek*, Aug. 27, 1990; G. L. Kelling, R. Wasserman and H. Williams, "Police Accountability and Community Policing," *Perspectives on Policing*, a publication of the National Institute of Justice, U.S. Department of Justice and the Program in Criminal Justice Policy and Management, John F. Kennedy School of Government, Harvard University, No. 7, Nov. 1988; M. H. Moore and R.C. Trojanowicz, "Policing and the Fear of Crime," *Perspectives on Policing*, a publication of the National Institute of Justice, U.S. Department of Justice and the Program in Criminal Justice Policy and Management, John F. Kennedy School of Government, Harvard University, No. 3, June, 1988; L. W. Sherman, "Patrols are Better Than Arrests," *The New York Times*, Sept. 22, 1990; T. A. Reppetto, "Put the Cop Back on the Beat," *The New York Times*, Sept. 22, 1990; and N. Meredith, "Attacking the Roots of Police Violence," *Psychology Today*, May, 1984.

p. 198. Being realistic about gun control: M. H. Moore, "The Bird in Hand: A Feasible Strategy for Gun Control," *Journal of Policy Analysis and Management*, Vol. 2, No. 2, 1983, pp. 185–195.

p. 198. The "Brady" bill requiring a 7-day waiting period before purchasing a handgun, see: W. King, "Sarah and James Brady Target: The Gun Lobby," *The New York Times Magazine*, Dec. 9, 1990, p. 42.

pp. 198–199. Information on the Wintemute/Teret initiative against gun manufacturers gathered during a phone interview with Stephen Teret in Dec. 1990.

pp. 199–201. "Creating A Comprehensive Family Policy," see: "A Vision for America's Future: An Agenda for the 1990's," Children's Defense Fund, Washington, D.C., 1989; and L. Schorr, *Within Our Reach*, Doubleday, 1988.

pp. 202–203. Clementine Barfield and SOSAD: Interview with Clementine Barfield conducted by author in Dec. 1990. SOSAD can be contacted at 453 Martin Luther King Blvd., Detroit, Mi. 48201. Telephone: (313) 833-3030.

APPENDIX I

THE IDEAL RELATIONSHIP BETWEEN PUBLIC HEALTH AND CRIMINAL JUSTICE IN PREVENTING VIOLENCE

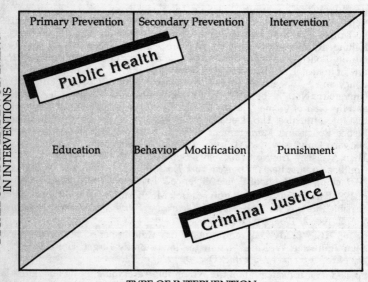

TYPE OF INTERVENTION

APPENDIX II

STATE-BY-STATE
ORGANIZATIONS

ALABAMA

Alethea House
P.O. Box 1514
Birmingham, AL 35201
(205) 324-6502

CONTACT: Chris Retan, Director

SERVES: Adult and Youth

STRATEGIES: The Alethea House has a 36-bed inpatient treatment program
providing services to addicted pregnant women. There is also an
outpatient program for pregnant women, women and their children, and a battered women treatment program. They also provide evening services. There is also an African-American family
strengthening service and a neighborhood prevention plan. The
Alethea house serves at-risk youth.

ARKANSAS

Tongass Community Counseling Center
222 Seward Street, #202
Vuneau, AK 99801
(907) 586-3585

CONTACT: Susan Chapman, MA, Clinical Director

SERVES: Domestic violence and sexual abuse perpetrators, adult and adolescent

STRATEGIES: Youth anger management program uses psycho-social education
on male roles, skill building on communication and conflict res-

olution issues, cognitive-behavioral approaches to behavior management, and a fundamental "empowerment" model as an alternative to violence.

CALIFORNIA

Alternatives to Violence
Alternatives Counseling Associates
3817 Atlantic Avenue, Suite 202
Long Beach, CA 90807
(213) 493-1161

CONTACT: Alyce LaViolette, Jean Fromm

SERVES: Victims and perpetrators of spouse abuse and other forms of family violence, rape and incest victims

STRATEGIES: Groups for batterers are unstructured, non time-limited, utilizing cognitive and behavioral strategies, education and investigation of sex roles, empathy training, anger management and so on. Individual counselling for survivors utilizing principles of feminist therapy, assertiveness, anger work, resource building, etc.

Center Against Abusive Behavior
131 N. El Molino
Suite 380
Pasadena, CA 91101
(818) 796-7358

CONTACT: L. John Key, Ph.d.

SERVES: San Gabriel Valley, East San Fernando Valley, Portions of Central and South Central Los Angeles

STRATEGIES: The bio-psycho-social approach in treating both the victims and the perpetrators of intra-family violence. They take a biological, psychological and sociological approach offering a multidimensional program of analysis and treatment.

Come Together Youth Workshops
9150 E Imperial Highway
Downey, CA 90242
(213) 940-2694

CONTACT: Mike Duran

SERVES: Teenagers

STRATEGIES: Adults from different human services fields come together with youth (male and female ages 14–17). The come-togethers are for three days or for one day. Three-day ones are held in the country.

The program includes large doses of human relationships, self-awareness, and self esteem building confrontations with self, recreation, and youth problems. One-day come-togethers are held in places such as TV studios. Breakfast is served as part of the program, as is lunch. Speakers make current events presentations; youth are involved in all sessions.

The Community Board Program, Inc.
149 Ninth Street
San Francisco, CA 94103
(415) 552-1250

CONTACT: Terry Amsler, Executive Director
Jim Halligan, Managing Trainer

SERVES: San Francisco neighborhoods, schools, and school districts nationwide; state and county agencies; juvenile rehabilitation centers and homes throughout the state of California.

STRATEGIES: Mediation and conciliation; prevention of violence through education and communication strategies at the elementary school level and throughout high school; working with referrals from Department of Social Services, et al.

Elementary School Conflict Managers Program
School Initiatives Program
Community Board Center for Policy and Training
149 9th Street
San Francisco, CA 94103

SERVES: Teachers and children

STRATEGIES: Five-day curriculum, using techniques of role-play and classroom discussion to teach conflict resolution and communication skills.

The HAWK Federation Manhood Development and Training Program
The Institute for the Advanced Study of Black Family Life and Culture Inc.
155 Filbert Street, Suite 202
Oakland, CA 94607
(415) 836-3245

CONTACT: William Cavil, Project Director

SERVES: African American males

STRATEGIES: Begun in 1987 with state department of education funds, this intervention works to affect the values, moral character, and positive development of young African American males so they may become "competent, confident, and conscious African American men." HAWK is an acronym for high achievement, wisdom, and knowledge.

International Association for the Study of Cooperation in Education
(ASCE)
Box 1582
Santa Cruz, CA 95061-1582
(408) 426-7926

CONTACT: Drs. Nan and Ted Graves, Executive Editors

SERVES: Teachers, administrators, staff developers and researchers

STRATEGIES: Cooperative small group learning strategies in the classroom and
in school governance. Includes: conflict resolution, problem solving strategies, and development of interpersonal skills while pursuing academic goals.

Learning the Skills of Peacemaking
45 Hitching Post Drive
Building 2
Rolling Hills Estates, CA 90274-4297
(213) 547-1240

CONTACT: Jalmar Press

SERVES: Teachers and children in elementary school

STRATEGIES: Series of 56 lessons, using playacting, creative writing, music,
and classroom discussion to teach communication skills, conflict
resolution skills, and understanding and accepting of cultural
differences.

National School Safety Center
Pepperdine University
16830 Ventura Boulevard
Suite 200
Encino, CA 91436
(818) 377-6200

CONTACT: Dr. Ronald D. Stephens

SERVES: Educators, law enforcers, and juvenile service professionals

STRATEGIES: Provides training and technical assistance in the area of school
crime prevention. In addition, NSSC publishes educational resources and produces training films in the areas of gangs, weapons in school, schoolyard bully prevention, crisis management
and safe school planning. The center serves as a national clearinghouse for school safety programs.

PACT (Policy Action Collaboration and Training) for Alternatives to
Violence and Abuse, Contra Costa County Health Services Department
(415) 646-6511

CONTACT: Larry Cohen or Pam Satterwhite

SERVES: Adolescents, parents, paraprofessionals and professionals in community colleges

STRATEGIES: To reach as many people as possible, the project has developed a community college training program for use in this and other educational settings; published a newsletter, and conducted a broad-based media campaign that includes, radio, television, and newspapers, to build a climate that supports violence prevention.

The Paramount Plan: Alternatives to Gang Membership
16400 Colorado Avenue
Paramount, CA 90723-2121
(213) 220-2121

CONTACT: Tony Ostos, Neighborhood Counselling Manager

SERVES: Hispanic youth and parents

STRATEGIES: Work with pre-teen youth and their parents via gang awareness classes in the school system and community meetings to prevent youth from joining gangs. Anti-gang individual family counselling is also offered. A fifth grade anti-gang/gang awareness curriculum has been developed, a second grade anti-gang/gang awareness curriculum is being piloted. Written curriculum and most media materials are culturally appropriate.

School Initiatives Program
Community Board Center for Policy Training
149 Ninth Street
San Francisco, CA 94103
(415) 552-1250

CONTACT: James Halligan, Managing Trainer

SERVES: Elementary and secondary school educators

STRATEGIES: In 1977, the Community Board Program in San Francisco began training community residents to help their neighbors resolve a range of disputes peacefully. Building on that work, the organization developed the School Initiatives Program in 1982 as a response to growing conflicts and violence in schools. The intervention consists of a conflict managers program and classroom curricula that prepare elementary and secondary school educators to plan, implement, and maintain school-based, student-to-student conflict resolution programs.

Senior Tutors for Youth
3640 Grand Avenue
Oakland, CA 94610
(415) 839-1039

CONTACT: Dr. Sondra M. Napell, Director/President

SERVES: Delinquent boys ages 13–18 sentenced by the juvenile court; adolescent boys and girls at a residential group treatment center for drug and alcohol abusers; 8th graders with below-normal basic skills (inner-city)

STRATEGIES: Utilizing elderly volunteers from a nearby retirement community. The Senior Tutors pair one-on-one for periods of 1–9 months. The pairs "bond" and discuss academic, social, emotional, vocational, and personal problems. The Senior Tutors undergo 1 hour of training (at which time listening skills, non-judgmental behaviors, and cultural differences are discussed and learned) in workshops prior to each week's tutoring session.

Stay on the Safe Side
Governor's Youth Crime Prevention Program
Center for Law-Related Education
4400 Cathedral Oaks Road
Santa Barbara, CA 03169-6370

SERVES: Teachers and children in grades K–4

STRATEGIES: Reduce victimization by increasing student knowledge of crime prevention and by encouraging positive attitudes toward law, rules, citizenship, and respect for self and others.

Youth and Family Services Bureau
Hayward Police Department
300 W. Winton Avenue
Hayward, CA 94544
(415) 293-7048

CONTACT: Art Elliott, Director

SERVES: All ages—City of Hayward; abusing and drug oriented families

STRATEGIES: Diversion programs for youth, petty theft, drugs, status offenses coordinated with gang suppression team and crime prevention.

COLORADO

Rocky Mountain Center for Health Promotion and Education
7500 West Mississippi Avenue, #230
Lakewood, CO 80226
(303) 934-1814

CONTACT: Mary A. Doyen, Executive Director
Bob Bongiovanni, Associate Director

SERVES: Public and private schools throughout Colorado and the U.S.

STRATEGIES: Promotion of comprehensive school health education, including the Teenage Health Teaching Modules, for grades 7–12. This includes the Violence Prevention Module. The agency provides workshop training for classroom teachers, along with ongoing technical assistance.

CONNECTICUT

Always on Saturday
Hartford Action Plan on Infant Health, Inc.
30 Arbor Street
Hartford, CT 06106
(203) 236-4872

CONTACT: Carolyn Delgado/Amos L. Smith

SERVES: Boys, ages 9–14 and 14–18

STRATEGIES: Weekly 2-hour small group sessions which include group activities with a focus on the development of each individual's social, emotional, and physical attributes. In addition to the adult group leader, male volunteers serve as adult advisors. There is a concerted commitment to broadening social exposure through field trips and other activities. One of the main goals of the program is the prevention of adolescent fatherhood.

DISTRICT OF COLUMBIA

Center to Prevent Handgun Violence
1225 Eye Street, NW
Suite 1100
Washington, DC 20005
(202) 289-7319

CONTACT: Barbara Lautman, Executive Director
N.T. Pete Shields, Chairman

SERVES: Students, teachers, school administrators, parents, law enforcement officers, health care providers, community organizations

STRATEGIES: Develops and implements handgun violence prevention with education programs (pre-K–12 grade curriculum), teacher training.

Institute for Mental Health Initiatives
Channeling Children's Anger
4545 42nd Street, NW
Suite 311
Washington, DC 20016
(202) 364-7111

CONTACT: Suzanne Stutman, MA, MSW, BCD, Executive Director

SERVES: Youth

STRATEGIES: Teaching anger-management skills, offering videotapes and a pamphlet on anger management skills to teens and their parents. Offered to individuals, schools, and communities nationwide.

Male Youth Health Enhancement Project
1510 9th Street, NW
Washington, DC 20001
(202) 332-0213

CONTACT: Andre Watson, Director

SERVES: Young males

STRATEGIES: Assisting young males in their transition from boyhood to manhood by providing activities stimulating their physical, emotional, and spiritual development.

Milton S. Eisenhower Foundation
Suite 504
1725 I Street, NW
Washington, DC 20006
(202) 429-0440

CONTACT: Lynn A. Curtis, President

SERVES: Youth and their families

STRATEGIES: The Eisenhower Foundation is a private sector recreation of the National Commission on the Causes and Prevention of Violence . . . a catalyst for youth self-help programs that strengthen families, reduce school dropouts, facilitate employment and economically develop neighborhoods . . . a sponsor of international exchanges, policy analysis and issue forums.

National Crime Prevention Council
1700 K Street, NW
Second Floor
Washington, DC 20006
(202) 466-6272

CONTACT: John Calhoun, Executive Director

SERVES: Youth, ages 10–20

STRATEGIES: Curriculum which attempts to reduce teen victimization; a project addressing social issues from child and drug abuse to literacy, teen pregnancy, and Teens as Resources Against Drugs and Students Mobilized Against Drugs: creates videos, skits, rallies, poster contests, etc.

Project Spirit
The Congress of National Black Churches, Inc.
600 New Hampshire Avenue, NW
Suite 650
Washington, DC 20037-2403
(202) 333-3060

CONTACT: Vanella Crawford, Director

SERVES: African-American pastors, parents and children

STRATEGIES: After-school tutoring and living-skills enhancement, parent education, and pastoral counseling training

FLORIDA

The Grace Contrino Abrams Peace Education Foundation, Inc.
3550 Biscayne Boulevard
Suite 400
Miami, FL 33137-3854
(305) 576-5075
(800) 749-8838

CONTACT: Warren S. Hoskins, Executive Director

SERVES: Preschool through middle school students

STRATEGIES: Creating text and student workbooks and audio/visual materials
for conflict resolution and peace education in schools and youth
intervention groups. Training of teachers and youth-related persons in skills for teaching conflict resolution and mediation to
children and youth.

Fighting Fair
Grace Contrino Abrams Peace Education Foundation, Inc.
P.O. Box 19-1153
Miami Beach, FL 33119

SERVES: Teachers and children in elementary school

STRATEGIES: Six classroom lessons using classroom discussion videos, art-
work, and rap music to focus on issues of cooperation, communication, social problem solving, empathy, behavioral intent, and
respect for self and others.

GEORGIA

New Way of Fighting
Department of Human Resources
Division of Public Health
878 Peachtree Street, NE
Atlanta, GA 30309
(404) 894-6617

CONTACT: Ronnie S. Jenkins, M.S.

SERVES: Minority youth

STRATEGIES: School-based conflict resolution education and violence prevention activities including a student sponsored "STOP THE VIOLENCE" campaign.

Wholistic Stress Control Institute
Project Stress Control
3480 Greenbriar Parkway
Suite 230
P.O. Box 42481
Atlanta, GA 30331
(404) 344-2021

CONTACT: Jennie Cook-Troffer, M.Ed., Executive Director

SERVES: African-Americans, whites, Hispanics, and Asians

STRATEGIES: Stress control curriculum for pre-school, K–5, and 6–12 educational materials. Videos, tapes, posters, puppets, songs, materials also available for adults. All materials include lessons on positive ways to reduce anger. Program models have won exemplary awards in prevention, mental health, juvenile delinquency prevention and substance abuse prevention.

HAWAII

Hawaii Mediation Program
University of Hawaii at Manoa
West Hall Annex 2, Room 222
1776 University Avenue
Honolulu, HI 96822

CONTACT: Mel Ezer, Director

SERVES: Students

STRATEGIES: Student Mediators are chosen by the entire school population (i.e. students, administrative and teaching staff, and support staff) which is asked to name three people they consider to be leaders. The final group chosen from those nominated who agree to participate is culturally diverse and equally divided between males and females. Intensive two-day trainings are then conducted in which trainees rotate between role-playing situations as mediators and disputants.

ILLINOIS

B.U.I.L.D., Inc.
(Broader Urban Involvement and Leadership Development)
1223 N. Milwaukee
Chicago, IL 60622
(312) 227-2880

CONTACT: Mr. Daniel W. Swope/Mr. David J. Yancy

SERVES: Youth ages 10–21

STRATEGIES: Prevention program taught in elementary schools; remediation programs where outreach is done on the streets with gangs and delinquent youth.

Chicago Intervention Network
510 North Peshtigo Court, 5B
Chicago, IL 60611
(312) 744-1820

CONTACT: Ronald W. Alston/Lillie Hudson

SERVES: Elementary schools, grades 4–8

STRATEGIES: Promoting positive awareness through the implementation of youth programs relating to self-esteem, gang and drug awareness. Providing positive role models via CIN in orchestrating a truth to life and its windfalls.

Chicago Police Department
Gang Crime Section
1121 S. State Street
Chicago, IL 60605
(312) 744-6328

CONTACT: Commander Sollie W. Vincent

SERVES: City of Chicago

STRATEGIES: Investigation and suppression of street gangs prone to violence through arrest, confiscation of their weaponry, and prosecution. Acts as a resource to other government agencies, private organizations, and community groups responding to the problem via the provision of data, education, and personnel coordination.

Project Image
765 E. 69th Place
Chicago, IL 60637
(312) 324-8700

CONTACT: Bob Warner, Executive Director

SERVES: African American males

STRATEGIES: This intervention is designed to strengthen the image, role, and presence, of African American males in the community through ecumenical, community-based programs which provide positive African American role models.

Project Peace
Chicago Housing Authority
Department of Resident Organizations and Youth Services
534 E. 37th Street
First Floor
Chicago, IL 60653
(312) 791-4768 (ext. 30)

CONTACT: R. Olomenji, Project Facilitator

SERVES: African American Youth

STRATEGIES: Project Peace is an educational intervention designed to deal with violence and conflict within the schools. The project uses a mentoring role-model component, an education component using the Violence Prevention Curriculum for Adolescents, and an intervention for young people at risk.

Viewpoints
University of Illinois
Department of Psychology
Chicago, IL
(312) 413-2626

CONTACT: Nancy Guerra

SERVES: Adolescents

STRATEGIES: Cognitive-behavioral (social problem solving)

Youth Development Project
Tri-City Mental Health
3901 Indianapolis Boulevard
East Chicago, IL 46312
(219) 398-7050

CONTACT: Carl Weissbradley
Sandy Appleby

SERVES: At-risk youth

STRATEGIES: The model is based on two projects that have successfully brought together a mental health center, recreation center, Hispanic community center, and city-sponsored community center to provide programming five days a week for high risk youth. Prevention strategies include drug and alcohol education, self-esteem-promoting activities, ALATEEN meetings, recreational programs, job-serve activities, tutoring, conflict resolution sessions, and cross-cultural specific events.

INDIANA

Victim Assistance
Fort Wayne Police Department
City County Building
One Main Street
Fort Wayne, IN 46802
(219) 427-1205

CONTACT: Patricia Smallwood

SERVES: Fort Wayne and Allen County—All crime victims—primary and secondary

STRATEGIES: We provide information, guidance, and emotional support for individuals and families victimized by crime. Direct services include crisis intervention, advocacy within the criminal justice system, and other follow-up services. We also provide community education concerning victimization issues, training for associated groups and agencies, and advocacy efforts for system changes.

KANSAS

Building Conflict Solving Skills for Adolescents
Kansas Child Abuse Prevention Council
715 West 10th Street
Topeka, Kansas, 66612
(913) 354-7738

CONTACT: Jenith Hoover

SERVES: 10–16 year old students

STRATEGIES: An eight-lesson curriculum is taught to students which highlights non-violent problem solving in interpersonal conflicts.

STOP Violence Coalition
8340 Mission Road, #205
Shawnee Mission, KS 66206

SERVES: Inmates and their families

STRATEGIES: *Reaching Out From Within* is a source book created by inmates to reduce the violence in their lives and the lives of others. This curriculum is the result of an inmate self-help group in a Kansas Co-correctional facility.

MARYLAND

Community Relations Service
U.S. Department of Justice
5550 Friendship Boulevard
Suite 330
Chevy Chase, MD 20815
(301) 492-5948

CONTACT: Daryl Borgquist, Media Affairs Officer
Gail Padgett, Associate Director, Office of Technical Assistance and Support

SERVES: Disputes involving race, color, and national origin

STRATEGIES: The community relations services conciliates and mediates racial disputes resulting from biases based on race, color and national origin. Racial incidents may be reported and services requested through CRS' tollfree hotline (1-800-347-HATE).

Educational Services for Children and Adolescents
The Hayward Pratt National Center for Human Development
6501 N. Charles Street, P.O. Box 5503
Baltimore, MD 21285-5503
(301) 938-3929
(301) 938-3908

CONTACT: Careen Mayer, Program Director

SERVES: Teachers, students and parents

STRATEGIES: "In Tune with Teens," a parent's guide; STAR—long-term intensive training for teachers dealing with at-risk students; LIVING SMART—programs about alcohol and drugs, primarily using theater—also programs about dealing with change and stress; "NO HANG UPS" adolescent educational phone-in audio tape library; CONFLICT MANAGEMENT AND MEDIATION— programs for training elementary and middle school students to mediate conflicts, primarily on the playgrounds.

Project 2000
Morgan State University
School of Education in Urban Studies
322 Jenkins Hall
Baltimore, MD 21239
(301) 444-3275

CONTACT: Dr. Spencer Holland, Founder

SERVES: African American boys in the first grade

STRATEGIES: Although project 2000 was designed to be an academic development program, practical considerations of the school and community environment, such as concerns about violence, resulted in its offering students training in such areas as conflict resolution.

MASSACHUSETTS

Agape
650 Greenwich Road
Ware, MA 01082
(413) 967-9369

CONTACT: Suzanne Belote Shanley

SERVES: Mostly Catholic schools from grades 4–12; college, teachers

STRATEGIES: Teaching non-violence from a gospel perspective, including examination of violence within (self-esteem issues); violence without (family, neighborhood, cultural; i.e. media), with scripturally-centered tools for non-violence conflict resolution.

Barron Assessment and Counseling Center
Parkman School Building
25 Walk Hill Street
Jamaica Plain, MA 02130
(617) 524-0176 or (617) 522-3841

CONTACT: Franklin A. Tucker, Director
Raffael DeGruttola, Assistant Program Director

SERVES: Elementary, middle, and high school students found in possession of a weapon in school; students exhibiting aberrant behavior and viewed as a safety concern

STRATEGIES: A non-punitive placement to meet and address the non-educational and emotional needs of students found in possession of a weapon in school or are exhibiting aberrant behavior in school.

Boston Conflict Resolution Program
Boston Area Educators for Social Responsibility
11 Garden Street
Cambridge, MA 02138
(617) 492-8820

CONTACT: William Kreidler

SERVES: Children age 12 or under

STRATEGIES: Teacher training and support; workshops for children addressing issues of prejudice, competition, communication, empathy, co-operation, and expression of emotion.

Child Assault Prevention Project
MASS/CAPP
Judge Baker Children's Center
295 Longwood Avenue
Boston, MA 02115

CONTACT: Starr Potts or Debbie Lewis

SERVES: Parents, teachers, and children preschool through grade 12

STRATEGIES: Parent programs, teacher and staff in-service training, classroom workshops for children that cover topics of assertiveness, peer support, and skills for telling trusted adults about assault experiences.

Community Youth Services for Elementary and Middle School Children
Camille O. Cosby Center
Judge Baker Children's Center
295 Longwood Avenue
Boston, MA 02115
(617) 232-8390 x 2200

CONTACT: Dr. Gloria Johnson-Powell

SERVES: Elementary and middle school children with a focus on girls

STRATEGIES: Recreational and educational services are provided along with early detection and intervention with violence. Prevention of the involvement of girls in gangs is the major focus.

Dating Violence Intervention Project
P.O. Box Harvard Square Station
Cambridge, MA 02238
(617) 868-8328

CONTACT: Carole Sousa/David Adams

SERVES: Teens

STRATEGIES: Providing preventative education to teens on dating violence and to empower youth to work on the issue of ending teen dating violence. Training people who work with youth and the above.

East Boston Neighborhood Health Center
10 Grove Street
East Boston, MA 02128
(617) 569-5800

CONTACT: Peter Stringham, M.D.

SERVES: Residents of East Boston and neighboring communities

STRATEGIES: Teaching non-violent, warm parenting; teaching pre-adolescents how to get out of fights; teaching adolescents the reasons others want to fight and concrete strategies for avoiding violence.

Educators for Social Responsibility Conflict Resolution Programs
23 Garden Street
Cambridge, MA 02138
(617) 492-1764

CONTACT: Larry Dieringer, Associate Director

SERVES: Teachers, school administrators, guidance counselors, social workers, and parents

STRATEGIES: ESR offers programs for elementary, middle and high schools. Services offered: staff development workshops, curriculum and other instructional resources including videotapes and implementation guides, training for implementation of peer mediation programs, teacher leadership development programs, consultation with school program coordinators about program implementation, follow-up programs that can include teaching demonstration lessons, observing classes and providing feedback to teachers, and facilitating discussions with participating teachers. Our programs will help teachers and students improve their understanding and skills in specific areas including: conflict resolution, violence prevention, prejudice reduction, communication, emotional expression and multicultural awareness.

EMERGE: A Men's Counseling Service on Domestic Violence
18 Hurley Street
Suite 23
Cambridge, MA 02141
(617) 547-9870

CONTACT: David Adams

SERVES: Men ages 18+ who have physically assaulted their wives or girlfriends

STRATEGIES: Group counseling, community education, preventive education.

Facing History and Ourselves National Foundation, Inc.
25 Kennard Road
Brookline, MA 02146
(617) 232-1595

CONTACT: Margot Stern Strom/Marc Skvirsky

SERVES: Educators, Jr. high, and high school students, university and community

STRATEGIES: Facing History is moral education. The target is hatred, prejudice, racism and indifference. The strategy is to reach young people with instruction in the history of the Nazi Holocaust and the Armenian Genocide as examples of what happens when morality breaks down. The plan is to reach our children's teachers who, with special training and innovative resources, can bring students through the understanding of terrible historical events to form the basis for maturity, marked by the practice of good citizenship. Facing history provides training for teachers, clergy, and other adult leaders.

The Good Grief Program
Judge Baker Children's Center
295 Longwood Avenue
Boston, MA 02115
(617) 232-8390

SERVES: Teachers, administrators, group leaders, and parents; children who have experienced the death of a friend

STRATEGIES: Crisis intervention for children experiencing grief and loss, inservice training and support for adult target population, maintenance of a resource library, and consultation services for schools and community groups.

Harvard Injury Control Center
Harvard School of Public Health
677 Huntington Avenue
Boston, MA 02115
(617) 432-1090

CONTACT: John Graham, Director

SERVES: Youth and the elderly

STRATEGIES: The Harvard Injury Control Center supports scientific research and training to improve injury control. A primary Center goal is to reduce the burden of trauma on the two most vulnerable populations: youth and the elderly. The Center promotes injury control through research proposals, internships, curriculum development, doctoral dissertation support and post-doctoral fellowships.

Harvard Negotiation Project
Building Bridges
Harvard Law School
Pound Hall, Room 513
Cambridge, MA 02138
(617) 495-1684

CONTACT: Professor Roger Fisher, Director
Douglas Stone, Manager of the High School Negotiations Project
Gail Jacobson, Project Administrator

SERVES: High school students, teachers both nationally and internationally

STRATEGIES: Building Bridges is a peer-taught curriculum for high school students on effective methods for handling conflict in their own lives, and a framework for the peaceful resolution of social and international conflict. Building Bridges' curriculum, geared both toward inner-city and suburban schools, is being developed by Harvard Law School and the Harvard Negotiations Project.

The Medical Foundation Prevention Center
Violence Prevention Project
95 Berkeley Street
Boston, MA 02116
(617) 451-0049

CONTACT: Paul Bracy, Violence Prevention Coordinator

SERVES: Youth and families

STRATEGIES: Training and education; coalition building. Peer leadership preventing violence is a youth leadership training and outreach program which provides youth involvement in prevention efforts in schools and community agencies. Training is available for professionals who are interested in developing violence prevention programs. Coalition building for community responses to violence prevention is an ongoing activity of the center.

My Family and Me: Violence Free
School Consultation and Treatment Program
Massachusetts Department of Mental Health
Boston, MA

CONTACT: Barbara Bond and Melania Bruno

SERVES: Teachers and children in grades 4–6

STRATEGIES: Twelve-session curriculum designed to teach about conflict resolution skills, stress management, decision-making skills, sexism, peer relationships, and social problem-solving skills

National Association for Mediation in Education
425 Amity Street
Amherst, MA 01002
(413) 545-2462

CONTACT: Annette Townley
Rachel Goldberg

SERVES: Educators, professionals, students, and youth

STRATEGIES: Development, implementation, and institutionalization of school-
and university-based conflict resolution programs and curricula.
NAME is the primary national and international clearinghouse
for information, resources, technical assistance, and training.

National Institute Violence Prevention
One Cleveland Park
Roxbury, MA 02119
(617) 427-0692

CONTACT: Joanne Taupier
Howard Spivak

SERVES: Service providers for families and youth

STRATEGIES: Training providers in violence prevention strategies, techniques,
and program development.

Program on Human Development and Criminal Behavior
Harvard School of Public Health
677 Huntington Avenue
Boston, MA 02115
(617) 432-1080

CONTACT: Dr. Felton Earls, Director

SERVES: Urban youth, infants to age 21, in two American cities (so far not
selected, but should be selected by December 1991)

STRATEGIES: Preliminary research underway

Resource Center for the Prevention of Family Violence and Sexual Assault
Massachusetts Department of Public Health
150 Tremont Street
Boston, MA 02111-1125
(617) 727-7222

CONTACT: Helene Tomlinson

SERVES: Statewide—adults, adolescents, children

STRATEGIES: Community education

School Consultation and Treatment Program (SCAT)
20 Vining Street
Boston, MA 02115
(617) 734-1300 x170

CONTACT: Ann Greenbaum, Margaret Goodwin, Harriet Epstein

SERVES: Elementary and middle school students attending 5 Boston public
schools

STRATEGIES: Individual and group therapy, family treatment, teacher consultation, staff training. Our classroom prevention program involves classroom intervention in areas including violence prevention, child abuse prevention, conflict resolution, cooperative activities and effective education.

School Mediation Associates
72 Chester Road, #2
Belmont, MA 02178
(617) 876-6074

CONTACT: Richard Cohen, Director

SERVES: Young people ages 12 and up/adults

STRATEGIES: Training young people and adults to mediate interpersonal and intergroup conflicts among their peers. Work with schools and other systems to implement peer mediation programs.

Trauma Prevention Procedures and Support Systems
Boston Public Schools
26 Court Street
Boston, MA 02108
(617) 726-6200 x5903

CONTACT: Stanley Swartz, Director, Student Support Services

SERVES: Boston school students K–12

STRATEGIES: It is the policy of the Boston Public schools to provide a full array of services for students, through the utilization of both the internal and external support resources, in order to promote their social and emotional growth and wellbeing.

Violence is a Choice—Youth Outreach
South Shore Women's Center (SSWC)
14 Main Street
Plymouth, MA 02360
(508) 746-2664

CONTACT: Susan Edwards, Maria Moscaritolo

SERVES: Grades K–12, Plymouth County

STRATEGIES: Education—violence prevention curriculum for grades K–12. Counseling (individual and group) for teens in abusive relationships; special group for parenting teens in abusive relationships and just-beginning group for children (under 12) in violent homes.

Violence Prevention Curriculum Project Grades 10–12
Educational Development Center, Inc. (EDC)
55 Chapel Street
Newton, MA 02160
(617) 969-7100

CONTACT: Renee Wilson-Brewer, Project Director
William DeJong, Research Director

SERVES: High school students in grades 10–12, primarily urban students

STRATEGIES: Acknowledge that anger is a normal and natural emotion; provide students with hard-hitting facts about the real risk they face as either the victims or the perpetrators of violence; create in students a need to find alternatives to fighting by discussing gains and losses; analyze the precursors of a fight and, through role-playing, practice their own means of conflict resolution.

The Violence Prevention Project
1010 Massachusetts Avenue, 2nd Floor
Boston, MA 02118
(617) 534-5196

CONTACT: Linda Hudson, Director
Joanne Taupier, Project Coordinator

SERVES: Teachers, social service personnel, law enforcement officials, youth workers, public health and medical professionals

STRATEGIES: Training and technical assistance for professionals and organizations involved with youth. Development of public service advertisements and educational materials.

MICHIGAN

Center for Peace and Conflict Studies
Wayne State University
2319 Faculty Administration Building
656 W. Kirby Street
Detroit, MI 48202
(313) 577-3453, 577-3468

CONTACT: Dr. Frederic Pearson, Director
Elizabeth Sherman, Secretary

SERVES: Metro Detroit and Southeastern Michigan

STRATEGIES: Community diagnosis through mapping rates of violence for the city of Detroit. We also serve as a source of information for a variety of local groups and agencies, like the Wayne County Task Force on Violence Reduction.

Center for Prevention and Treatment of Psychological Trauma
Detroit Receiving Hospital and University Health Center
4201 St. Antoine
Detroit, MI 48201
(313) 745-4811

CONTACT: James F. Zender, Ph.D., Director

SERVES: Primarily 18 and older; 75% African American; 25% Caucasian

STRATEGIES: Hospital-based response center and community. Referrals from
              victim services; individual trauma-focused psychotherapy, com-
              munity crisis response team coalition: improve victim and psy-
              chological trauma services.

Institute-Trauma and Loss in Children (TLC)
New Center
2051 W. Grand Boulevard
Detroit, MI 48208
(313) 895-4000

CONTACT: Bill Steele, MA, MSW
             Roberta Sanders

SERVES: Core-city

STRATEGIES: Educational video programs designed for school use.

SOSAD
453 Martin Luther King Boulevard
Detroit, MI 48201
(313) 833-3030

CONTACT: Clementine Barfield

SERVES: Families and youth

STRATEGIES: Founded by a woman whose 16-year-old son was killed, SOSAD
             provides grief counseling for families; youth empowerment and
             development activities; as well as a 24-hour crisis hotline. SOSAD
             is not just an organization. It is a growing movement to stop the
             violence.

VIP (Violence is Preventable) Program
6000 John E. Hunter Drive
Detroit, MI 48210
(313) 935-1582
(313) 895-4800

CONTACT: Rev. Priscilla Carey Tucker

SERVES: Youth ages 8–20

STRATEGIES: Providing services to youths in trouble including: drug addicts, drug dealers, prostitutes, youths with criminal records, and the general population.

STRATEGIES: There is a course that runs for 6 weeks, approximately 4 hours per day, taught by Rev. Carey Tucker. This course is offered to public high schools and churches, and includes videos, written tapes, counseling, and field trips.

Wayne State University Center for Prevention and Control of
Interpersonal Violence
Wayne State University School of Medicine
540 E. Canfield Avenue
Detroit, MI 48201
(313) 577-6690

CONTACT: John B. Waller, Jr., Dr. P.H.

SERVES: Metropolitan Detroit

STRATEGIES: Community diagnosis and mapping

Where Have All The Children Gone?
New Center Community Mental Health Services
2051 West Grand Boulevard
Detroit, MI 48208
(313) 895-4000

CONTACT: Roberta V. Sanders, Director

SERVES: Students

STRATEGIES: Violence prevention training for classroom use that focuses on awareness of the problem of violence and problem-solving skills development, with an emphasis on cross-cultural issues. It consists of a 26-minute videotape, "Where Have All The Children Gone?" and a workbook with five 50-minute sessions.

MINNESOTA

Fighting Invisible Tigers
Free Spirit Publishing Co.
123 N Third Street, Suite 716
Minneapolis, MN 55401
(612) 338-2068

CONTACT: Connie Schmitz

SERVES: High school teachers and teenagers

STRATEGIES: Twelve-part curriculum for use by teachers, covering topics of stress management, communication, assertiveness training, peer relationships, and social support systems.

Skills for Violence-Free Relationships
Domestic Violence Prevention Curriculum
Minnesota Coalition for Battered Women
Physicians Plaza Building
570 Asbury, Suite 201
St. Paul, MN 55104
(612) 646-6177

CONTACT: Denise Gamachie

SERVES: Teachers and children in grades 4 through 6

STRATEGIES: Twelve-session curriculum designed to teach conflict-resolution skills, stress management, decision-making skills, sexism, peer relationships, and social problem-solving skills.

Wilder Child Guidance Clinic—North Suburban Branch
CLIMB Theatre
Wilder Clinic
2480 White Bear Avenue
Maplewood, MN 55109
CLIMB Theatre, 500 N. Robert St. #220, St. Paul, MN 55101
(612) 770-1222 (Wilder)
(612) 227-4660 (CLIMB)

CONTACT: Nancy Westrell—Wilder
Peg Wetli—CLIMB

SERVES: Children and their families, ages up to 17

STRATEGIES: Outpatient mental health (Wilder). Theatre for persons with disabilities and for addressing social issues.

MISSOURI

Kansas City Urban Interpersonal Violence Injury Control Project
Kansas City Department of Health
(816) 274-9100

CONTACT: Mary Weathers or Mark Mitchell

SERVES: Youth

STRATEGIES: The program includes conflict resolution, anger control, problem solving, and alternatives to violence, using role-playing and simulations, as well as discussions and written materials. There is also a witness hotline, a youth drug and violence hotline, and an anti-violence billboard, donated by a billboard company. A mass media public education effort, delivered via minority-oriented radio and television programs, and a speakers bureau contribute to building a climate that opposes violence and seeks other alternatives to resolving disputes.

Urban Interpersonal Violence Project
Sponsored by: The Ad Hoc Group Against Crime
2360 E. Linwood
Kansas City, MO 64109
(816) 861-9100

CONTACT: Mary Frances Weathers, Director
             John Samuels, Outreach Specialist

SERVES: African Americans, ages 14–39 who are at high risk of becoming victims or perpetrators of violent crimes or assaults. Metropolitan Kansas City Community.

STRATEGIES: Referrals are accepted from schools, youth serving agencies, police, the Juvenile Justice System, and courts. Intervention focuses on the conflict resolution training (analysis of problem situations, and decision making).

NEW HAMPSHIRE

Children at Risk
New Hampshire

SERVES: Parents identified as high-risk by local community agencies

STRATEGIES: Parent aides provide home visits, transportation, and telephone contact with high-risk parents to help with situational problems, increase parenting skills, and identify psychosocial problems.

NEW MEXICO

New Mexico Center for Dispute Resolution
510 Second Street, NW
Suite 209
Albuquerque, NM 87102
(505) 247-0571

CONTACT: Melinda Smith, Director
             Sarah Keeney, Director School Mediation

SERVES: Elementary, junior, and senior high school students in 10 northern and southern rural counties; families in conflict crisis, juvenile offenders and their victims (correctional staff), outreach programs, including Colorado and Texas

STRATEGIES: Child/parent mediation, services for runaways, restoring relationships between juvenile offenders and their victims, creating mediation programs and outreach programs, including help in developing programs for other communities.

Youth Development, Inc.
6301 Central N.W.
Albuquerque, NM 87105
(505) 831-6038

CONTACT: Augustine C. Baca, Executive Director

SERVES: Youth ages 6–26

STRATEGIES: Outreach counseling, scholarships, youth motivation projects, GED prep, AIDS training, stay in school project, youth employment system.

NEW YORK

Alternatives to Violence Project
15 Rutherford Place
New York, NY 10003
(212) 477-1067

CONTACT: Ms. Paddy Lane, State Administrator; Fred Feucht, President

SERVES: Prisons, community groups. AVP is beginning to experiment with programs for youth.

STRATEGIES: AVP presents 2½–3-day workshops which help participants learn creative and caring ways of dealing with conflict. The workshops build a sense of community and trust through exercises focusing on affirmation of self and others, communication skills, cooperations, and conflict resolution.

Boys and Girls Clubs of America
771 First Avenue
New York, NY 10017
(212) 351-5900

CONTACT: James Cox, Director of Urban Services
Roxanne Spillett, Director of Program Services

SERVES: 1.52 million youths in 1,200 local facilities nationwide with special emphasis on inner-city youth

STRATEGIES: Boys and Girls Clubs provide a safe, professionally-staffed environment where youths are involved in programs that promote healthy self-esteem, positive intra-group behavior, and positive problem solving.

Florence V. Burden Foundation
630 Fifth Avenue
Suite 2900
New York, NY 10111
(212) 332-1150

CONTACT: Barbara R. Greenburg, Executive Director

SERVES: Non-profit agencies and institutions

STRATEGIES: The Foundation is a private grantmaking foundation that funds research and demonstration programs in the field of crime and justice. The Foundation's priorities are twofold: programs that teach young children how to avoid violence and conflict with the law, and programs that strengthen and nurture relationships between children and their incarcerated mothers.

Children's Creative Response to Conflict
523 N. Broadway, Box 271
Nyack, NY 10960
(914) 358-4601

CONTACT: Priscilla Prutzman, Mitchell Clark

SERVES: Teachers, students, others who work with children

STRATEGIES: Cooperation, communication, affirmation, conflict resolution, mediation bias awareness.

Contemporary Issues
Girl Scouts of the U.S.A.
830 Third Avenue
New York, NY 10022
(212) 940-7500

SERVES: Girls aged 5–18

STRATEGIES: Age-appropriate activities designed to increase self-esteem and develop decision-making skills.

Grant Middle School Conflict Resolution Training
2400 Grant Boulevard
Syracuse, NY 13208
(315) 435-4433

CONTACT: Rudy Duncan, School Social Worker

SERVES: Public middle school students

STRATEGIES: In addition to teaching conflict resolution strategies, the school-developed curriculum deals with issues of self-esteem, ego, and cultural diversity.

Andrew Glover Youth Program, Inc.
Manhattan Criminal Court Building
100 Center Street, Room 1541
New York, NY 10013
(212) 349-6381

CONTACT: Angel Rodriquez, Executive Director

SERVES: At-risk teens to young adults from Manhattan's Lower East side

STRATEGIES: Counseling, intervention, court advocacy, and supervision services for non-advocacy clients; short-term legal service, literacy tutoring, homework help, work readiness, rap sessions.

New York City Department of Juvenile Justice
365 Broadway
New York, NY 10013
(212) 925-7779

CONTACT: Rose W. Washington, Commissioner

SERVES: Children ages 7–15

STRATEGIES: In detention, DJJ has implemented a case management system that assesses each child's needs and creates an individualized service plan. Education, medical care, mental health counseling, recreation and substance abuse prevention. The aftercare program links children with services mentioned above.

Resolving Conflict Creatively Program (RCCP)
163 Third Avenue, #239
New York, NY 10003
(212) 260-6290

CONTACT: Linda Lantieri, Coordinator; Tom Roderick, Executive Director

SERVES: Cross-section of New York City school children, pre-kindergarten through 12th grade, teachers and parents.

STRATEGIES: Classroom instruction in conflict resolution and intergroup relations, training for parents and teachers, peer mediation programs for students.

NORTH CAROLINA

Local Violence Prevention/Intervention
Mecklenburg County Health Department
2845 Beattis Ford Road
Charlotte, NC 28216
(704) 336-6443

CONTACT: Barbara Pellin

SERVES: School-based youth and their families

STRATEGIES: Training personnel and community human service providers to facilitate and implement the Violence Prevention curriculum at the Program for Excluded Students in Charlotte. Also, an intervention to reduce the participation of youths 10–18 residing in two targeted neighborhoods who are in youth gangs and abuse drugs.

SAVE (Students Against Violence Everywhere)
West Charlotte Senior High School
2219 Senior Drive
Charlotte, NC 28216
(704) 343-6060

CONTACT: Gary Weart, Advisor

SERVES: Students and communities

STRATEGIES: Promoting non-violence in the school and community environment. SAVE provides education about the effects and consequences of violence and provides safe extracurricular activities for students. Membership is open to all students. SAVE may be established at any school to help bring about an end to senseless violence in communities across the land.

West Charlotte Fighting Back Project
700 East Stonewall Street, Suite 345
Charlotte, NC 28202
(704) 336-4634

CONTACT: Ahmad Daniels, M.Ed., Project Director

SERVES: County commission District Two—an African-American neighborhood.

STRATEGIES: Decrease the demand for alcohol and other drugs through the utilization of existing service agencies coupled with new initiatives.

OHIO

Child Abuse Program
Columbus Children's Hospital
700 Children's Way
Columbus, OH 43205
(614) 461-6888

CONTACT: Charles Johnson, M.D., or intake worker on call

SERVES: Franklin County, Ohio and southern tier of counties to West
Virginia

STRATEGIES: Medical, nursing, psychological crisis intervention, diagnosis.
The Family Support Program offers individual group therapy for
victims of sexual abuse and adolescent and pre-adolescent perpetrators. Physical abuse therapy from children's hospital mental
health clinics.

Society for Prevention of Violence (SPV)
3109 Mayfield Road, Room 207
Cleveland Hts., OH 44118
(216) 371-5545

CONTACT: Ruth Begun, Executive Director

SERVES: Children ages 3–15

STRATEGIES: SPV provides holistic education using the structured approach of
social skills training. This method of education will build self-
esteem and character and create life values. It is based on skills
needed to make proper responses to conflicts and temptations.
Role play is part of the training.

OREGON

Oregon Youth Study
207 E. Fifth Street
Suite 202
Eugene, OR
(503) 485-2711

CONTACT: Will Mayer

SERVES: Families of antisocial children, working class and welfare

STRATEGIES: Information—primarily a research agency, some training for social learning approach to family treatment.

PENNSYLVANIA

Addison Terrace Learning Center
2136 Elmore Square
Pittsburgh, PA 15219
(412) 642-2081

CONTACT: Stephanie Griswold-Ezekoye, Executive Director
Catherine McGee, Program Coordinator

SERVES: Children of alcoholics and their families, adolescent parents, adolescent chemical abusers and their families

STRATEGIES: New-image, culture-specific passage program, personal growth and development program, right start parenting program, group intervention process, individual intervention process, in-home outreach program, homework assistance program.

Bringing Black Males to Manhood
200 Ross Street
Pittsburgh, PA 15219
(412) 261-1130

CONTACT: Robert Carter

SERVES: African-American males between the ages of 10 and 17

STRATEGIES: Self-esteem building, group activities, use of successful African-American role models, cultural and recreational activities.

House of UMOJA Boystown
1410 North Frazier Street
Philadelphia, PA 19131

CONTACT: Sister Falaka Fattah, Executive Director

SERVES: High risk African-American males ages 15–18

STRATEGIES: Surrogate parenting, afrocentric rights of passage, violence prevention through conflict resolution.

Philadelphia Injury Prevention Program
Medical Examiners Office
321 University Avenue, 2nd Floor
Philadelphia, PA 19104
(215) 823-7493

CONTACT: Rudolph L. Sutton, M.P.H., Director

SERVES: 70,000

STRATEGIES: Community safe blocks, where homes on each block are visited and interventions are initiated. School-based violence curriculum. A post-intervention program in a major hospital counseling victims of violence.

Pittsburgh Peace Institute
116 S. Highland Avenue
Pittsburgh, PA 15206
(412) 361-5900

CONTACT: Kathleen Guthrie, Liane Norman
SERVES: Pittsburgh, S.W. Pennsylvania, E. Ohio, W. Virginia
STRATEGIES: Education. Theory and practice of conflict resolution and violence
            prevention.

TENNESSEE

Boys and Girls Club of Franklin/Williams County
1116 Columbia Avenue
Franklin, TN 37064
(615) 794-4800

CONTACT: Carter Julian Savage, Executive Director
            Harold Bennett, Program Director
SERVES: 600 youths, 160 member neighborhoods
STRATEGIES: Providing intervention through guidance-oriented programming
            geared toward youth (7–17 years old). Personal and education
            development, cultural enrichment, environment education, lead-
            ership and citizenship development, health and physical educa-
            tion, social recreation, African American perspective.

Boys Club of Memphis
Central Office
189 South Barksdale
Memphis, TN 38104
(901) 278-2947

CONTACT: Jim McGalla, Director of Services
SERVES: Boys, ages 7–17
STRATEGIES: Providing professional guidance to boys to help them be contrib-
            uting human beings.

TEXAS

Texas Women's University
College of Nursing
1130 M.D. Cinderson Boulevard
Houston, TX 77030
(713) 794-2138

CONTACT: Dr. Judith McFarlane

SERVES: Adults in schools and teen clinics

STRATEGIES: 10-minute video—Prevention of Battering During Pregnancy

Teen Dating Violence Project
Center for Battered Women
P.O. Box 19454
Austin, TX 78760
(512) 928-9070

CONTACT: Leslie Letiecq-O'Shea

SERVES: Five Austin high schools, 60–80 teen girls

STRATEGIES: Psycho-education support groups for high school girls experiencing teen dating violence. Some individual counseling and
classroom/community presentations.

VIRGIN ISLANDS

Virgin Islands Department of Health
Charles Harwood Memorial Hospital
Estate Richmond
Christiansted, St. Croix
U.S. Virgin Islands 00820
(809) 773-6551 or 773-2030

CONTACT: Donna Green, M.D.

SERVES: 106,000

STRATEGIES: Working with schools and churches to implement antiviolence
curriculum. Working with agencies to increase availability of positive programs for young people.

WASHINGTON

Second Step, A Violence Prevention Curriculum
Committee for Children
172 20th Avenue
Seattle, WA 98122
(206) 322-5050

CONTACT: Kathy Beland (author), Theresa Jeannot (orders, information)

SERVES: Preschool–grade 8

STRATEGIES: Curriculums presented by teachers in a photograph/lesson-card
format. (Four separate curriculums: preschool-kindergarten,
grades 1–3, grades 4–5, and grades 6–8)

WISCONSIN

Delinquency Prevention/Gang Intervention
1028 So. 9th Street
Milwaukee, WI 53204
(414) 384-3100

CONTACT: Gary Graiko, Coordinator of Youth Alternatives

SERVES: At-risk and gang-associated youth (primarily Hispanic between the ages of 10–21)

STRATEGIES: Job placement, alternative education, counseling, court advocacy, anti-gang school presentations, etc.

National Crisis Prevention Institute
3315-K North 124th Street
Brookfield, WI 53005
(800) 558-8975
(414) 783-5787

CONTACT: Linda Steiger, Director
Lisa Keehn, Associate Director

SERVES: Any population of individuals in need

STRATEGIES: CPI has a comprehensive crisis intervention program that gives staff confidence in a safe, therapeutic approach.

INDEX

A

Abrams (Grace Contrino) Peace Education Foundation 235
Abuse, child 153–54
Academic performance 57, 162–67
Acquaintance homicides 21–22, 137
Ad Hoc Group Against Crime 252
Adams, Mukiya 80, 82
Addison Terrace Learning Center 258
Adolescence 48–63
    See also Young persons
    gangs and 96–97, 105–10
    violence and 23–24
Adults See also Parents 58–59, 93, 94
Afro-American gangs 104–5
Agape (organization) 241
Aggression See also Violence
    biological aspects of 7–9
    child abuse and 153–54
    as learned behavior 44–45
    mass media models of 41–44
    psychiatric aspects of 5–6
    stability of 43
Alabama agencies 227
Alcohol See also Drunk driving 9, 115
Alethea House 227
Ali, Shakur 157–58
Alternatives Counseling Associates (firm) 228
Alternatives to Violence Project 253
Always on Saturday (program) 233
Andrew Glover Youth Program 255
Anger
    free-floating 1–10
    object lesson on 131
    in violence prevention curriculum 177–78, 183
Anti-smoking campaign 141–42, 162
Anti-social children 152–56
Arkansas agencies 227–28
Assault statistics 20–21
Athletics 91
Autonomy, personal 52

B

B.U.I.L.D., Inc. 237
Bailey, Richard 12

Barfield, Clementine 202–3
Barron Assessment and Counseling Center 241
Behavior modification 141
Behavior reinforcement 154–55
Bell, Carl 69
Beyond 911 (Moore, Sparrow and Kennedy) 196
Biden, Joseph 13
Biological sciences 7–9
Bishop, Ann 181, 182
Black gangs 104–5
Black youth
    mentoring for 176
    police and 122–24
    poverty and 64–79
    school performance of 162–67
    self-perception of 93–94
Bloods (gang) 104, 117
Boston
    gangs in 81
    police in 86, 87
    Stuart murder case and 122
    violence prevention curriculum pilot project in 187–91
Boston Area Educators for Social Responsibility (organization) 241
Boston City Hospital 189
Boston Conflict Resolution Program 241
Boston Public Schools 247
Bourg[e?]ois, Philippe 124
"Box, The" 172
Boys 78–79, 158–59
Boys and Girls Club of Franklin/Williams County 259
Boys and Girls Clubs of America 253–54
Boys Club of Memphis 259
Bracy, Paul 38–39, 187
Brady Amendment 198
Brain function 7–9
Bringing Black Males to Manhood (organization) 258
Broader Urban Involvement and Leadership Development, Inc. 237
Bronx County 19
Brooklyn Public School 321, 173–75
Brown, Claude 53–54, 62, 150–51

Brown, Lee 27, 195
Brown, Reggie 73–75
*Building Conflict Solving Skills for Adoles-
cents* 239
Bukuras, Mark 187
Bulhan, Hussein 92
Burden (Florence V.) Foundation 254
Burke High School 80–94
  discipline in 168
  gangs and 106–7
  violence prevention curriculum and
    134, 137
Bush, George 31
Butler, Denise 111
Buttler, Jeffrey 26

C
California agencies 228–32
Camille O. Cosby Center 242
Canby, Vincent 29, 30
Carlsson-Paige, Nancy 35
Cartoon programs 36
Castle Hill Houses project 112
Cathedral High School 134, 137
Center Against Abusive Behavior 228
Center for Battered Women 260
Center for Law-Related Education 232
Center for Peace and Conflict Studies
    248
Center for Prevention and Treatment of
    Psychological Trauma 249
Center to Prevent Handgun Violence
    233
Centers for Disease Control 16, 136–37
Centerwall, Brandon 17
Chambers, Robert 32, 34
Channeling Children's Anger 233
Cher 31
Chicago Housing Authority 238
Chicago Intervention Network 237
Chicago Police Department 237
Child abuse 153–54
Child Abuse Program 257
Child Assault Prevention Project 242
Children
  anti-social 152–56
  in crack trade 115–16
  education of 161–83
  intelligence of 164–66
  in Kauai 58–59, 159–60
  moral development of 59–62
  raising of 146–57
  of single-parent families 73
  statistics on 144
  television and 38–41, 46–47
  of the underclass 77–78
  violence and 69
  weapons and 19
Children at Risk (organization) 252
Children's Creative Response to Conflict
    (organization) 254
Children's Defense Fund 77
Church-going 43–44
Cities*See also*Urban neighborhoods
  crack use in 126
  homicide rates in 16
  underclass populations of 73

Clark, Joe 168
Clark, Reginald 169, 171
Clemens, Roger 173
CLIMB Theater 251
Clothing 85
Coalition for Violence Prevention 192–94
Cocaine 102, 118–19
"Cocaine Kids" (gang) 101–3
Coercive family processes 154–55
College education 163–64
Colorado agencies 232–33
Columbus Children's Hospital 257
Come Together Youth Workshops 228–
    29
Comer, James 166
Communities
  collapse of 75–76
  police relations with 121–24, 194–97
  underclass and 71–73
  violence prevention in 184–203
Community Board Center for Policy
    Training 231
Community Board Program 229
Community Relations Service 240
Community Youth Services for Elemen-
    tary and Middle School Children
    (program) 242
Competence 57–58
Compliance 148–49
Conference on Violence as a Public
    Health Problem 138
Confessions of Berhard Goetz, The (film) 32
Conflict resolution programs 173–75
Congress of National Black Churches
    235
Connecticut agencies 233
Consumer Produce [Product?] Safety
    Commission 199
Contemporary Issues (program) 254
Contingent requests 149–50, 151
Corbet Crew 95
Corporate gangs 101
Cosby (Camille O.) Center 242
Cottle, Thomas J. 57
Crack cocaine 113–17, 126, 128–29
Crews (gangs) 101
Crime Control Institute 19
Criminal justice system 4–5, 107–8
Crips (gang) 104, 117
Current Affair, A (T.V. program) 34

D
Dangerous Society (C.S. Taylor) 99
Dash, Leon 119–20
Dating Violence Intervention Project 242
Death, adolescent perception of 110
Delinquency Prevention/Gang Interven-
    tion (organization) 261
Depression, mental 136
Detroit 99–100
Detroit Receiving Hospital and Univer-
    sity Health Center 249
Developmental tasks 50
Die Hard 2 (film) 29
Discipline of children 147–52, 155
Diseases 135
Disinhibition 45

District of Columbia
  drug traffic in 119–20
  homicides in 117–18
  social agencies of 233–35
Domestic Violence Prevention Curriculum
  251
Dorchester, Mass. 88–89
Drama 180–81
Driving, drunk 143
Drop-outs 164
Drug dealers
  earnings of 128–29
  gangs as 100–101, 105
  as role models 90, 116
  in Washington, D.C. 119–20
Drugs, illicit *See also* Cocaine; Crack cocaine
  in Dorchester 88–89
  homicides and 24–25
  students and 86
  violence and 9, 65–66, 119
Drunk driving 143

E
East Boston Neighborhood Health Cen-
  ter 242–43
Eazy E (musician) 37, 38
Economic displacement 71
Education *See* Higher education; Learn-
  ing; Schools
Educational Services for Children and
  Adolescents (program) 240
Education[al?] Development Corporation
  192, 194, 248
Educators for Social Responsibility Con-
  flict Resolution Programs 243
Efficacy Institute 169–72
Eisenhower (Milton S.) Foundation 234
Elementary School Conflict Managers
  Program 229
EMERGE (organization) 56, 243
Emergency rooms 1–3, 28, 133, 189–90
Empathy 77, 159
Erikson, Erik 56
Eron, Leonard D. 43–44, 152
Ervin, Frank 8–9
Escalante, Jaime 168–69
Ethnic pride 92–93
Evans, David L. 163
Experimentation, adolescent 63
Extracurricular activities 57

F
"F— tha Police" (song) 37
Faces of Death (film) 31–32, 41
Facing History and Ourselves National
  Foundation 243–44
Fairness 61–62
Families
  adolescent separation from 51–54
  illicit drugs and 124–28
  national policy on 199–203
  single-parent 72–73
  therapeutic intervention in 156
  violence prevention and 145–60
Fathers 78–79, 158–59
Favorite Son (T.V. program) 32–33

Federal Bureau of Investigation 13, 24,
  27, 37
Ferguson, Ron 93, 94, 176, 179
Fighting *See* Violence
Fighting Fair 235
Fighting gangs 100, 104
Fighting Invisible Tigers 250–51
Films 29
Firearms *See also* Handguns
  adolescent grandiosity and 120–21
  control of 197–99
  homicides and 14–15
  students on 84
Florence V. Burden Foundation 254
Florida agencies 235
Folgert, Emmett 47
Foot patrols 195–96
Fort Wayne Police Department 239
Fox, Jamie 42
Free-floating anger 1–10
Future goals of youths 56–59

G
Gangs 95–110
  in Boston 81
  clothing and 85
  crack trade and 117
  homicides and 24–25
  police and 121–24
  violence and 65–66
Gangs, Cops and Drugs (T.V. program)
  106
Gender factor
  in crack use 114, 126
  in gang membership 98–99
  in homicides 16–17
  in violence 9–10
Gender identification 79
Generational conflict 52–53
George, Nelson 38
Georgia agencies 236
Gerbner, George 46
Ghettos *See* Urban neighborhoods
Girl Scouts of the U.S.A. 254
Glory (film) 31
Glover (Andrew) Youth Program 255
Goetz, Bernhard 32
Good Grief Program 244
Government services *See also* Social
  agencies 75–76
Governor's Youth Crime Prevention
  Program 232
Grace Contrino Abrams Peace Education
  Foundation 235
Grandiosity, adolescent 120–21, 125
Grant Middle School Conflict Resolution
  Training 254–55
Group membership 96–97
Guns *See* Firearms; Handguns
Guns N'Roses (musical group) 37
Gunshot wounds 20

H
Haloperidol 7–8
Handguns 15, 17–20
Hartford Action Plan on Infant Health,
  Inc. 233

Harvard Injury Control Center 244
Harvard Negotiation Project 244–45
Harvard School of Public Health 244, 246
Harvard University 163–64
Hau[s?]man, Alice 187, 188
Hawaii Mediation Program 236–37
HAWK Federation Manhood Development and Training Program 229
Hayes, Roy 117
Hayward (Calif.) Police Department 232
Hayward Pratt National Center for Human Development 240
Head injuries 9
Head Start program 201
Health care providers See also Physicians 189–90
Health Promotion Project 186, 191
Heavy metal music 36–37
Helping agencies 75–76, 227–61
Henningfield, Jack 115
Henry Horner Homes housing project 66–67
Heroin 113
Herzog, James 158
Hesse, Petra 36
Hicks, Suzanne 192, 193
High school students
   in Boston 82–94
   in Little Rock 193
   violence prevention curriculum and 134
Higher education 163–64
Hill, Holliday, Connors, and Cosmopulos (firm) 190
Hinckley, John 41
Hispanic-Americans 66, 93, 104
Holland, Albert 81, 167
Homicides
   among acquaintances 21–22, 137
   in Los Angeles 66
   statistics on 13–17, 24, 65
   "victim precipitated" 136
   in Washington, D.C. 117–18
Hospital emergency rooms 1–3, 28, 133, 189–90
House of UMOJA Boystown 258
Houston 196–97
Howard, Jeffrey 165, 169–72
Humor 182

I
Illegitimacy 72
Illinois agencies 237–39
Immigrants 70
Imprisonment 109, 163
Indiana agencies 239
Individuation 51–54
Infants 126–28
Inner city neighborhoods See Urban neighborhoods
Institute for Mental Health Initiatives 233–34
Institute-Trauma and Loss in Children 249
Intelligence 164–66, 170–71

International Association for the Study of Cooperation in Education 230
International homicide rates 14
Interpol 15
Isolation, personal 90
Israeli schools 169–70

J
Jackson, Derrick 162
Jackson, Jesse 83
Japanese schools 169–70
Jeremiah E. Burke High School 80–94
   discipline in 168
   gangs and 106–7
   violence prevention curriculum and 134, 137
Johnson, Tony 95–96
Journalism 33–34
Judge Baker Children's Center 242, 244
Junior high school students 193
Justice 61
Justice Department 126
Juvenile murderers 153

K
Kansas agencies 239–40
Kansas Child Abuse Prevention Council 239
Kansas City Urban Interpersonal Violence Injury Control Project 251–52
Kelling, George 187
Kennedy, David 196
Knives 19–20
Kohlberg, Lawrence 60–62
Kotlowitz, Alex 64, 67
Kunjufu, Kawanza 165–66

L
Latino gangs 104
Learning 44–45, 162–68
Learning the Skills of Peacemaking 230
Levin, Diane 35
Levin, Jack 42
Lewis, Dorothy Otnow 153
Limbic system 7–8
Link Valley neighborhood 196–97
Little Rock, Ark. 192–93
"Living After Murder" program 68
Local Violence Prevention/Intervention (program) 256
"Locura" 100
Los Angeles
   gangs in 104–5
   Hispanic homicides in 66
   police brutality in 123–24

M
McClain, Diante 64, 68
Mack, John 36
McKinley, James C. 11
MADD 143
Male Youth Health Enhancement Project 234
Males, young See Young men
Manchild in the Promised Land (C. Brown) 53, 150–51

Mark, Vernon 8–9
Maryland agencies 240–41
Maslin, Janet 30
Mass media 29–47, 87, 103–4, 107
Mass murders 42
MASS/CAPP 242
Massachusetts agencies 241–48
Massachusetts Department of Mental
    Health 245
Massachusetts Department of Public
    Health 246
Matthews, Rod 41
"Mean world syndrome" 45–46
Mecklenburg County Health Depart-
    ment 256
Media 29–47, 87, 103–4, 107
Mediation 175
Medical costs 20
Medical Foundation Prevention Center
    245
Men, young See Young men
Mental health professions 5–6
Mentoring programs See also Re-
    parenting 176
Metenkephalin 8
Mexican-American gangs 104
Michigan agencies 248–50
Miller, Walter B. 103
Milton S. Eisenhower Foundation 234
Milwaukee schools 162–63
Minnesota agencies 250–51
Minnesota Coalition for Battered
    Women 251
Missouri agencies 251–52
Mr. Rogers (T.V. program) 45
Modeling See Role models
Monroe, Marilyn 42
Moore, Mark 196
Moore, Tiffany 84
Moral development 59–62, 109–10
Morgan State University 240–41
Mortality See also Death 135–36
Mothers
    addicted 126–28
    as role models 89
    teenagers as 77–78
Mothers Against Drunk Driving (organi-
    zation) 143
Murderers, juvenile 153
Murders, mass 42
"Mushrooms" (bystanders) 25–26, 30
Music 36–38
My Family and Me 245

N
N.W.A. (musical group) 37
Narcissism
    of gang members 109–10
    grandiosity and 120–121
    respect and 179
    rituals and 97
    teenage motherhood and 77–78
    violence and 55
National Association for Mediation in
    Education 245
National Crime Prevention Council
    234

National Crisis Prevention Institute 261
National Institute [for?] Violence Pre-
    vention 246
National Institute of Justice 116
National Rifle Association 198
National School Safety Center 230
Neighborhoods, urbanSeeUrban neigh-
    borhoods
New Center Community Mental Health
    Services 250
New Hampshire agencies 252
New Mexico agencies 252–53
New Mexico Center for Dispute Resolu-
    tion 252–53
New Way of Fighting 236
New York City Department of Juvenile
    Justice 255
New York State agencies 253–55
Non-violence See also Violence preven-
    tion 76, 130–32
North Carolina agencies 256

O
Ohio agencies 257
Olweus, Dan 9, 152
"Operation Cold Turkey" 122
"Operation Hammer" 123
Oppression, internalized 92
Oregon Social Learning Center 147–48,
    149, 154, 156
Oregon Youth Study (organization)
    257

P
PACT (organization) 230–31
Paige, Nancy Carlsson 35
"Parallel value system" 120
Paramount Plan (organization) 231
Parenthood (film) 157
Parents See also Re-parenting
    of adolescents 49, 53
    child-raising skills of 148
    illicit drugs and 125–26
    retraining of 156–57
    as role models 22–23, 89, 145
    school involvement of 169
    surrogate 159–60
Parker, Tanya 184–85, 186
Patterson, Gerald 147–48, 150, 151, 152,
    154, 156
"Peacemakers" program 173–75
Peer groups 53, 61–62, 90
Peer mediation 175
Pennsylvania agencies 258–59
Pepperdine University 230
Philadelphia 122
Philadelphia Injury Prevention Program
    258
Physicians 135
Pierce, Glen 33, 73
Pittsburgh Peace Institute 259
Police
    Black suspicion of 5
    in Boston 86, 87
    brutality of 122–24
    community relations with 121–24,
        194–97

Police (*cont.*)
  in Los Angeles 123–24
  in rap music 37
  in violence prevention 27
Policy Action Collaboration and Training
  for Alternatives to
Violence and Abuse (organization) 230–
  31
Post traumatic stress syndrome 68
Poverty
  homicides and 16–17
  smoking and 141–42
  young men of color and 64–79
Pratt (Hayward) National Center for
  Human Development 240
Pregnancy 126–28
Press (journalism) 33–34
Prevention strategies 140, 189
Prevention of violence *See* Violence pre-
  vention
Pride 109–10, 148
Prisons 109, 163
Prize fights 42
Program on Human Development and
  Criminal Behavior 246
Project Image 238
Project Peace 238
Project Spirit 235
Project Stress Control 236
Project 2000 240–41
Public health 26–28, 130–44
Public School 321 (Brooklyn) 173–75
Public service announcements 190–91
Publicity 42–43, 107
Punishment *See also* Prisons 4, 61

R
Ramey, Louis 6
Rap music 37–38
Re-parenting *See also* Mentoring pro-
    grams
  by Ali 157–58
  rehabilitation and 108
  by surrogates 159–60
Reading ability 40
Reagan, Ronald 30–31, 41
Rehabilitation programs 4, 108
Religion 43–44
Resolving Conflict Creatively Program
  255
Resource Center for the Prevention of
  Family Violence and Sexual As-
  sault 246
Respect *See also* Self-esteem 179
Revenger (novelty) 31
Rice, Pat 106
Rimer, Sara 74
Risk-taking 62–63
Rites of passage 52
Rituals 97
Rivera, Geraldo 32
Roach, Mickey 156
Roache, Francis M. 27
Robert Taylor Homes housing project
  69–70
Robocop 2 (film) 29
"Rockefeller Laws" 115–16

Rocky Mountain Center for Health Promotion and Education 232
Role models
  drug dealers as 90, 116
  fathers as 79, 159
  in learning 44–45
  parents as 22–23, 89, 145
  theory of 147
  unrelated adults as 58–59
"Role plays" 180–81
Rosenberg, Mark 20, 42, 137
Roxbury, Mass. 187–91

S
Sack, Kevin 111
Save our Sons and Daughters (organiza-
  tion) 202–3, 249
SAVE (program) 256
SCAT (program) 246–47
Scavenger gangs 100
Schizophrenia 8
School Consultation and Treatment Pro-
  gram 246–47
School Initiatives Program (San Fran-
  cisco) 231
School Mediation Associates 247
Schools 19–20, 57, 161–83
Schorr, Lisbeth 152, 201
Schwarzenegger, Arnold 29, 30
"Search on sight" policy 122
Seattle 18
Second Step 260
Seedat, Mohamed 68–69
Seizures 8–9
Self-determination 52
Self-esteem *See also* Pride; Respect
  athletes' 91
  Black sons' 79
  boys' 159
  children's 173
  ethnic pride and 93
  gang membership and 106
  young woman's 92
Self-hatred 6
Self-protection 90
Senate Judiciary Committee 13
Senior Tutors for Youth (program) 231–
  32
Sesame Street (T.V. program) 45
Sex factor
  in crack use 114, 126
  in gang membership 98–99
  in homicides 16–17
  in violence 9–10
Sexual identity 54–56, 79, 108
Simmons, Preston 111–13
Single-parent families 72–73
Skills for Violence-Free Relationships 251
Slaby, Ron 31–32, 40, 194
Smith, Amos 201–2
Smoking 141–42, 162
Social agencies 187–88, 227–61
Social groups 76, 96–97
Socialization 9–10
Society for Prevention of Violence 257
Songs 36–38
SOSAD 202–3, 249

South Boston, Mass. 187–91
South Shore Women's Center 247
Spanking 150–51
Sparrow, Malcolm 196
Spivak, Howard 186, 187, 191
Sports 91
State organizations 227–61
Statistics
    on assault 20–21
    on children 144
    on homicide 13–17, 24, 65
    on mortality 136
Stay on the Safe Side (program) 232
Stemmerman, Sean 12
Stewart, Billy 110
Stop the Violence movement 38
STOP Violence Coalition 239–40
"Straight Outta Compton" (song) 37
Stringham, Peter 182, 191
Stuart, Charles and Carol 33–34, 122
Students
    in Boston 82–94
    in Little Rock 193
    violence prevention curriculum and
        134
Students Against Violence Everywhere
        (program) 256
Stutman, Robert M. 127
Suicides 42
Superhero cartoon programs 36
Surgeon General of the United States
        27–28, 136, 138
Surrogate parents 159–60

T
Tabloid television 34
Taupier, Joanne 191
Taxi Driver (film) 41
Taylor, Carl S. 99
Teachers 165–66, 168–69
Teen Dating Violence Project 260
Teenage Mutant Ninja Turtles (film) 35
Teenagers See Adolescence; Young per-
        sons
Television 32–34, 39–41, 43, 44–47
Tennessee agencies 259
Teret, Stephen 198–99
Territorial gangs 100, 104
Tersignis, Raymond 12
Testosterone 9
Texas agencies 259–60
Texas Women's University 259–60
Therapy, family 156
Tongass Community Counseling Center
        227–28
Total Recall (film) 29, 30
Toys 31, 35
Trash television 34
Trauma Prevention Procedures and Sup-
        port Systems (program) 247
Traylor, Napier 26
Tri-City Mental Health (organization)
        238–39

U
Underclass 69–75
Unemployment 72–73

United States Consumer Produce [Prod-
        uct?] Safety Commission 199
United States Department of Justice 240
United States Federal Bureau of Investi-
        gation 13, 24, 27, 37
United States Justice Department 126
United States Senate Judiciary Commit-
        tee 13
United States Surgeon General 27–28,
        136, 138
University education 163–64
University of Hawaii at Manoa 236–37
University of Illinois 238
Urban Interpersonal Violence Project 252
Urban neighborhoods
    collapse of 75–76
    underclass and 71–73
    violence prevention in 184–203

V
Vancouver 18
Veterans 68
Victim Assistance (program) 239
"Victim precipitated" homicide 136
Viens, Robert and Thomas 13
Vietnam veterans 68
Viewpoints (organization) 238
Violence See also Aggression
    adolescence and 23–24
    child raising and 151
    cocaine and 118–19
    cost/benefit analysis of 178–79
    drug traffic and 65–66, 119
    gangs and 96–98, 109–10
    narcissism and 55
    of police 122–24
    psychological impact of 67–69
    young women on 94
Violence is a Choice 247
Violence is Preventable Program 249–50
Violence prevention See also Non-
        violence
    in communities 184–203
    public health methodology and 26–28,
        132–35, 136–38
    in schools 161–83
Violence prevention curriculum
    in communities 186–91
    first version of 4
    goals of 161–62
    Rosenberg and 137–38
    in schools 134, 175–83
Violence Prevention Curriculum Project
        Grades 10-12 248
Violence Prevention Project 186–91, 248
VIP Program 249–50
Virgin Islands Department of Health 260

W
Walton family 66–67
War Play Dilemma, The (Carlsson-Paige
        and Levin) 35
Washington, D.C.
    drug traffic in 119–20
    homicides in 117–18
    social agencies of 233–35
Washington State agencies 260

Wayne State University 248, 250
Weapons *See also* Firearms; Knives 19–20
Werner, Emmy 58–59, 159
West, Carl 12
West Charlotte Fighting Back Project 256
West, Percy 12
Where Have All the Children Gone? 250
White, Donald 12–13
Wholistic Stress Control Institute 236
Wilder Child Guidance Clinic 251
Williams, Arnulfo, Jr. 11–12
Williams, Johnny 11
Williams, Terry 101, 102, 125
Willis, Bruce 29, 30
Wilson, William Julius 17, 70–71
Winsten, Jay A. 143
Wintemute, Garen 198–99
Wisconsin agencies 261
Within Our Reach (L. Schorr) 152, 201
Women heads of family 72–73
Women, young *See* Young women
World Health Organization 15

Y
Young men 13–14
Young men of color
  mentoring for 176
  police and 122–24
  poverty and 64–79
  school performance of 162–67
  self-perception of 93–94
Young persons 135–36, 152
Young women
  in gangs 98–99
  as mothers 77–78
  on peer pressure 90
  sexual relations of 56
  on violence 94
Youth agencies 187–88
Youth and Family Services Bureau 232
Youth Development, Inc. 253
Youth Development Project 238
Youth gangs *See* Gangs

Z
Zamora, Ronald 41

ABOUT THE AUTHORS

Dr. Prothrow-Stith is currently Assistant Dean at the Harvard School of Public Health. She served for two years as the Massachusetts Commissioner of Public Health—the first woman and second African-American to be appointed to the position. The author is known for her work in preventing youth violence and for her work in adolescent health. Issues in the forefront of Dr. Prothrow-Stith's agenda include school health, violence prevention, universal health insurance, and AIDS. Her position at Harvard gives her the opportunity to address the public health issues that concerned her as state public health commissioner. She will work as a liaison between academic public health and government and community.

Michaele Weissman is a freelance writer who lives and works in Newton, Massachusetts. She has been working with Dr. Prothrow-Stith on the issue of adolescent violence for three years. Her first book was a narrative history of women in America.